IMAGES of America

THE NAPA RIVER

On the Cover: The *St. Helena* appears on the Napa River in the early 1900s. Riverboat captain Albert Hatt owned the steamer *St. Helena*, which was a rival of the *Zinfandel* because its accommodations were considered superior. The vessel consists of three levels with several windows lining the sides. (Courtesy of the University of Southern California, USC Libraries.)

IMAGES
of America

THE NAPA RIVER

Nancy McEnery with the Napa County Historical Society
Foreword by Moira Johnston Block

ARCADIA
PUBLISHING

ISBN 978-0-7385-9504-7

Published by Arcadia Publishing
Charleston, South Carolina

Printed in the United States of America

Library of Congress Control Number: 2012930402

For all general information, please contact Arcadia Publishing:
Telephone 843-853-2070
Fax 843-853-0044
E-mail sales@arcadiapublishing.com
For customer service and orders:
Toll-Free 1-888-313-2665

Visit us on the Internet at www.arcadiapublishing.com

To Rick

Contents

Acknowledgments

There are so many people to acknowledge in this book project. I would like to thank Napa County Historical Society executive director Nancy Levenberg, researcher-archivist Alexandria Brown, and research coordinator Jules Evans-White. Their generosity in allowing me to use historical photographs in their collection made this book possible. Jules and Alex were also instrumental in checking for the historical accuracy of the captions. Kristie Sheppard of the Napa Valley Museum contributed photographs as well. Jim Kern, director of the Vallejo Naval and Historical Museum, read the manuscript and provided expert advice and suggestions, as did Bernhard Krevet and Shari Gardner of Friends of the Napa River (FONR). Bernhard also provided some fantastic images of the river that are included in this book. I am so grateful to Moira Johnston Block, founding president of FONR, for her tireless work on behalf of the river and her graciousness in editing this book and writing the foreword. Jason Bell deserves thanks for his research help. Thanks goes to Chris Malan, executive director of the Institute for Conservation Advocacy, Research and Education, for her suggested additions to the book. I want to also acknowledge my editor at Arcadia, Amy Perryman, for her encouragement, creativity, and great advice. Unless otherwise noted, all images appear courtesy of the Napa County Historical Society.

Ten percent of the author's royalties will be donated to groups supporting the health and history of the Napa River.

Foreword

I am delighted to introduce Nancy McEnery's book on the history of the Napa River. This is a book to sit down with and savor, for it captures what few know about this modest waterway: its story is an epic drama that runs through the heart of the history of Napa Valley. Evoking the romance of the river, it reminds us that long before this became a world-famous valley of great wines, it is also the Napa River Valley—our "Royal Road." It was a lifeline and reliable feast for the native Wappo living on its banks; the artery that opened the valley to settlers, shipping, and industrial fortune; and a dynamic living thing that knew eras of triumph, abandonment, survival, struggle, and currently vibrant renaissance. This book could not be timelier, for we are witnessing a river healing and transforming in plain sight, playing new roles in our lives. For those who love to walk and explore surviving traces of our history, *The Napa River* will be welcomed as a richly informed guidebook. With a trove of rare photographs, here are the ships, the captains, the riverside industry that brought damage as well as prosperity, and the parade of changing transportation from trains to highways, which left Napa City bypassed and the river a derelict dumping ground in the 20th century. Finally, an effort to heal the river began in 1993 in my living room as a group of river enthusiasts ("river rats") formed into Friends of the Napa River. In 1998, we shared an unprecedented community collaboration that achieved the Napa River Flood Project, a pioneering model for controlling floods while restoring a river. I want to thank Nancy for a rigorously researched historical document that brings the story right up to date, permitting today's river rats to share the vivid panorama we missed. I am sure our precious "Living River" speaks its thanks, too, as it flows out to the bay.

—Moira Johnston Block
Founding President
Friends of the Napa River

Introduction

The "Y" shape of the sparkling wine flute describes perfectly the flow of water down the east sides of the Palisades and west sides of the forested Mayacamas Mountains into the Napa River Valley. During the rainy season, 53 tributaries bulging with water flow throughout the watershed, carrying soils and cobble that distribute throughout the basin. The water flows into a 55-mile-long river that begins atop the 4,300-foot Mount St. Helena to the north and empties into the San Pablo Bay at sea level. Water does not gush down the creeks year-round, only in the winter and early spring. While insignificant in summer, the creek beds do not remain bone dry. At its northern beginnings, the river is little more than a creek with ancient oaks, conifer, and willows lining its banks. Laurel, bay, buckeyes, and alders can also be found. The upper portion of the Napa Valley is less than a mile wide near Calistoga. As the river moves south, the valley widens to five miles across, and the river is marginally navigable only by dredging as it passes through wetlands. North of Trancas Street in Napa, a full 17 miles before it reaches the San Pablo Bay, the river is a tidal estuary system. In the summer, the salinity of the river in central Napa may be 10 percent, yet in the winter, it is brackish. Along the way, this watercourse runs through a heavily farmed and partially urbanized valley. The cities of Calistoga, St. Helena, Rutherford, Oakville, Yountville, Napa, American Canyon, and Vallejo all share a bank with the Napa River.

The evolution of the Napa River from a pristine riparian habitat and tidal estuary to a highly valued waterway in the mid-19th century is the main subject of this book. The vibrant riverboat captains and early entrepreneurs and industrialists who created the city of Napa took advantage of the river's bounty, but eventually, mercury mining, logging, population growth, farming, cattle, and industries severely polluted the river. The riverboat captains played an integral role in the material history of Napa. In fact, these stories illustrate how people coming from far and wide, who built their livelihoods and their town's identity in tandem, settled not only Napa, but also the West.

By the 20th century, as shipping gave way to rail transport, the Napa River's importance as the horsepower for the industry began to wane, but the damage had been done. Once home to 34 species of native fish, including Coho salmon, the river had become a toxic mix of chemicals, a danger to human health, and a smelly waterway filled with sewage and algae. Surging its banks and defying all efforts to control its floodwaters, the Napa River threatened the very towns it helped to create. Over the past 160 years, the perpetual construction of levees, dikes, and flood walls left the towns vulnerable to flooding.

In the mid-1990s, abandoning a traditional approach, a coalition of community members and organizations came up with an extraordinary plan to allow the river to regain some of its historical floodplain and prevent flooding through a blend of engineering and ecology. Napa County, along with the US Army Corps of Engineers, carried out the plan. The Napa River Flood Management Project makes it possible for the river to begin meandering in some areas. New marshes and wetlands are emerging. The Napa River is undergoing a renaissance. The city of Napa and St. Helena are beneficiaries of a revitalized river, as visitors to Napa discover the new urban river trail and walk lively, flood-protected streets. Much is still to be done to restore water quality and make the river as healthy as it once was.

One

Early Napa River Valley
Wetlands and Wildlife

Picture the area north of San Francisco in the early 1800s. It was an area where tule elk, pronghorn antelope, and grizzly bears roamed freely. The Napa River basin supported thousands of spawning steelhead and Coho and Chinook salmon in its clear waters. In the valley's lowlands, there were thousands of acres of seasonally wet meadows surrounded by pockets of tall tule marsh. The river divided and reunited, creating natural islands. Many tributaries did not connect directly to the river but spread into valley wetlands. Native American people built pole houses and fashioned obsidian into shafts, spear points, and arrowheads. The Wappo and Patwin Indians made the valley their home. They sailed on rafts of tule bundles and caught fish and waterfowl from the maze of marshlands at the river's mouth. The group known as Mayakmah, meaning "water going out place," lived in the southern tidal areas of Napa and Sonoma Valleys.

The actual derivation and meaning of *Napa* remains unclear. Some speculate that Napa was a Patwin word meaning "a meeting place, particularly a fishing colony." New arrivals to the land, the Spanish and then the Mexicans, settled along the river's shore. The Americans who followed also located their homes and businesses along the river and brought ships up the estuary to Napa City. They reclaimed the marshland by constructing levees and isolating islands for farming.

In the upper valley, the river provided irrigation water to the fields and turned the wheels of the gristmill in St. Helena. Coastal temperate rainforest and dryland habitats, such as oak savanna and grasslands, were found not far from the wet marshes. The rich harvest of the valley originated from the fertile floodplain soils of the river's making.

At the southern end and widest part, the Napa Valley receives the cool sea breezes that blow through the Golden Gate and up San Francisco and San Pablo Bays. In the south, a delta formed by the Napa River, and the Sonoma and Tolay Creeks created a vast area of tidal marshland. This rich alluvial plain extends between the present-day cities of Napa and Sonoma. Birds of all kinds are plentiful along the river, such as mallards, green-winged teals, mergansers, herons, egrets, kingfishers, clapper rails, grebes, and quail. Birds that migrate south spend winters in the open water of San Pablo Bay and find protection in its marshes. Additionally, other animals such as minks, muskrats, raccoons, deer, gray foxes, bobcats, and mountain lions are found.

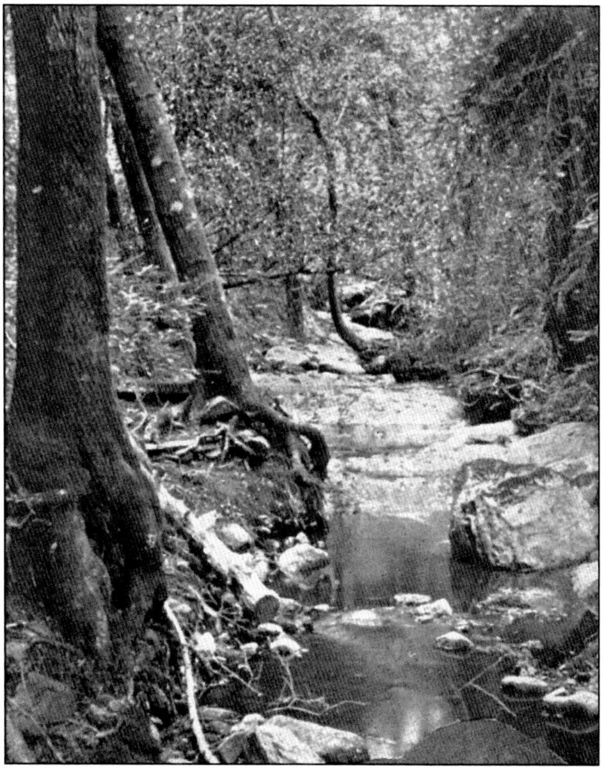

In what is now the city of Napa, and further north along the foothills of the Mayacamas Range, redwood trees and mixed-evergreen forests grew undisturbed. It was likely that wooded tributaries had frequent logjams, creating deep pools that sustained fish throughout the warm summers.

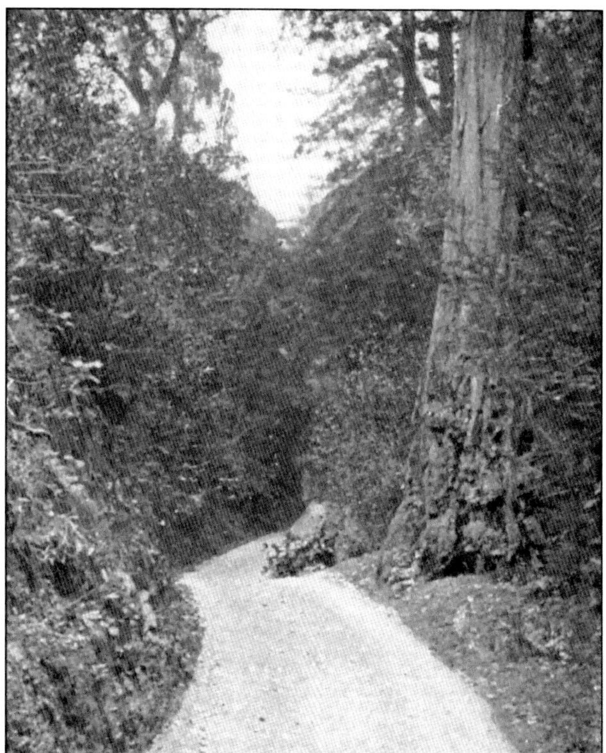

In early Napa, trails were laid out following the routes of old, well-established Native American trails, like this narrow road through the Mayacamas Mountains, or those that appeared most suitable for travel by horseback between ranchos. It was not until around 1851 that an existing, well-traveled route was created when the first county road became authorized and was situated in the center of the Napa Valley. Transporting goods over mountains by horse and wagon was burdensome and often treacherous. The price of lumber was exorbitant before sawmills were established, nearing $300 per 1,000 feet.

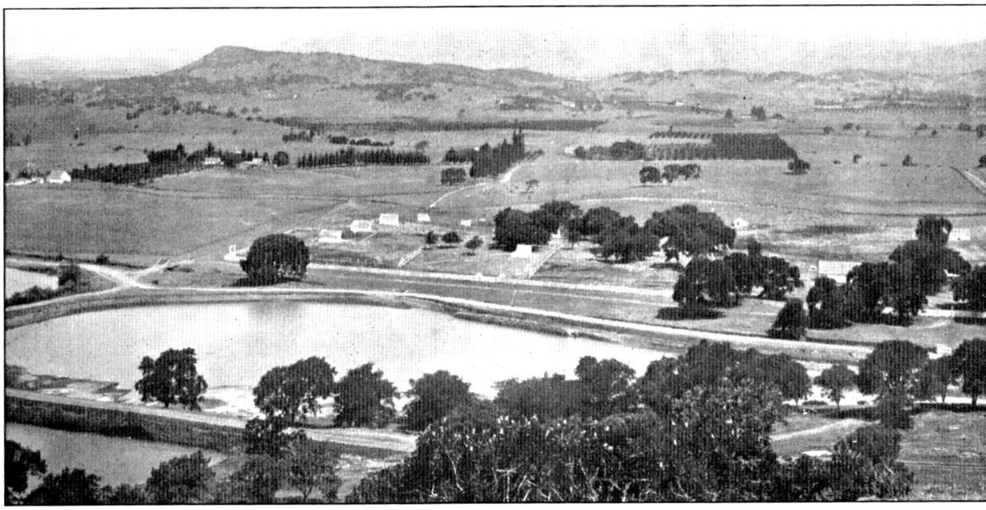

By the early 1840s, the primary land uses in the Napa Valley were agricultural, including timber production, grazing, and field crops. Looking west from Napa State Hospital lands, the Mayacamas Mountains can be seen on the horizon in the background. Sonoma is directly beyond to the west. Vineyards were later developed in the 1860s. In the *History of Napa and Lake Counties*, Harry Gunn notes, "In 1847 there was not a house in the county except for a few adobes, one occupied by Nicholas Higuerra and the other by Cayetano Juarez. There was not a store, hotel, saloon, church or school within the limits of the county. There were neither roads nor bridges nor fences." Oddly enough, this account does not mention George Yount, one of the earliest settlers to enter the Napa Valley, who built a rancho just north of Napa City.

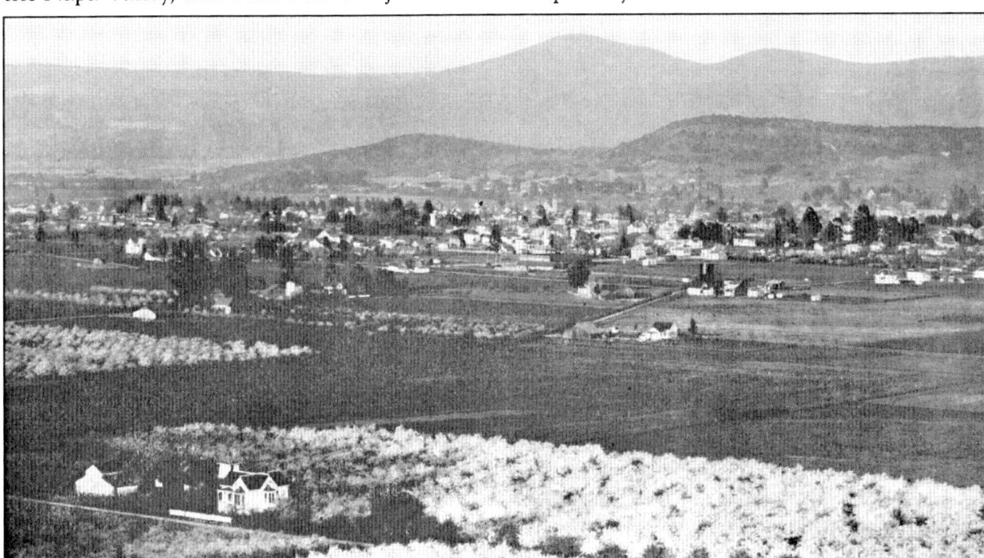

The Napa River runs through the center of the valley near the base of Alta Heights. The Vaca Range, which includes Mount George, appears to the east of Napa. The location and growth of Napa City were integrally related to the Napa River. Many businesses located near the river for easy shipping of their goods. Shipments of grain, (oats, corn, and wheat), flour, barrels of wine, animals, and hides were sent downriver, while finished products such as sewer pipes, machinery, dry goods, and apple boxes came from San Francisco. Some outgoing ships held whole flocks of sheep or a fortune in quicksilver from the mines at Knoxville or Lake County.

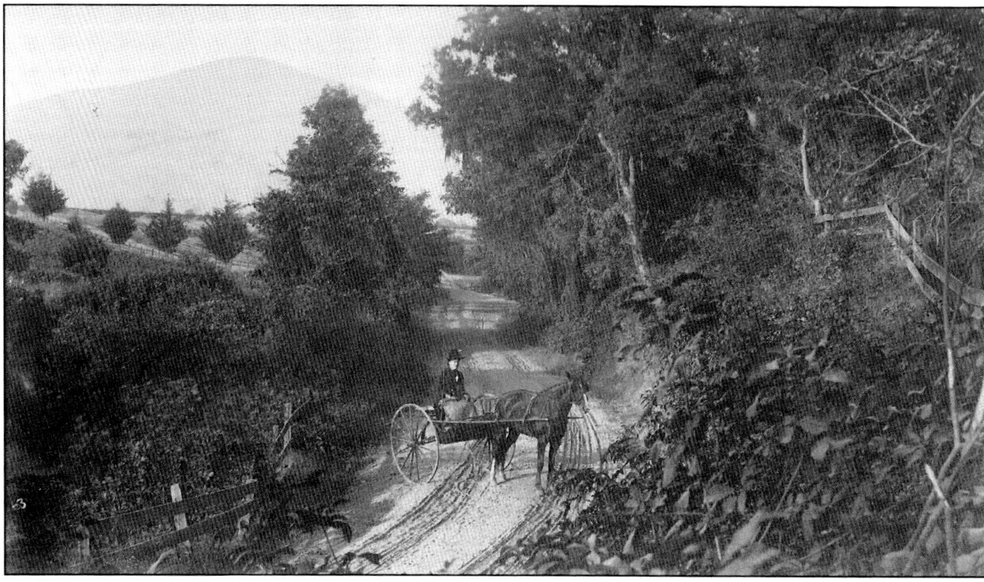

Early transportation in and around Napa City was by horse and carriage. (Courtesy of Napa Valley Museum.)

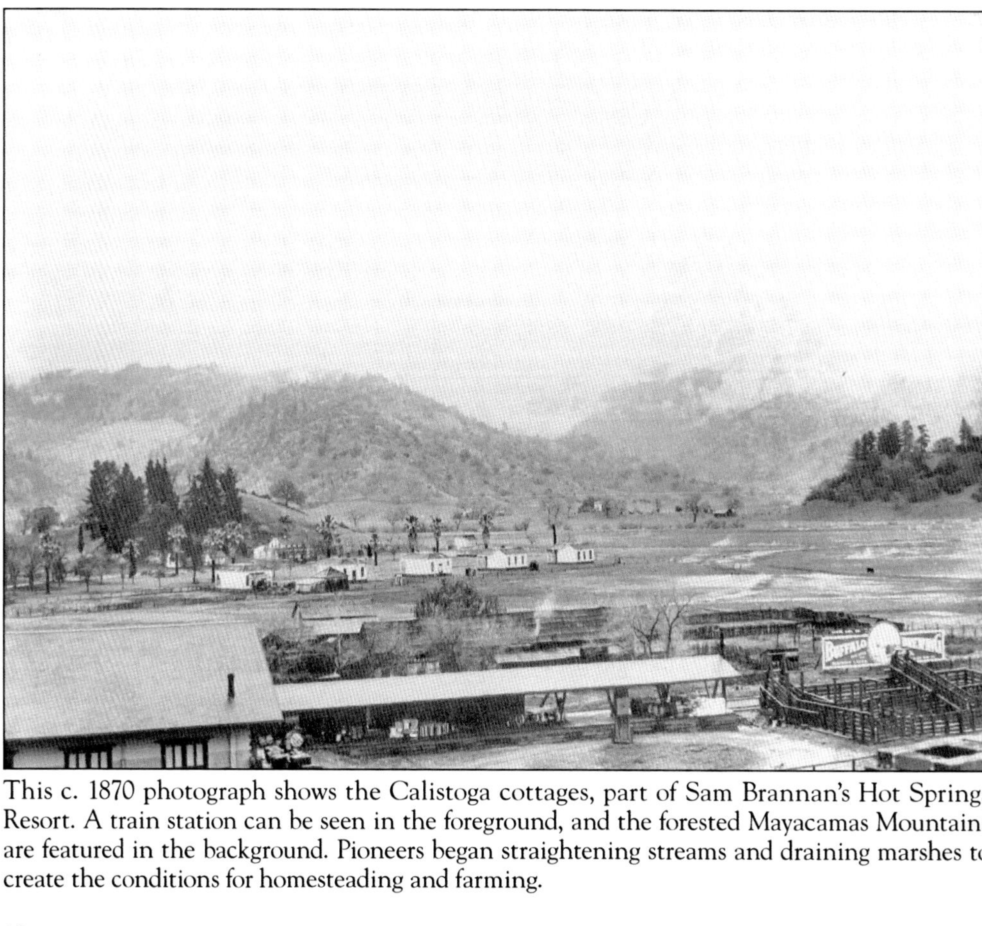

This c. 1870 photograph shows the Calistoga cottages, part of Sam Brannan's Hot Springs Resort. A train station can be seen in the foreground, and the forested Mayacamas Mountains are featured in the background. Pioneers began straightening streams and draining marshes to create the conditions for homesteading and farming.

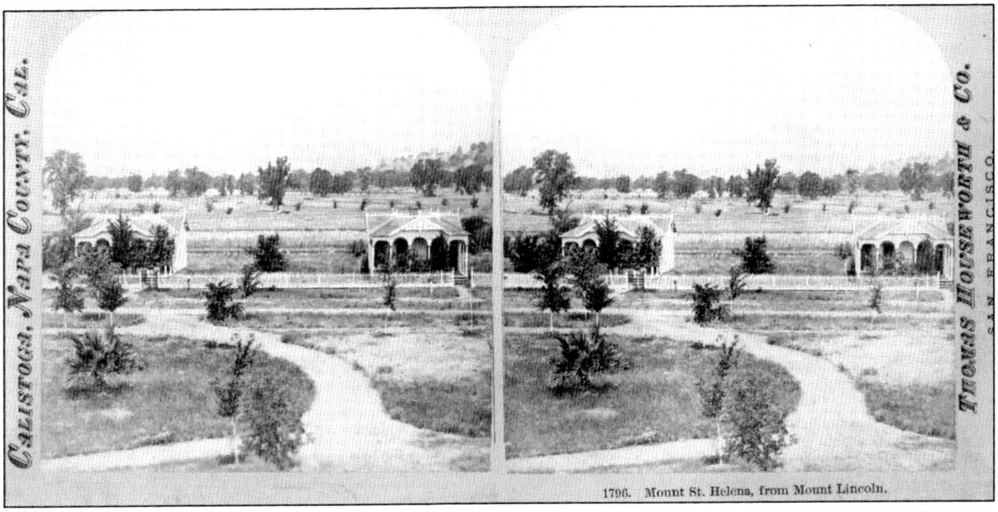

The Calistoga cottages provided a quiet setting away from bustling San Francisco. Note Mount St. Helena in the background. (Courtesy of Library of Congress.)

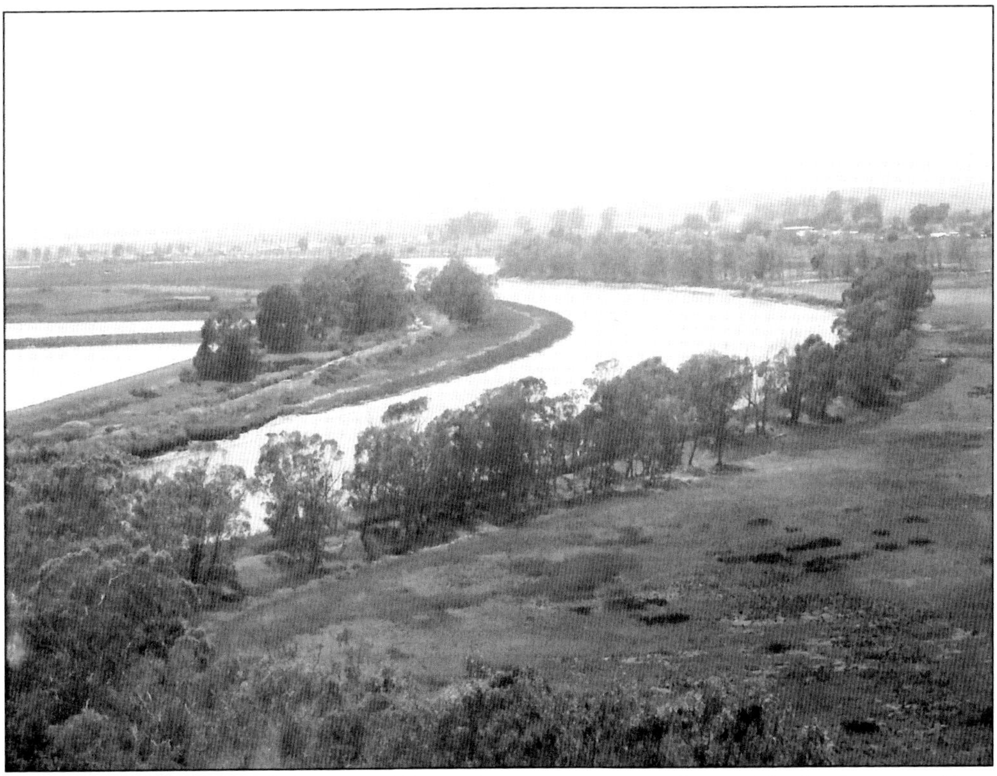

Looking northeast toward the city of Napa, the river narrows substantially. In the upper Napa Valley, it becomes a single-thread channel with a narrow adjacent riparian corridor. Due to erosion, the riverbed at some Upvalley locations is as much as 20 feet below what it was in the 1850s. (Courtesy of Bernhard Krevet, FONR.)

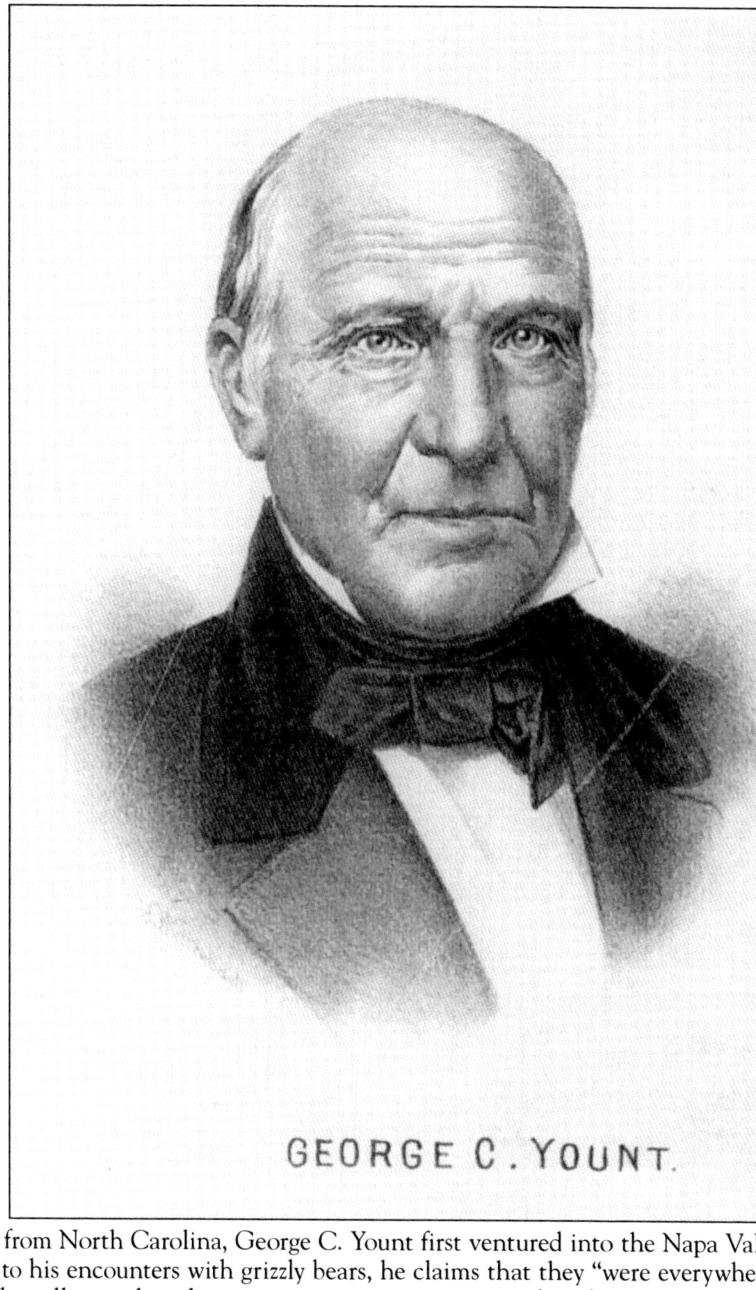

Originally from North Carolina, George C. Yount first ventured into the Napa Valley in 1831. In regards to his encounters with grizzly bears, he claims that they "were everywhere upon the plains, in the valleys and on the mountains, venturing even within the camping grounds, so that I have often killed as many as five or six in one day, and it was not unusual to see fifty or sixty within the twenty-four hours." California was a Mexican province until 1848. In 1836, Yount was given the first Mexican land grant in the valley: 11,000-acre Caymus Rancho near present-day Yountville. Later, in 1841, Julian Pope of Kentucky traveled on an expedition to the Napa Valley along with friends, including William Knight and William Gordon. Crossing the Carquinez Strait in a rowboat, they hired native people to take them up the Napa River. According to historian Lauren Coodley, they made camp at Yount's Rancho Caymus, and when they split up, each claimed a valley for his own. (Courtesy of Napa Valley Museum.)

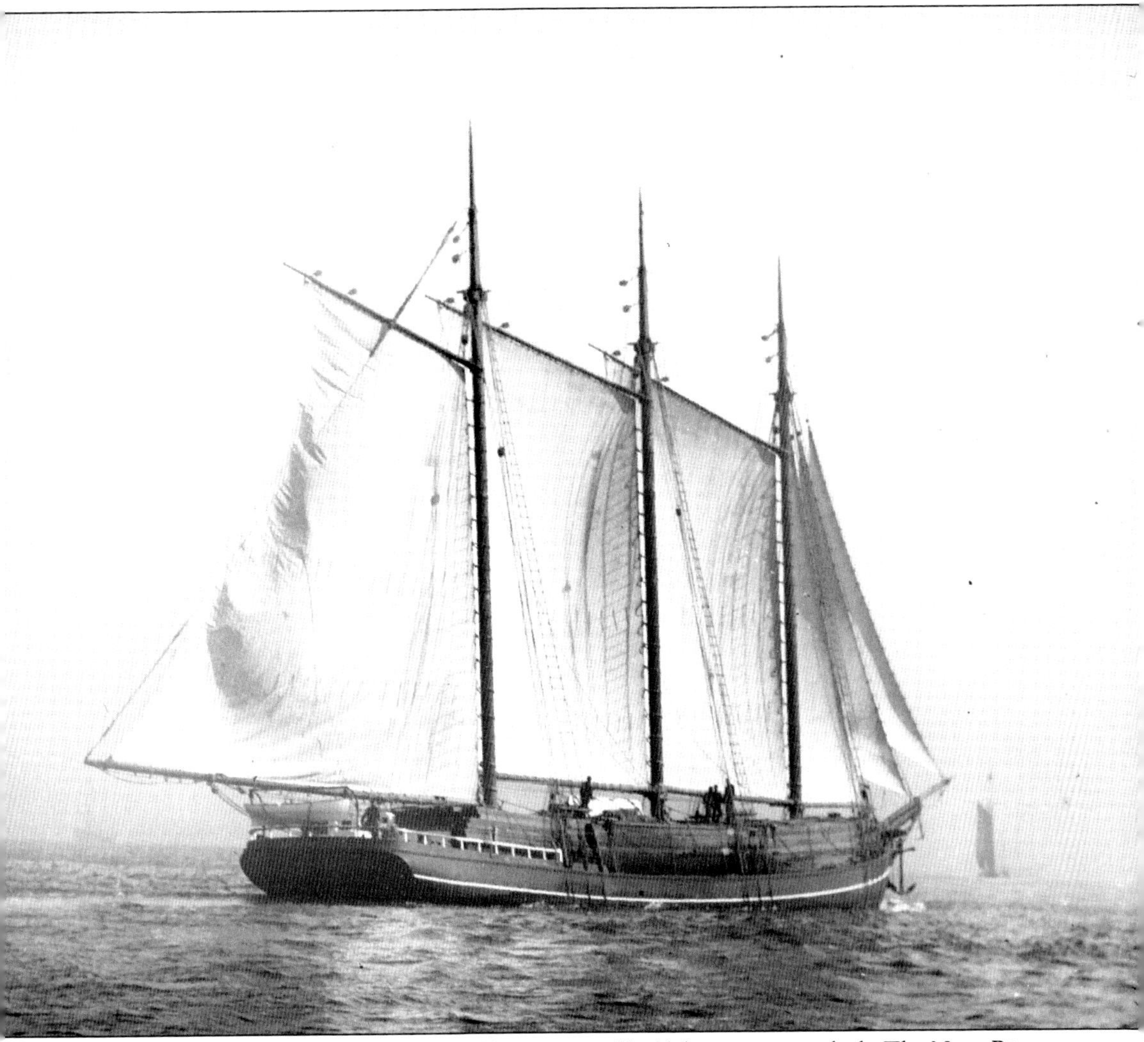

Lumber schooners like the *Sadie*, pictured here, carried half their cargo on deck. The Napa River was formally designated a navigable waterway by the state legislature on May 17, 1853. According to California law at the time, an estuary branch having a depth of only two feet at low tide but a depth at high tide of from seven to eight feet was considered navigable because it had the capacity to admit large vessels at any stage of the tide. Scow schooners were one of two types of sailing vessels found on the Napa River; they were blunt-nosed, center-board, two-masted schooners. These vessels rarely drew more than 20 to 22 inches of water, even when fully loaded. They were the true workhorses of the bay and typically carried hay, sand, coal, lumber, and other bulk goods. The second type, lumber schooners, specialized in hauling lumber, posts, and tan bark. They were typically short, wide, and of shallow draft. These features gave them excellent maneuverability. (Courtesy of San Francisco Maritime Historic Park.)

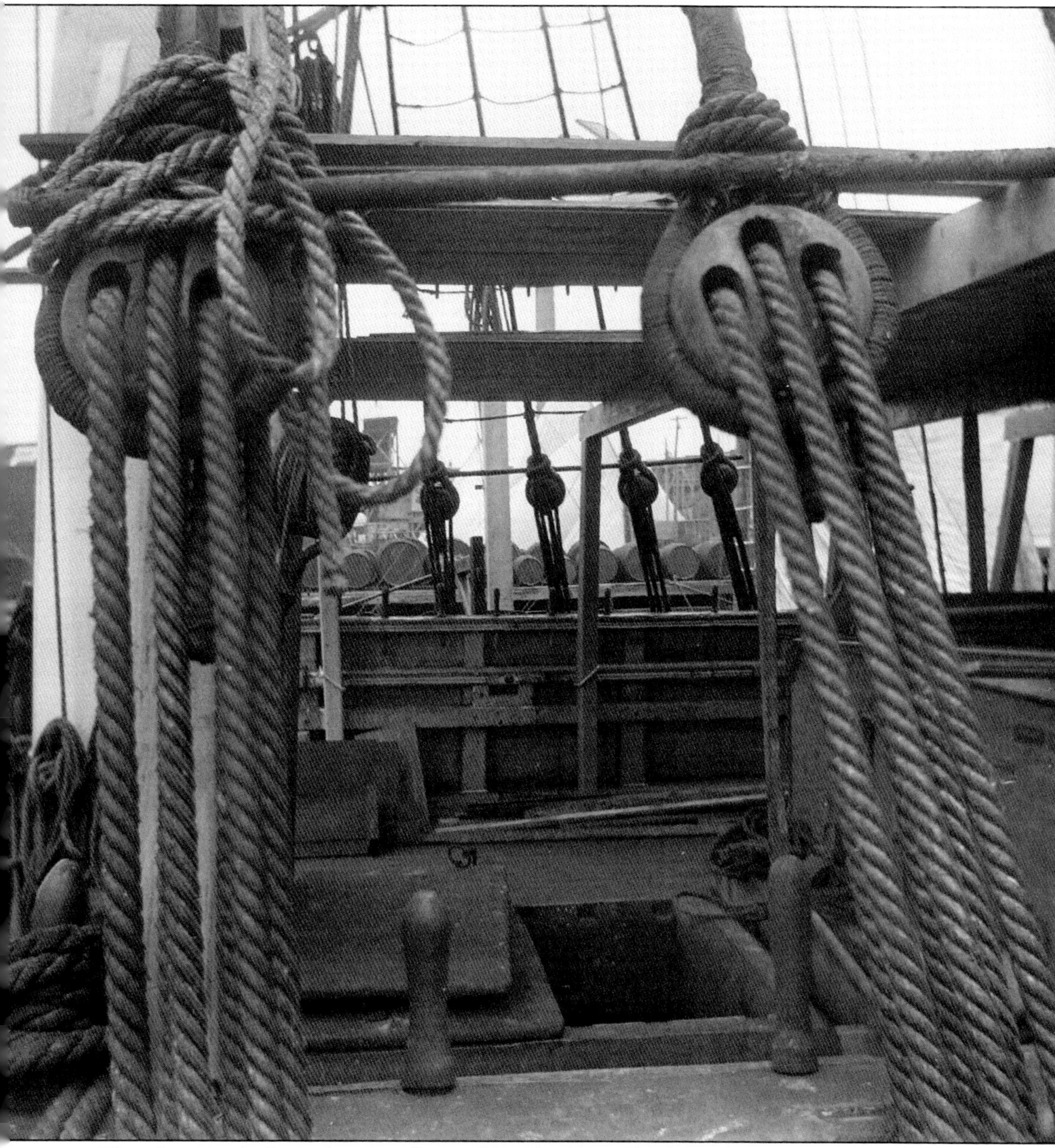

This photograph shows the ropes (lanyards) and cabling (deadeyes) used in rigging the sails of early schooners. The first record of a vessel on the Napa River is attributed to John Calvert Davis, an English ship carpenter and blacksmith who came to California in 1839. According to Bancroft's *History of California*, in November 1841, "He built in Napa Creek a schooner called the *Susana*. Davis asked the Mexican Government for permission to use the Mexican flag and sailed her up and back to Mazatlan in 1842–43." (Courtesy of New Bedford Whaling Museum.)

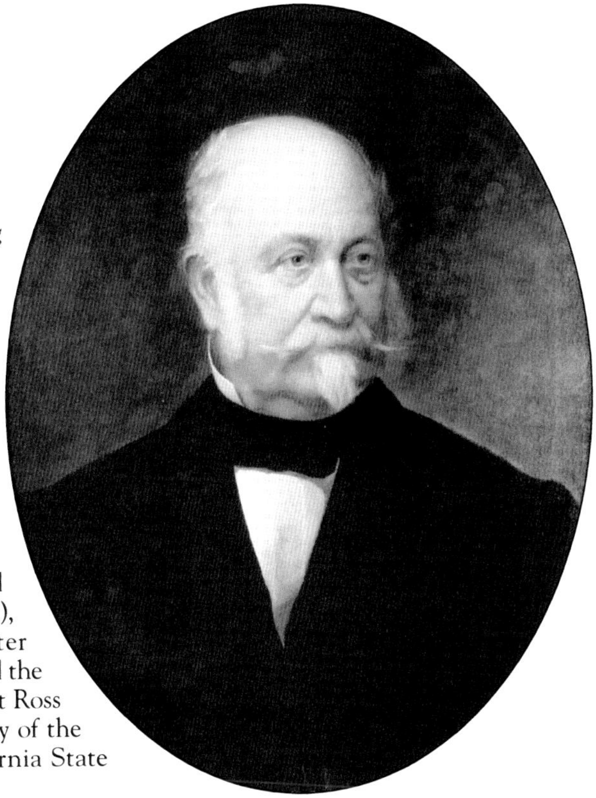

The first documented landing from another port occurred in 1844 when Gen. Johann Sutter's schooner *Sacramento* arrived from Sutter's Fort, pictured below. He had sailed up the Embarcadero de Napa, where present-day Division Street meets the river. Among the passengers Sutter carried on this journey were William Baldridge, Joseph Ballinger Chiles, Bartlett Vines and his wife Frances (who was a daughter of George Young and Elizabeth Cambridge Wilds Yount), and Yount's unmarried daughter Elizabeth Ann. Sutter had acquired the schooner with the purchase of Fort Ross from the Russians. (Both, courtesy of the California History Room, California State Library, Sacramento, California.)

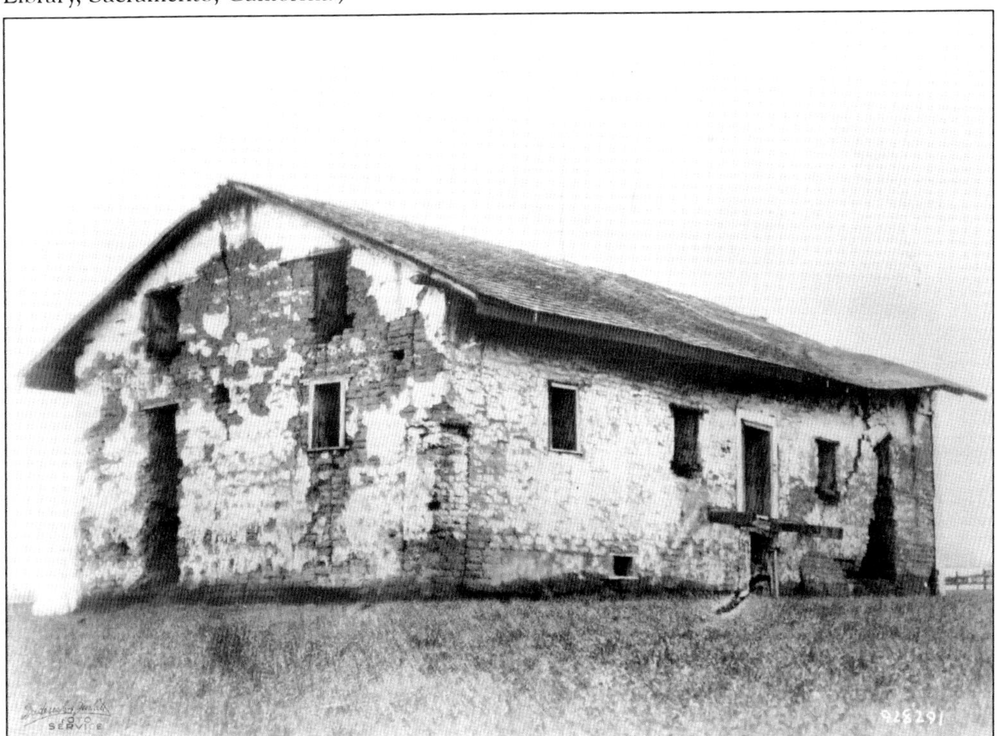

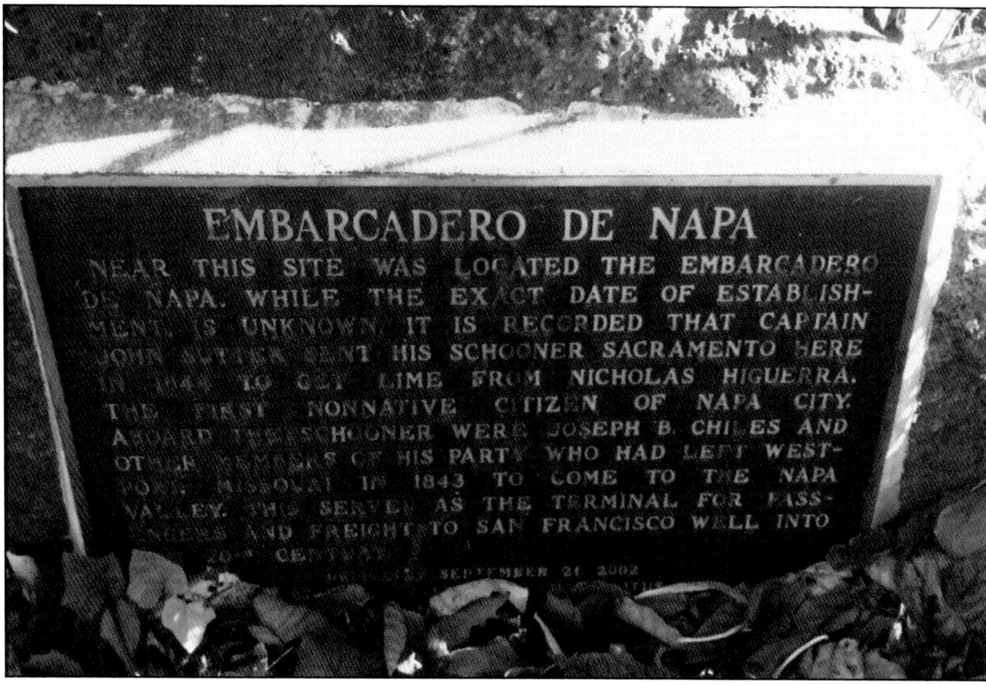

All that can be seen today of the Steamboat Wharf are marble slabs and a few pilings jutting out of the riverbank. C.A. Menefee explains that Napa first appeared in the press on February 12, 1848 in the *California Star.* James Hudspeth's map of 1848 calls it Nappa City. The ship *Malek Adhel* had passed up the Napa River to pick up lumber (redwood clapboards) from the Bale & Kilburn's mill for transhipment to Benicia and found plenty of navigable water to reach Embarcadero de Napa. This embarcadero, or landing, at the head of navigation and the ford just above it determined the eventual location of the town. It is likely that this landing was located just south of First Street. A plaque identifying the Embarcadero de Napa is located at the end of Division and Brown Streets. This terminus became a steamboat landing. (Author's collection.)

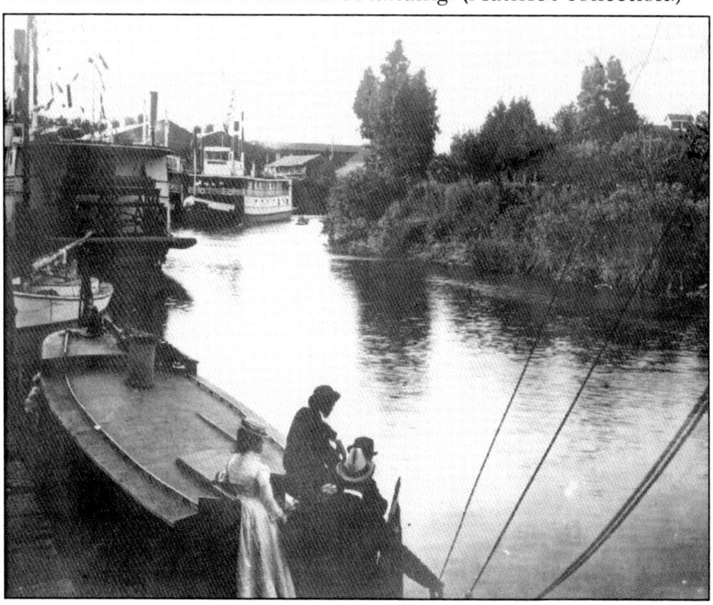

The three steamboats docked at Steamboat Landing are likely the *Zinfandel* in the foreground, with the paddle wheel visible, and the *St. Helena* and *Emma* facing forward. Capt. Nelson H. Wulff owned and ran the *Zinfandel*, and Capt. Albert Hatt owned the *St. Helena.* The smaller crafts are unidentified. Captain Hatt eventually purchased the *Zinfandel* and ran her on the river from 1907 to 1911.

Two

A City by the River
Settlers Come from Far and Wide

In 1845, Nathan Coombs chose Nappa City due to the navigation point of the river and its location as a former Native American village, likely Patwin. The new downtown was just below a ford that was passable during low tide. Previously, at high tide, men swam their horses across before the ferry was established. Since the only way to reach Napa City was by boat or horse, this proved essential to the city's location. William Russell and a partner established the first ferry service at Third Street in 1848.

Lumber was very expensive to cut and haul in the early 1840s. Like an early IKEA, buildings were often shipped already framed from Norway and the Eastern United States. It must have been quite a site to see the frames of these buildings being off-loaded from ships at Embarcadero de Napa. Imported buildings included Gregg & Seawell's store (located at the corner of Brown and First Streets), a portion of the old courthouse, the Napa Stable, and a small store for Lawrence & Kimball. Ferry traffic brought customers. All along the river, enterprising men found ways to make money. In 1851, J.B. Horrell built a toll bridge as a franchise above Vernon Mills. As early as 1852, the ferry at Suscol did big business as a franchise operated by H. Lutten. By 1857, the ferry franchise was granted to E.W. Thurber. In 1862, it was given to Valentine Hathaway, whose license was renewed by city council in 1867 and again in 1868. Napa historian Richard Dillon imagines that the Suscol ferryboat, like Napa's, was probably "a small, flat-bottomed barge or scow that was rowed, poled or towed across the river. It could even have been attached to a rope cable using the stream's current for the crossing, or even powered by a horse walking a treadmill." From these early ferryboats, more ornate and commodious vessels made their way to Napa City. Often, these beautiful white ferries resembled layer cakes as they carried passengers and freight to build a new life.

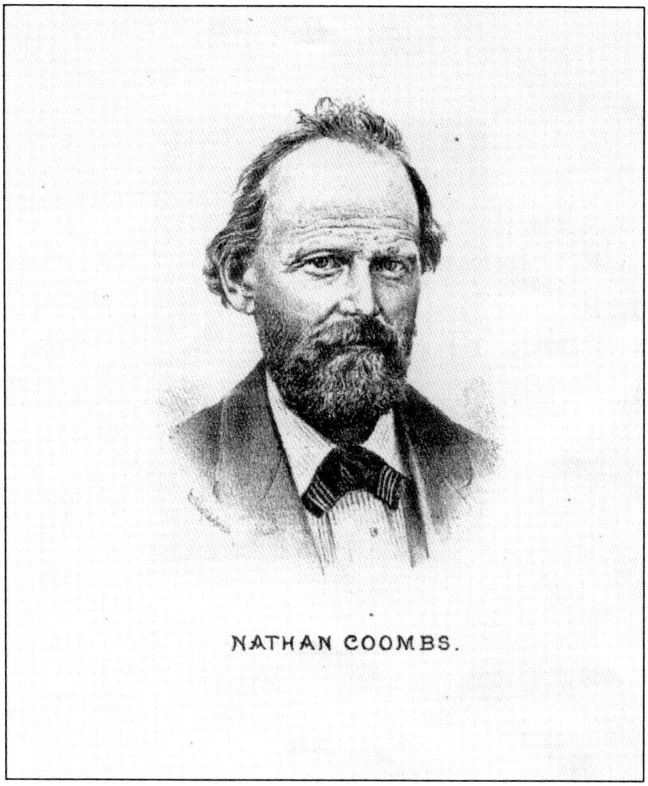

Napa City began small; it was only a few acres in size. In 1845, Nathan Coombs and Capt. John Grigsby did carpentry work for Nicholas Higuerra on his new adobe, and they received land, including the site of Napa City, as payment. Coombs bought Grigsby's portion and an additional parcel known as the Commons. (Below, courtesy of Bob Graham.)

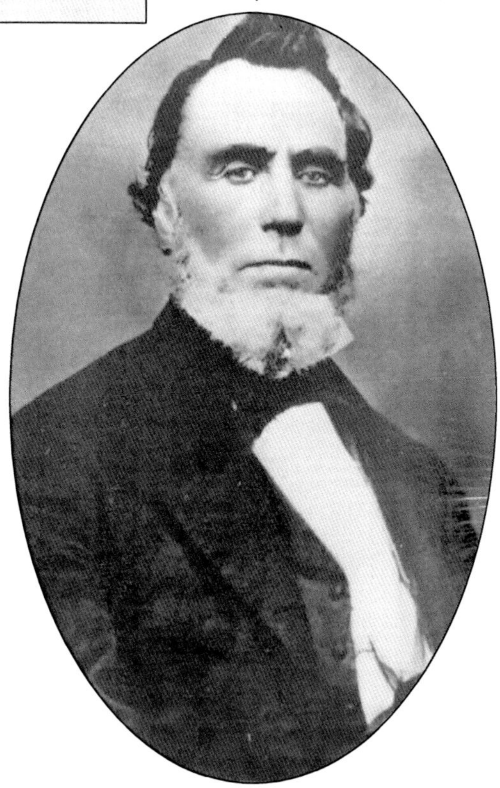

Coombs laid out the plan for the new city in the spring of 1847. It consisted of two blocks and five cross streets: First through Fifth Streets. A survey of Napa City by James Hudspeth would reveal that it was bounded to the east by the river and to the west by Brown Street. Thirty lots in all, it extended only 600 yards from the river to a steamboat landing later constructed in 1878.

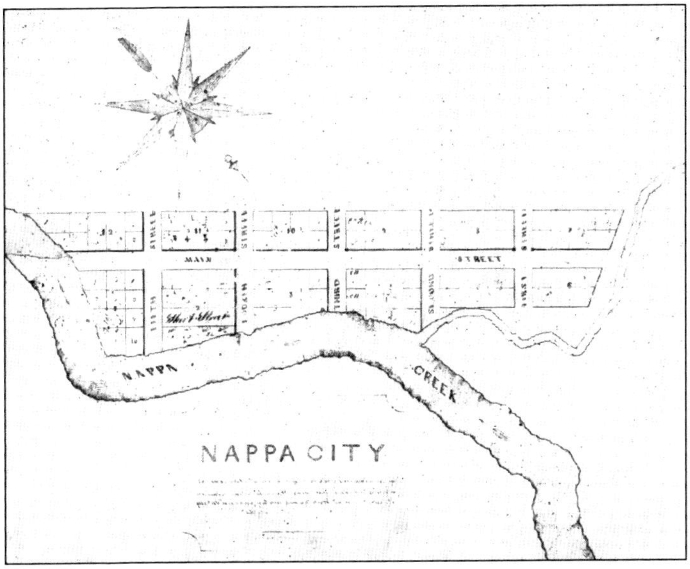

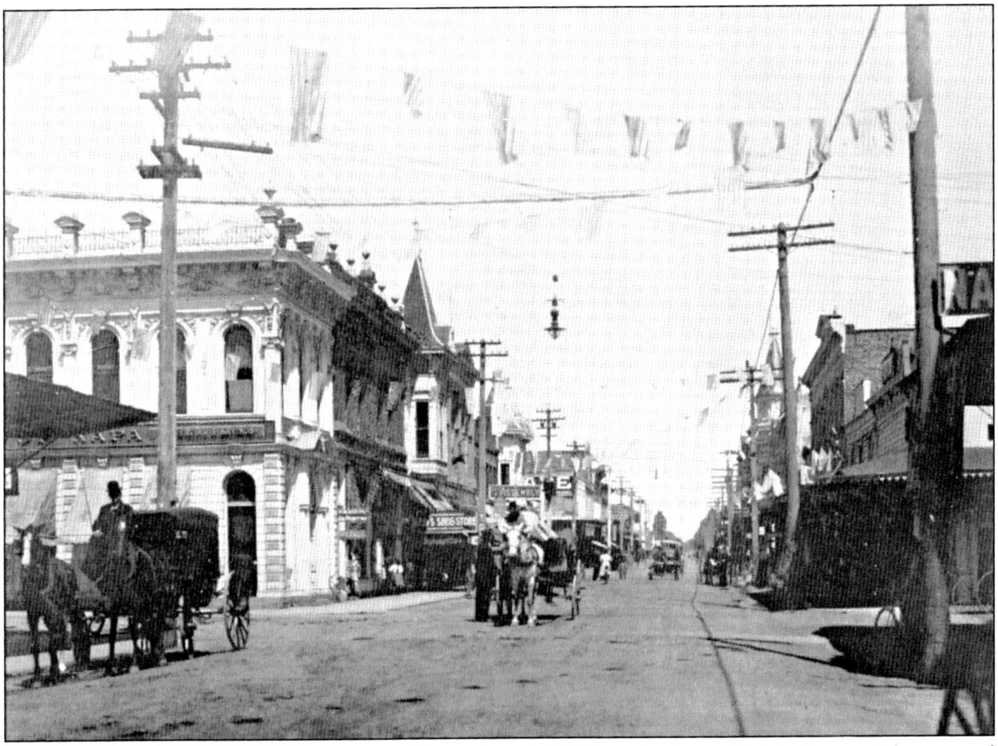

J.P. Thompson opened the first store in Napa City in 1848 at the foot of Main Street. The second store to open, located at the junction of Napa Creek and the river, was built by General Vallejo and his son-in-law Capt. John B. Frisbie; it was known as Vallejo & Frisbie's. The population of Napa City and County really took off between 1849 and 1854. Land in the agriculturally rich valley was fenced and put under cultivation by recent immigrants. The town was divided into Napa Alta (upper) and Napa Abajo (lower), and the split between the two was renamed from Union Street to Division Street. In this 1910 photograph of Main and First Streets, the downtown area is fully developed.

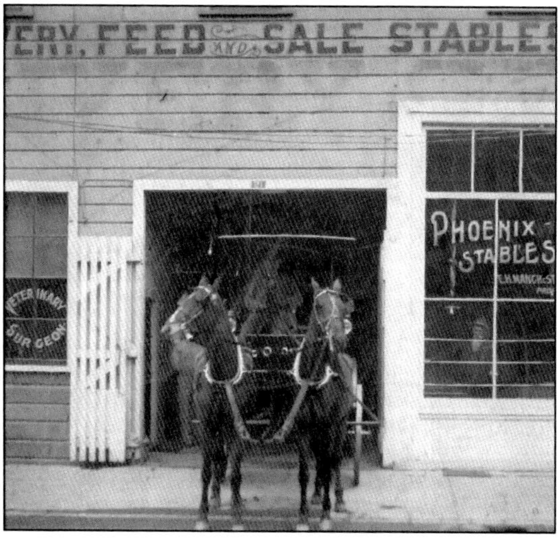

Resembling the Phoenix Stables pictured here, the wood-framed Napa Stable was one of the early imported structures. The small hamlets of Imola and Suscol emerged in South Napa. Harrison Pierce erected the first building in Napa City in 1848—a saloon. Only 18 feet by 24 feet, it was located near the river on the south side of Third Street. The lumber for the saloon was derived from land two miles above St. Helena and furnished by Ralph Kilburn, Harrison Pierce, and William H. Nash at Bale & Kilburn's mill. Kilburn had arrived in Napa Valley in 1842 and settled near Calistoga. Six years later, the price of lumber had dropped to $40 per 1,000 feet.

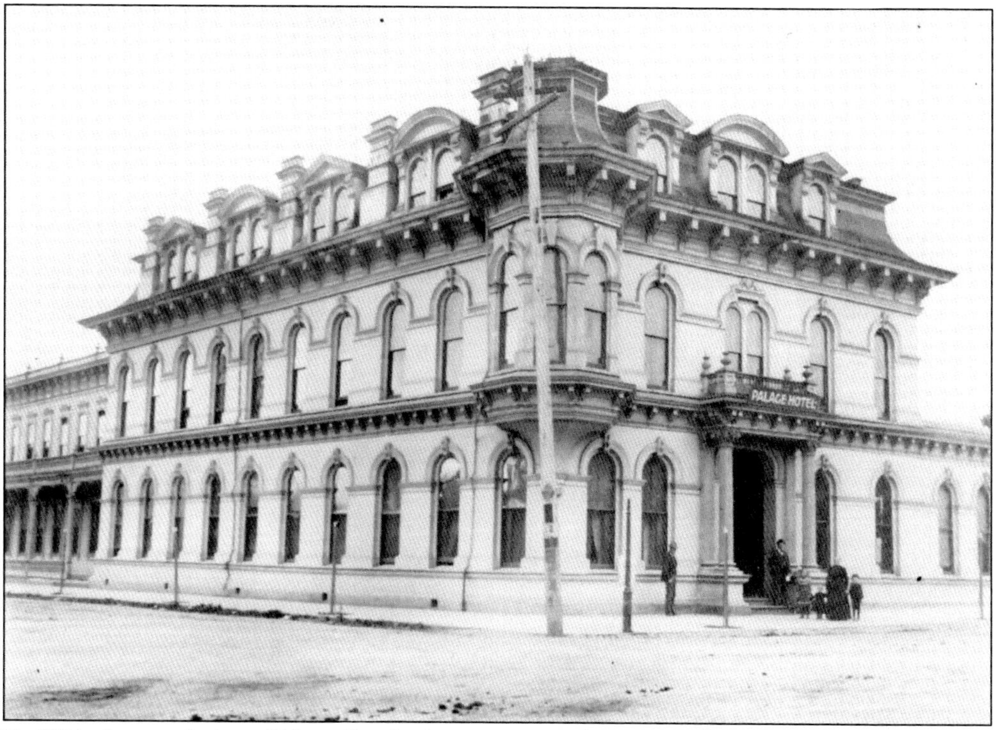

By 1854, the population of Napa City had grown to nearly 400 people and roughly 40 buildings, many of them primitive and temporary. It was not until 10 years later that the first bank, established by J.H. Goodman & Company, would serve the community and help fund further business and industry. According to Harry Gunn, as small as the place was, Napa was one of the business centers in the state; vast quantities of goods were sold at high prices. As visitors came to Napa, hotels like the Palace Hotel, shown here, were built. Restaurants and lodging houses opened in close proximity to saloons. A blacksmith shop sat on First Street near the corner of Main Street, and a butcher shop with a restaurant below it once occupied the corner where Wells Fargo Bank is located today.

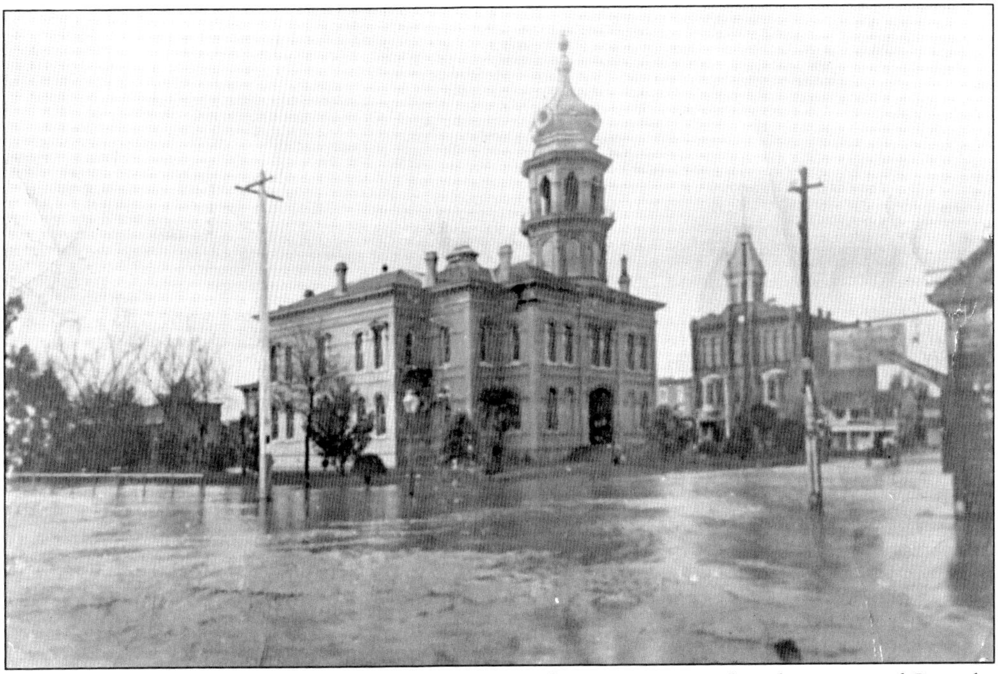

With the organization of the county in 1851, a courthouse was erected at the corner of Coombs and Second Streets. This photograph was likely taken during the flood of 1890.

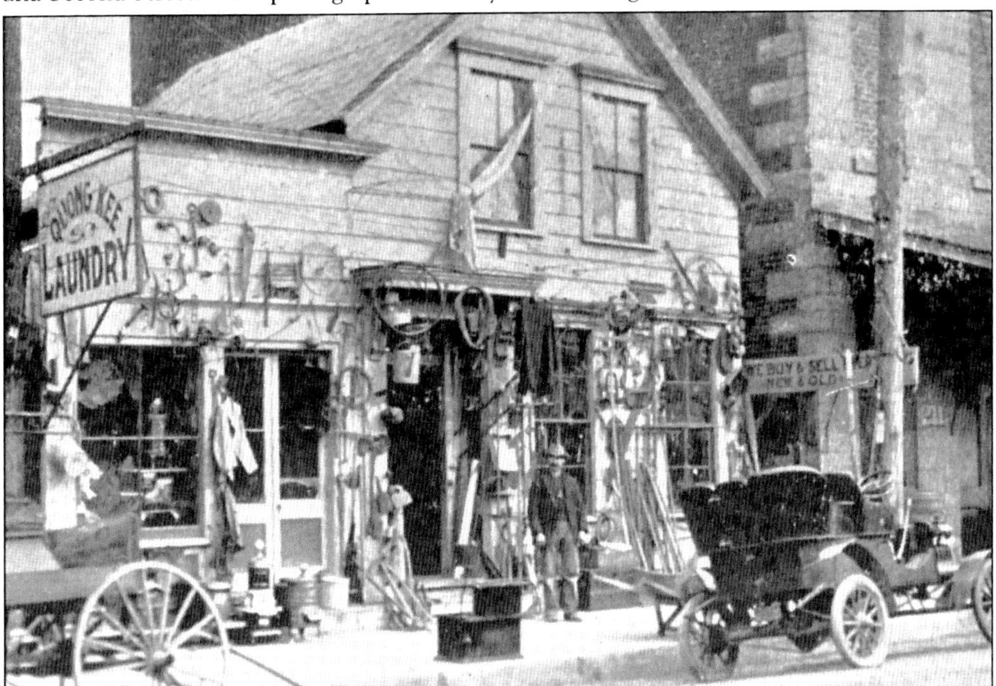

Chinese workers came to Napa after the Gold Rush to work in factories and construct levees on the river. Many opened businesses like the Quangkee Laundry in Napa's Chinatown. Their large numbers survive in only a few places such as in the Pfeiffer Building, located at 1245 Main Street. It was the Sam Key Laundry during Prohibition and remained so for over 40 years.

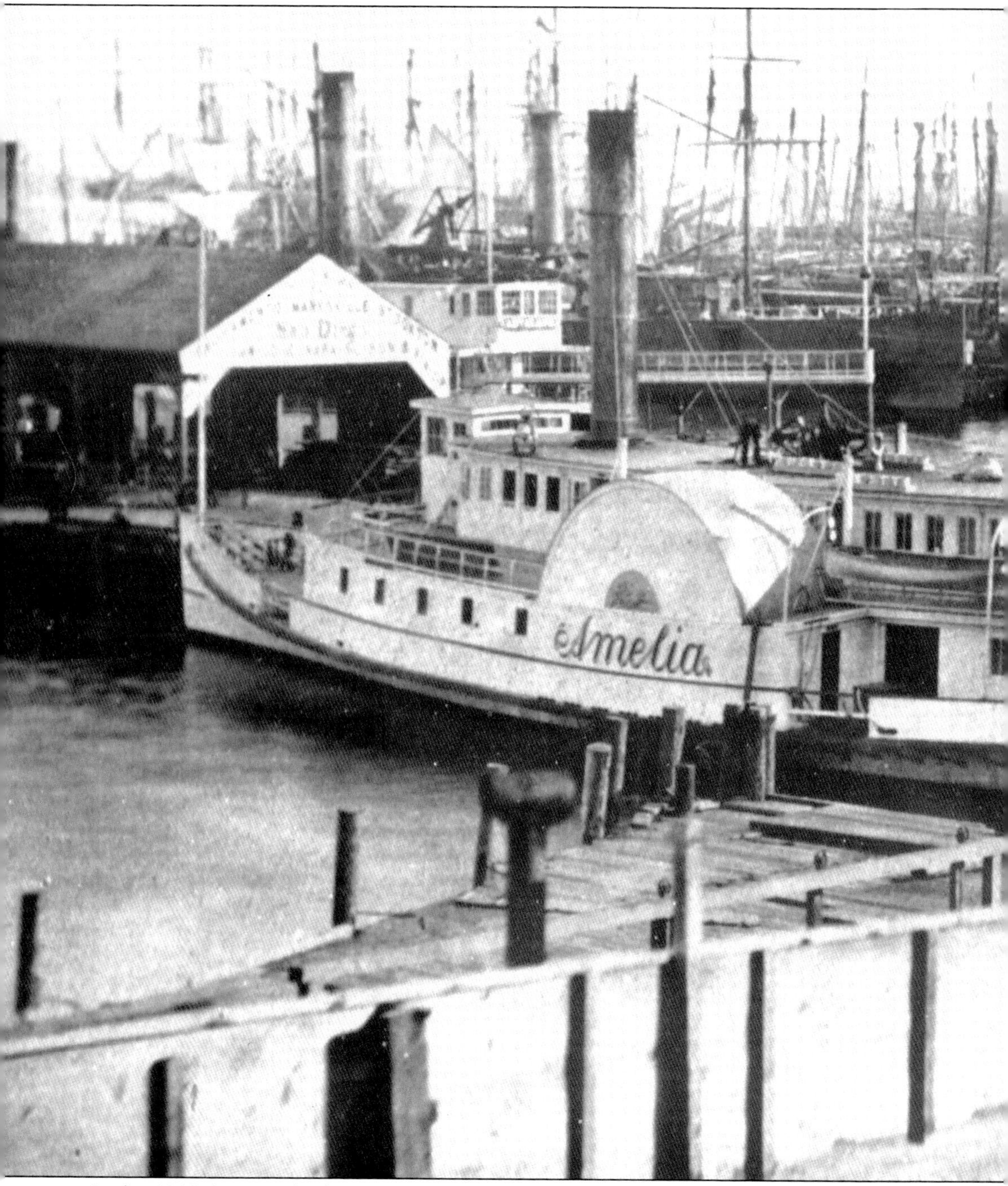

In this 1866 photograph, three Napa riverboats are docked at the Broadway Street Wharf in San Francisco. Behind the *Amelia* are the *Antelope* (left) and the *Paul Pry*. In addition to schooners and scow schooners, one could also find steam packets on the San Francisco Bay and Napa River. A packet is defined as a boat, usually a coastal or river steamer, that plies a regular route and carries passengers, freight, and mail. Side-wheelers were vessels with their paddle wheel on the side, and in contrast, Stern-wheelers had their paddle at the rear or stern. All of these vessels were integral to Napa City's growth and development. Steamers, side-wheelers, and stern-wheelers

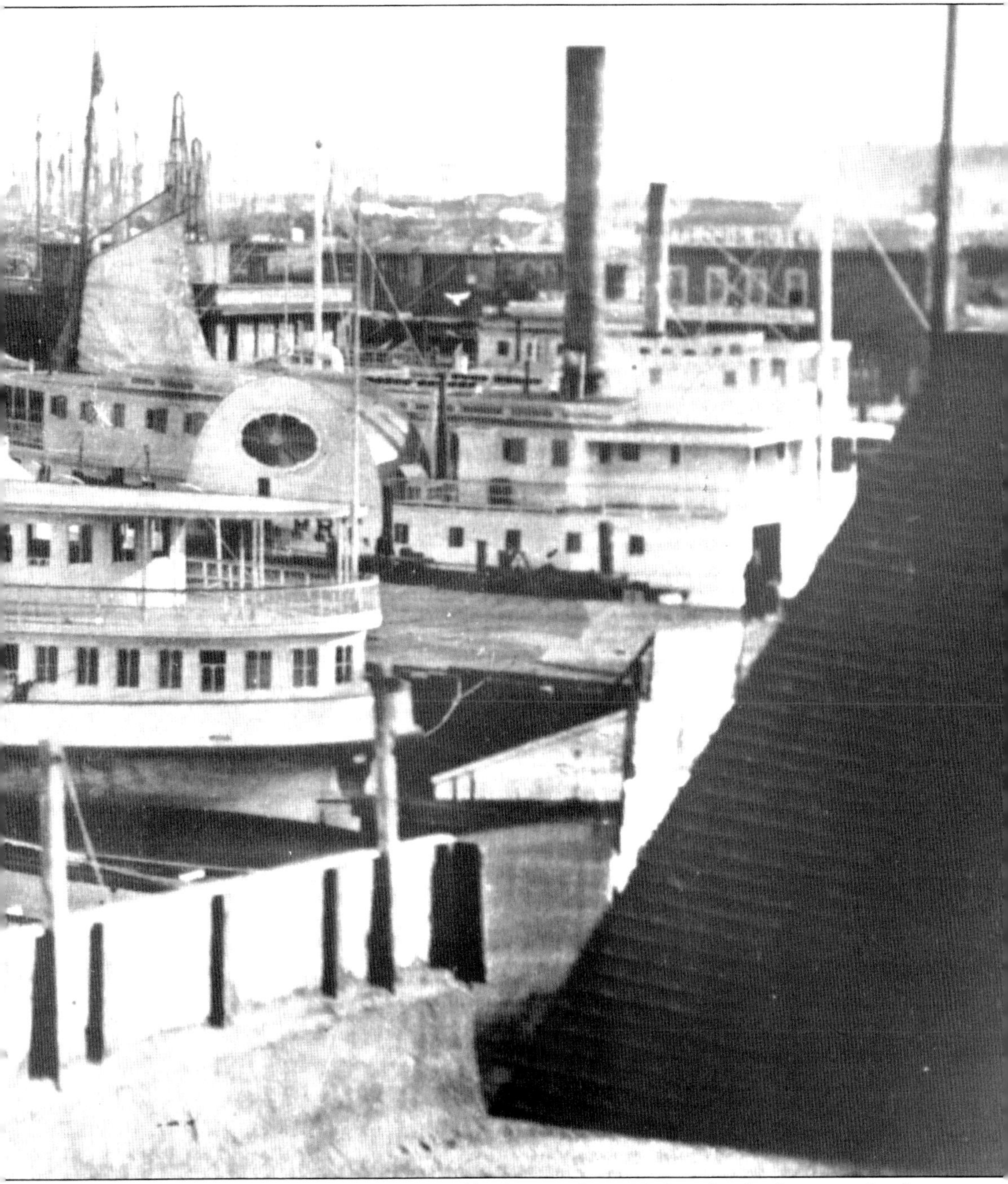

hauled freight from Napa to San Francisco and back again. By 1865, the side-wheel steamer *Amelia* traveled between Napa and San Francisco. She was 147 feet long, weighed 386 tons, and was built by Harry Owens at Potrero Point in San Francisco for Captains Curry and Jones in 1863. According to Charles Loring's article "Early Steam Navigation on the Napa River," she was the largest and most commodious steamer ever to ply the waters of the Napa River regularly. She was larger than either the *Zinfandel* or the *St. Helena*, the prides of the Napa River during a later era. (Courtesy of the San Francisco Maritime, NHP.)

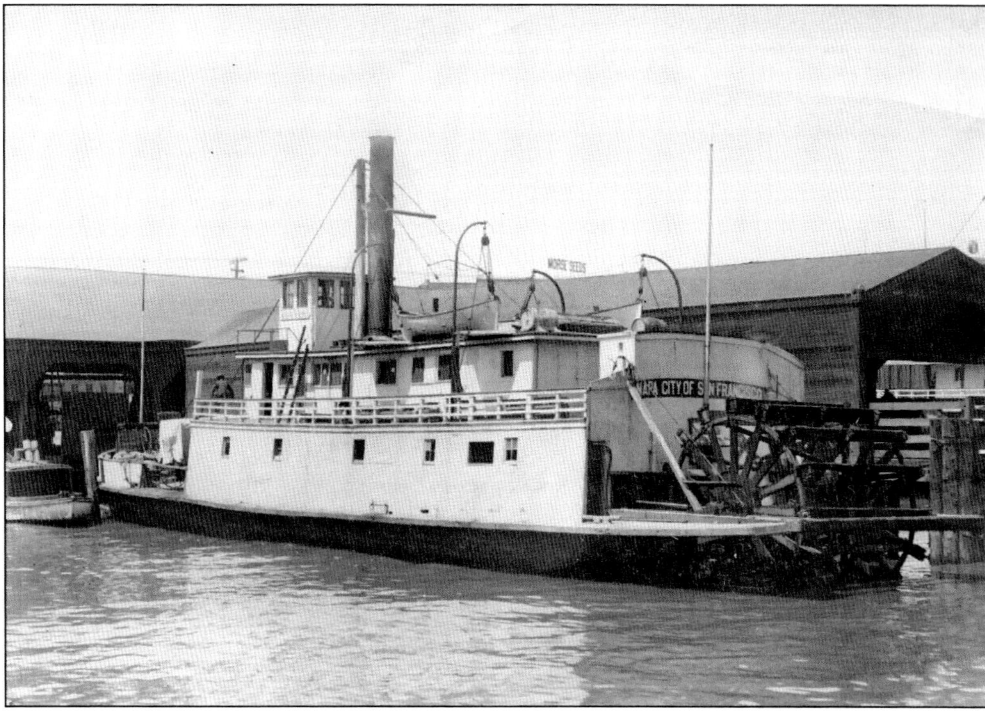

Because they were better able to navigate the twists and turns of the river, side-wheelers were preferred for their maneuverability. Vessels with too large a draft had to put in at Suscol Wharf to the south of Napa City. The *Napa City*, built in 1891, was a stern-wheeler occasionally challenged by the river's course. (Courtesy of the San Francisco Maritime, NHP.)

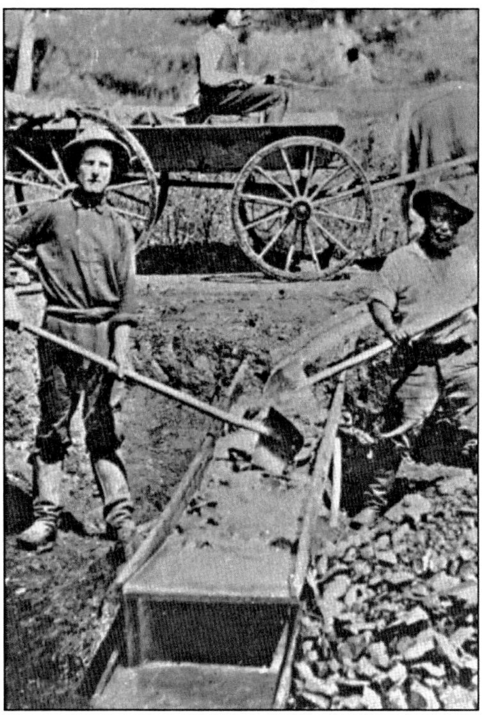

Gold was discovered in Coloma on January 24, 1848. By May 1849, many had left Napa for the newly discovered gold fields in the Sierra Foothills. Napa became a favorite resort for miners as they sought refuge from severe winter storms. Newly panned gold was the currency, and gold scales stood on every counter. Gambling, drinking, and hourly fights were the order of the day. A tent city comprised of itinerant miners arose along Main Street in late 1850. According to Janice Marschner in *California 1850*, many miners found work in sawmills and on cattle ranches throughout the valley. (Courtesy of Highway49.com.)

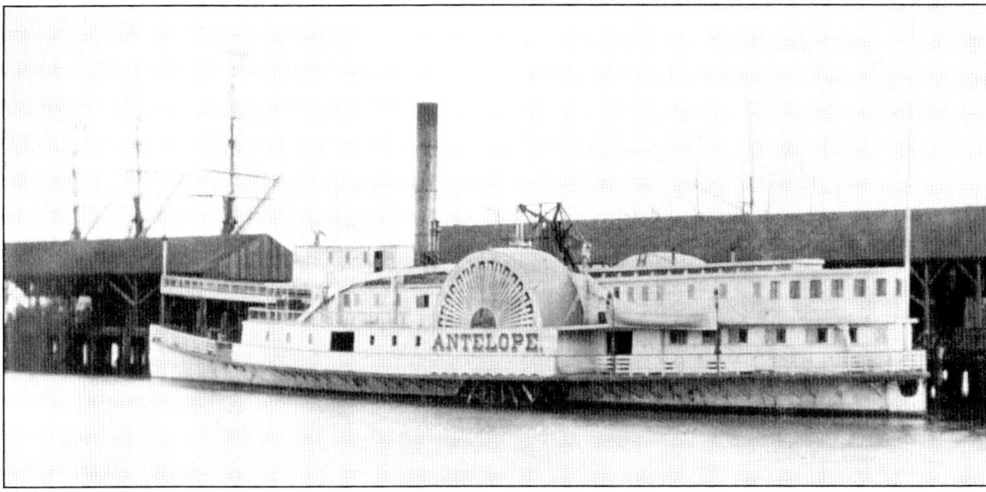

The *Antelope* was one of the most famous steamers of the time. In 1860, she ferried the first Pony Express rider and his horse from Sacramento to San Francisco, carrying gold bullion down the Sacramento River to San Francisco. When put into service in Napa City, the *Antelope* was renovated and given a fancy upper compartment for passengers. (Courtesy of the Society of California Pioneers.)

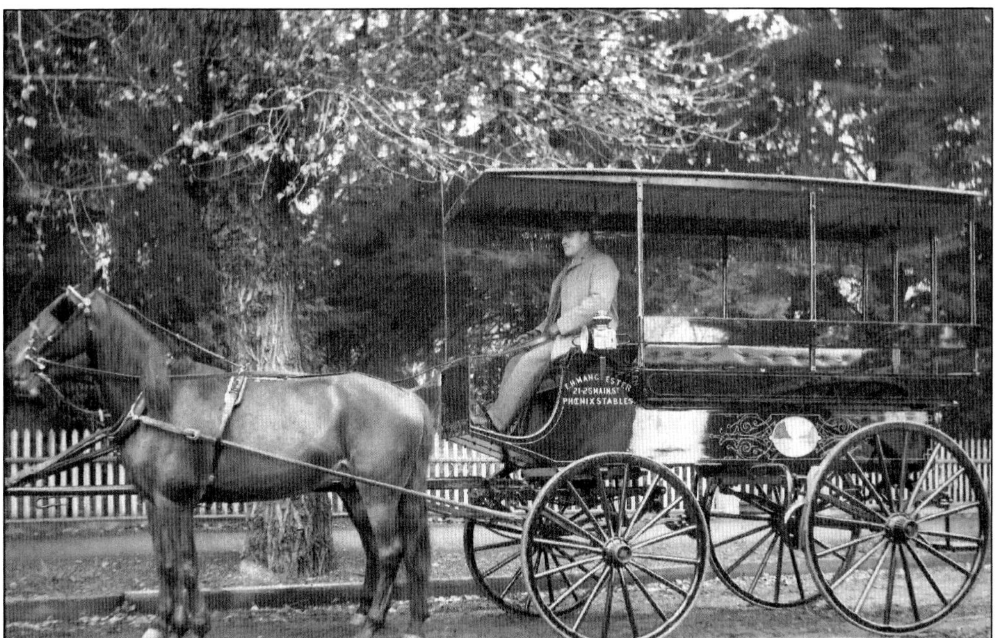

The first advertisement regarding a regular steamboat line between San Francisco and Napa City appeared in the *Daily Alta California*, a San Francisco newspaper, on April 20, 1852. The steamer *Jack Hayes* left Central Wharf in San Francisco on Tuesdays and Saturdays at 9:00 a.m. for Napa City, with stops at Vallejo and Suscol. Daily passenger service from Napa was not available as late as 1859, making a trip to San Francisco agonizingly long. If traveling on an off day, travelers had to hire a horse-drawn buggy to Benicia, cross Carquinez Strait, and catch a train to Oakland to make the last ferryboat to San Francisco. The Napa ferry schedule typically involved ships going downriver every other day and returning on alternate days.

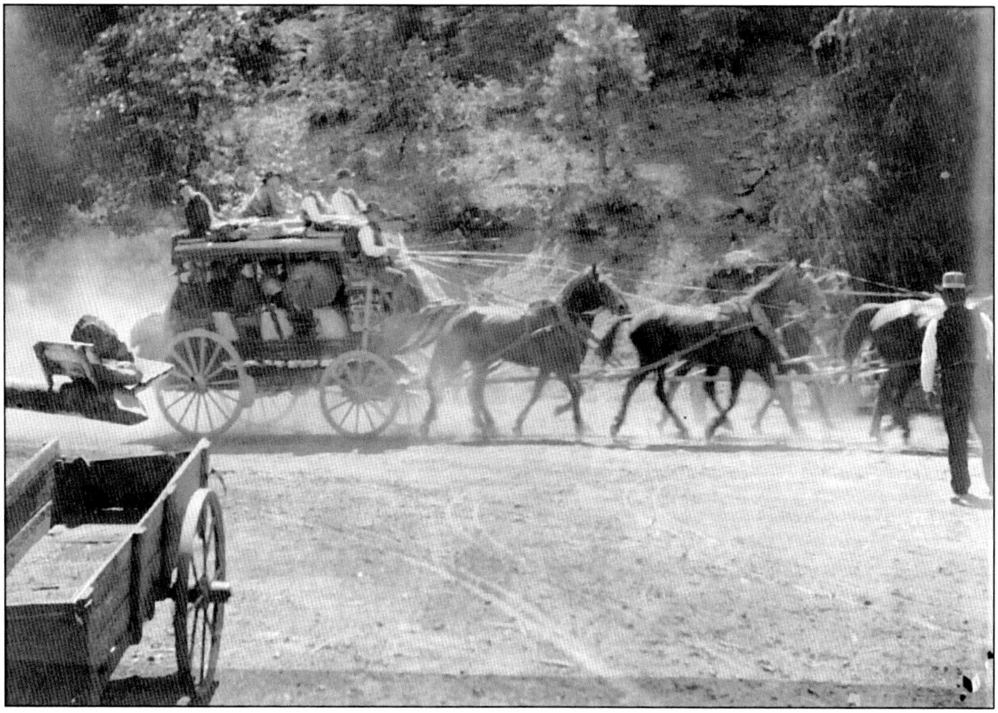

This trip from Napa City to Calistoga in 1864 was by stagecoach. It could be a dusty journey, as evidenced by the umbrella used by a female passenger. Sam Brannan and Nathan Coombs owned and ran a 24-passenger coach. Coombs also had a stagecoach line between Napa City and Vallejo. (Courtesy of Napa Valley Museum.)

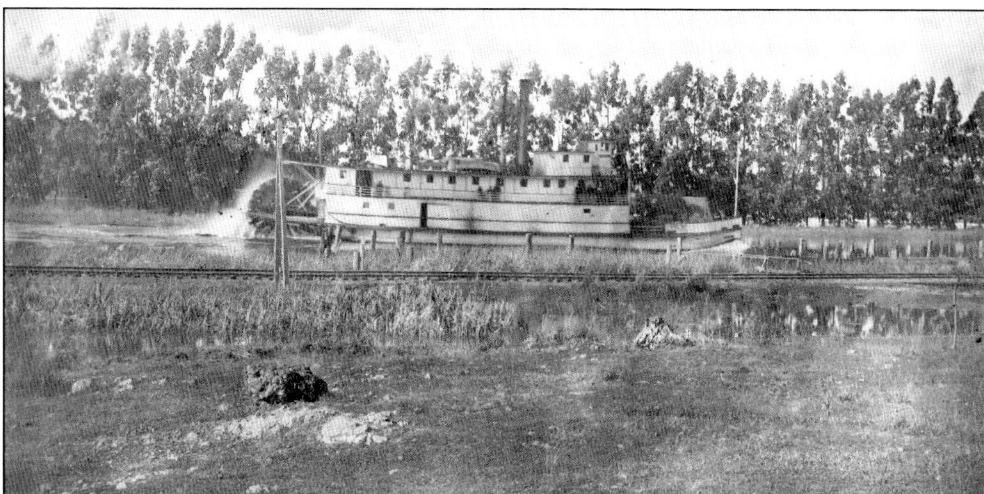

Suscol was the site of a river ford and served as a ferry, schooner, and steamer debarkation point. Suscol was also a site that Gen. Mariano Vallejo suggested to Nathan Coombs for a possible city on the river because larger vessels could more easily turn around there. In this image, the *Zinfandel* is on its way to Suscol Wharf. While probably just a dock on the muddy riverbank, the old ferry landing was originally built to serve Petaluma–Sacramento stages. While Steamboat Wharf was one of the main wharfs in Napa City serving the western side of the river community, a wharf in the small hamlet of Suscol served businesses and settlers to the southeast.

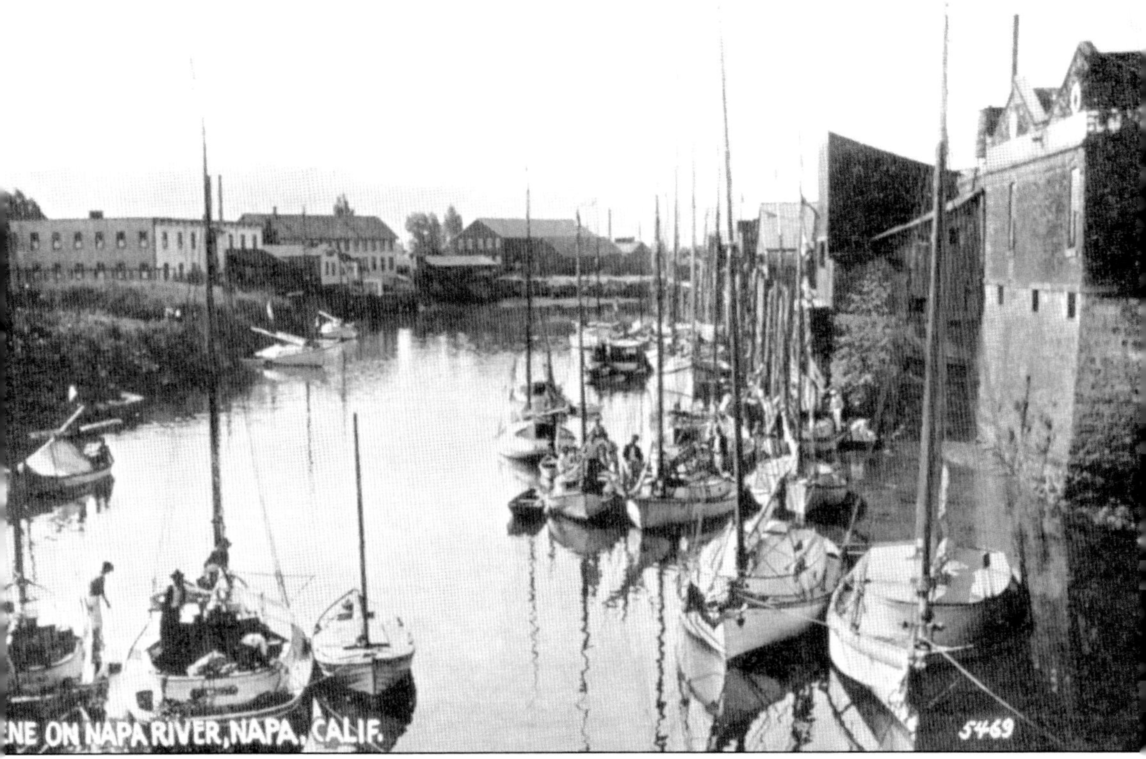

In this early-1900s photograph, sailing vessels crowd the waters near Steamboat Wharf; Uncle Sam's Winery is situated on the right. In May 1858, Thomas H. Thompson had secured a franchise for 20 years to construct a wharf at Suscol on the east side of the river, beginning at the ferry dock and extending southward 500 feet. Thompson, along with his brother Simpson Thompson, held sway in the community because of his connection to ranching, farming, and horticulture in the Suscol area. Wharfs were lucrative businesses, and the rights to collect rates for incoming cargo had to be agreed to by the board of supervisors. Historian Jack R. Greig cites the *Napa County Reporter* of August 15, 1862, to illustrate the rates for Boone Fly's new wharf, located in the Carneros District on the west side, south of Suscol: steamboats, $1 per landing; sailing vessels, 50¢ per hour; fruit and produce of all kinds, 25¢ per load; live cattle, mules, horses, etc., 5¢ each; grain, 20¢ per load; hay, 50¢ per ton; posts, $3 per 1,000; and lumber, 25¢ per load.

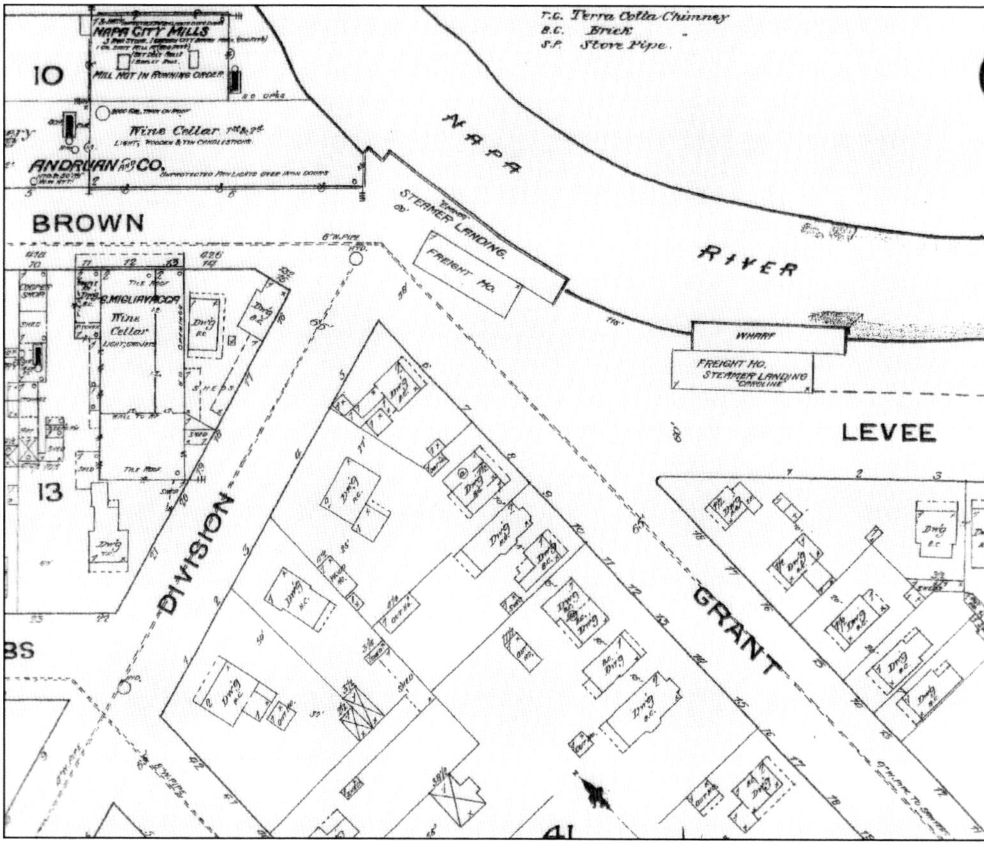

This 1885 map shows Levee Street (now Riverside Street) and Grant Street (now Brown Street) with the steamboat landing for the steamship *Emma* clearly identified, as is the steamship landing for the vessel *Caroline*. Eventually, seven wharfs would occupy the banks of the Napa River: Bennet's Wharf, Boreo's Wharf, Fly's Wharf, Suscol Wharf, Stanley's Wharf, Steamboat Wharf, and Zinfandel's Wharf.

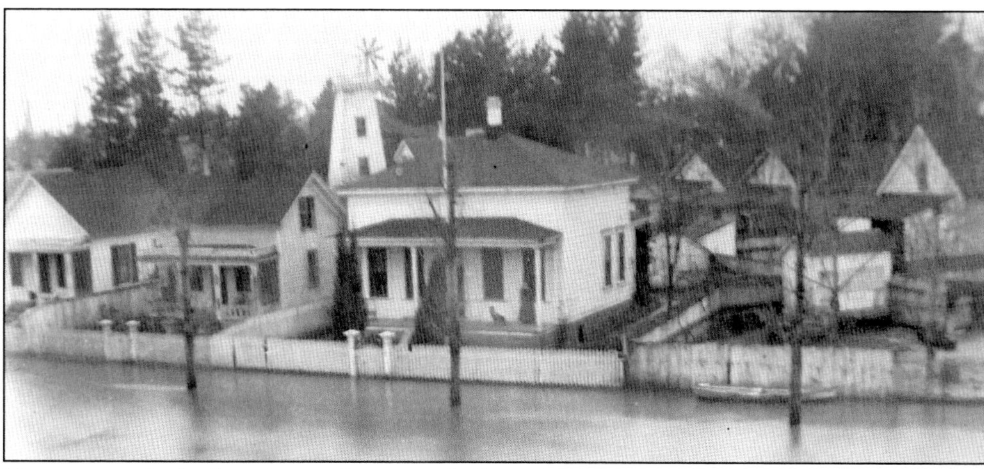

Houses were built along Levee Street with the main living quarters on the second floor to protect residents from flooding, as demonstrated in this 1890s photograph. (Courtesy of Napa Valley Museum.)

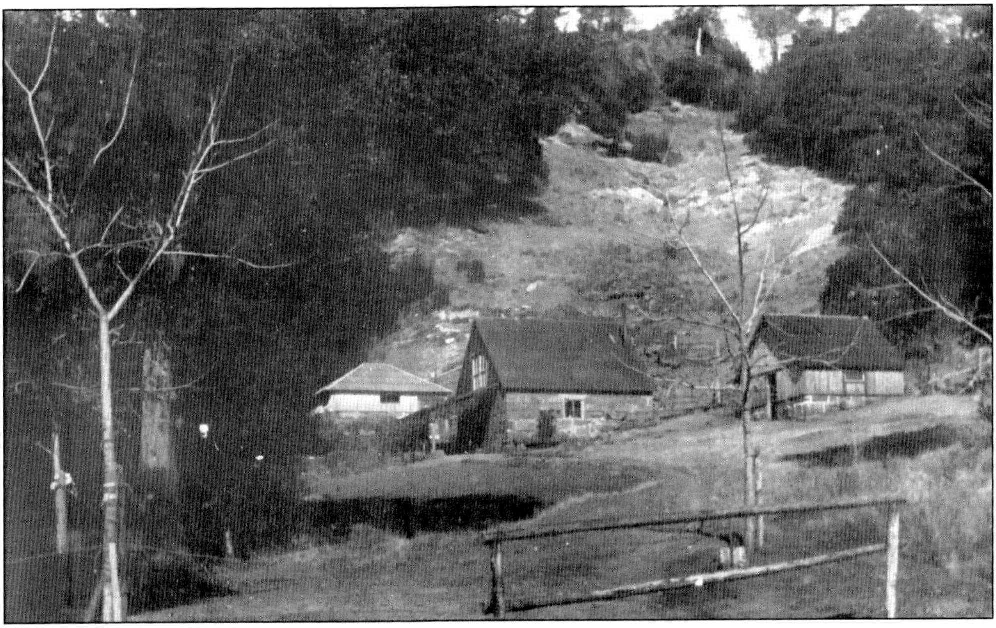

Karl Gustov Holm, a Finnish settler in the late 1890s, created a homestead located near the top of Oat Hill Mine Trail, shown here in the center. Foundations of the buildings remain at the location where the Oat Hill Mine and Palisades trails meet, high above Calistoga. During the Gold Rush, Napa's Oat Hill Mine was one of the leading producers of the ore cinnabar. When processed, cinnabar produces quicksilver, more commonly known as mercury. In addition to gold mining, mercury mining brought people to the Napa Valley.

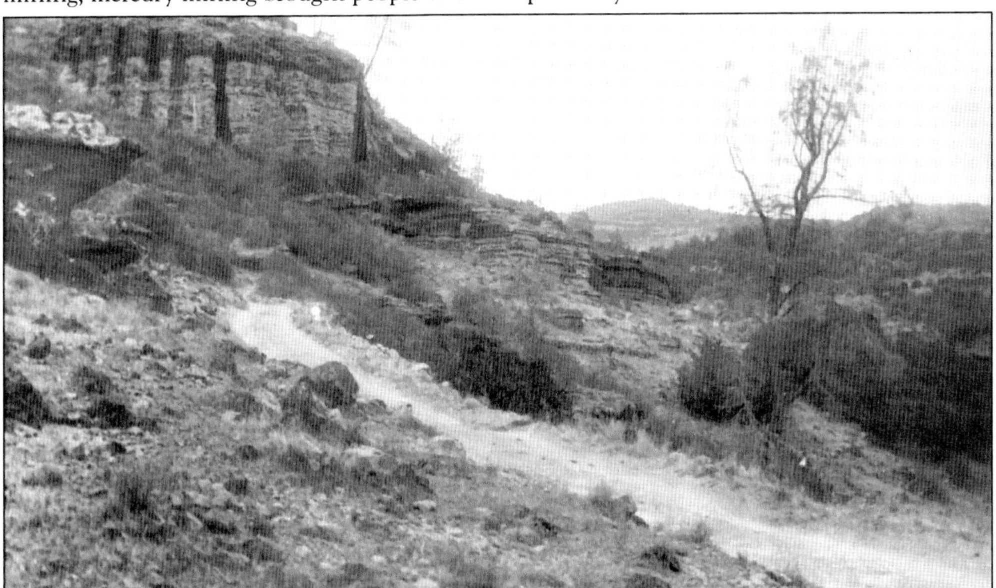

Mining in the Palisades occurred in 1858, with the peak years being in the 1860s and 1870s. The most famous silver mine was Silverado on the southeastern slope of Mount St. Helena. It was here that Robert Louis Stevenson brought his bride for their honeymoon in 1880. The Silverado trail began from Napa City and extended along the eastern side of the valley to the mines above Calistoga.

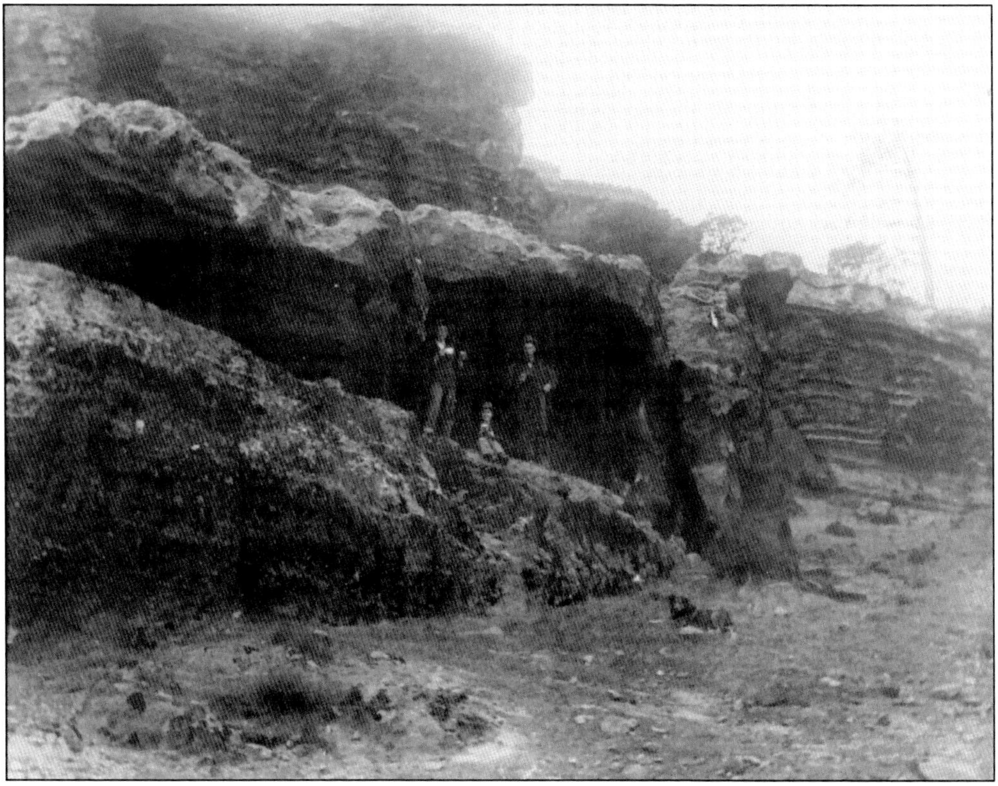

Two men and a boy enjoy a bit of shade on their walk in the Palisades.

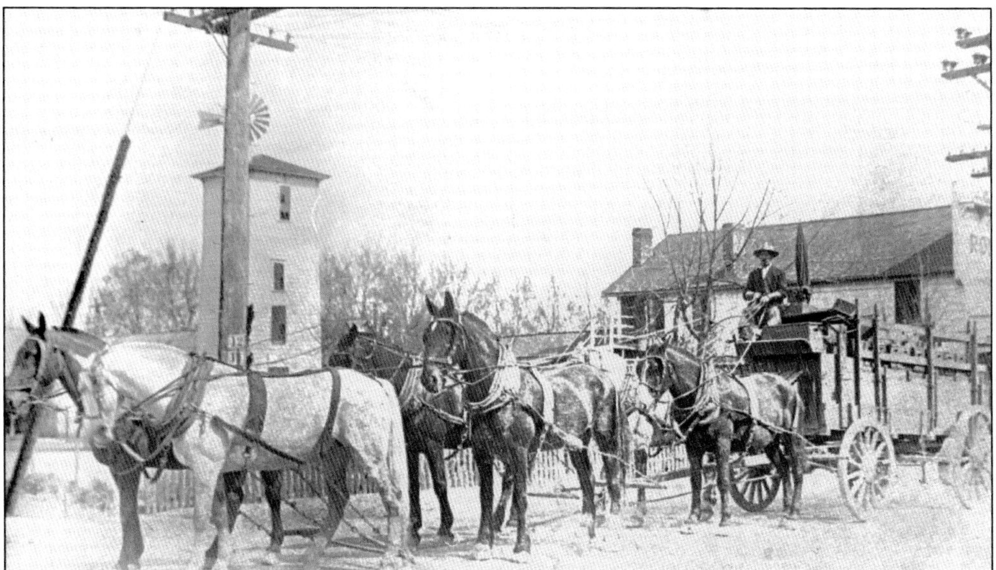

Wagons, like this one in Calistoga, were used to transport supplies to the miners.

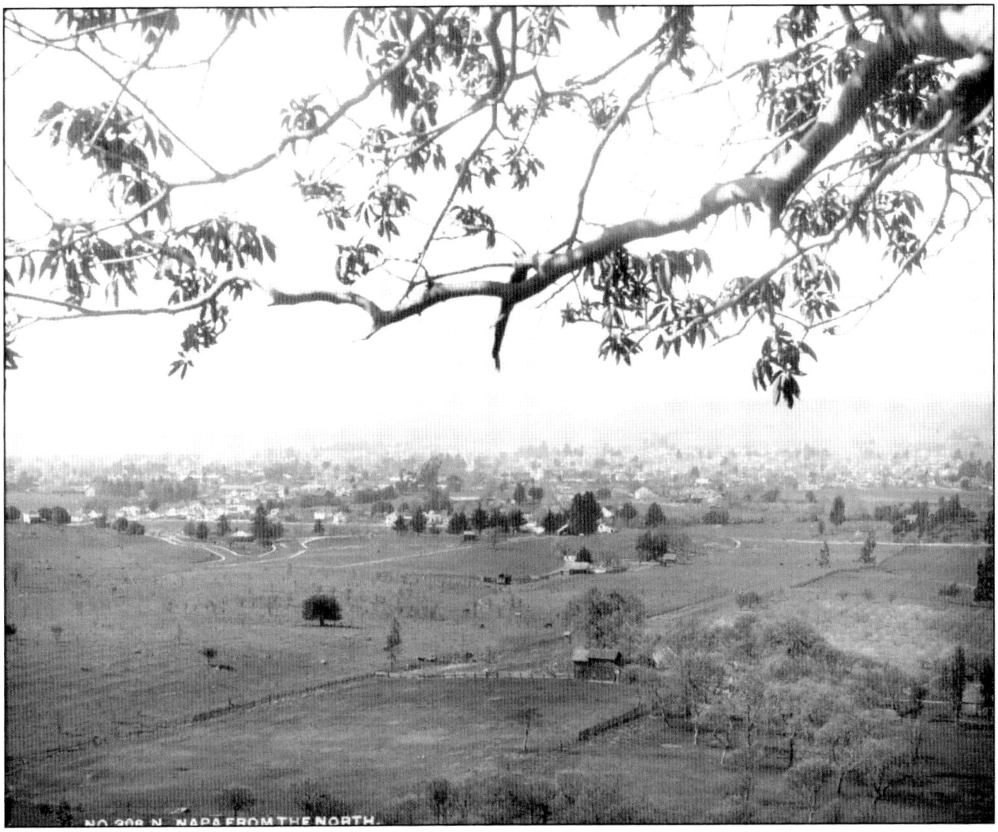

Napa was an ideal getaway for city dwellers in the 1870s. The country air and beauty drew visitors from far and wide.

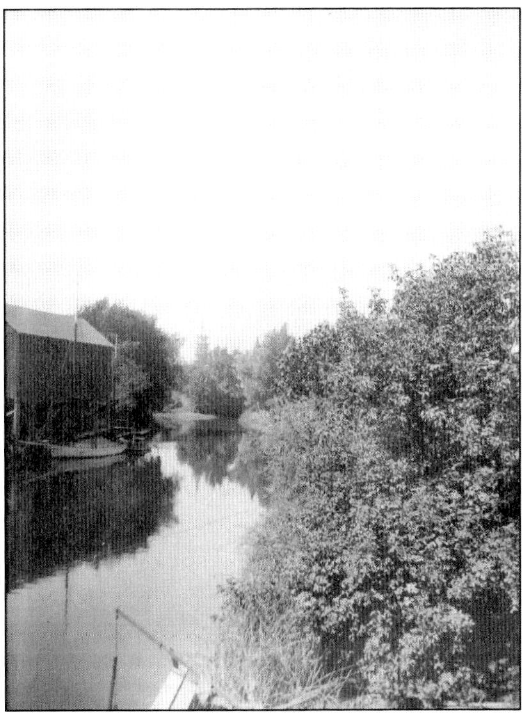

Many enjoy sailing on the Napa River, pictured here.

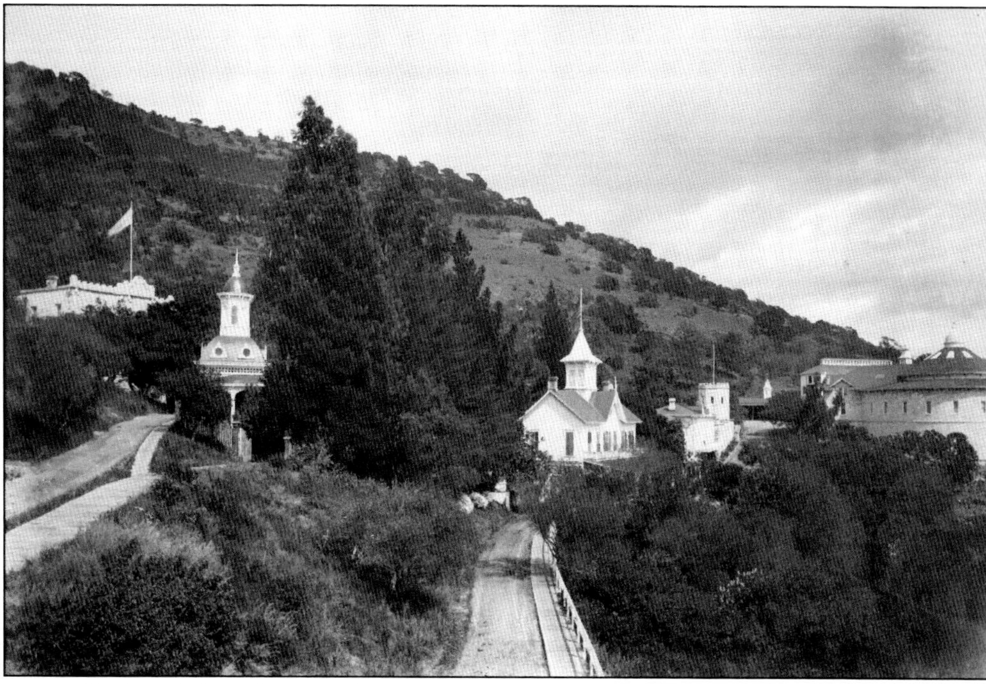

Resorts like Napa's Soda Springs, which contained Lemon Springs (a spring that tasted of lemons) and Pagoda Springs (a spring over which a pagoda was constructed) attracted many visitors in the late 1860s. Soda Springs and mud baths would become popular. (Courtesy of California History Room, California State Library, Sacramento, California.)

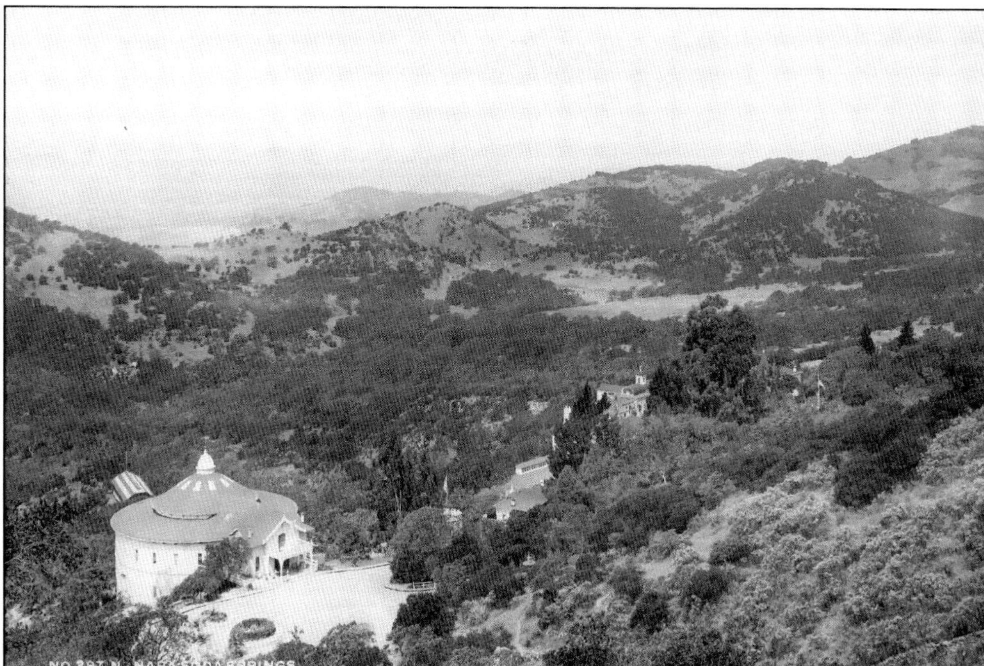

Napa's Rotunda at Soda Springs was touted as a vacation destination in the *San Francisco Call* newspaper.

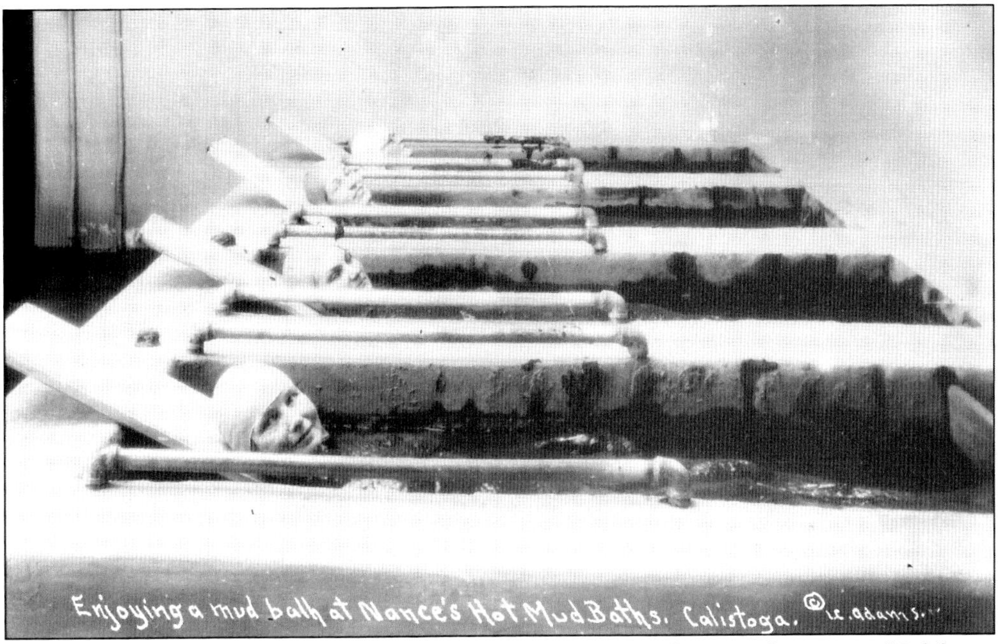

In the 1930s, "Nance's Hot Mud Baths" in Calistoga was a thriving business. (Courtesy of California History Room, California State Library, Sacramento, California.)

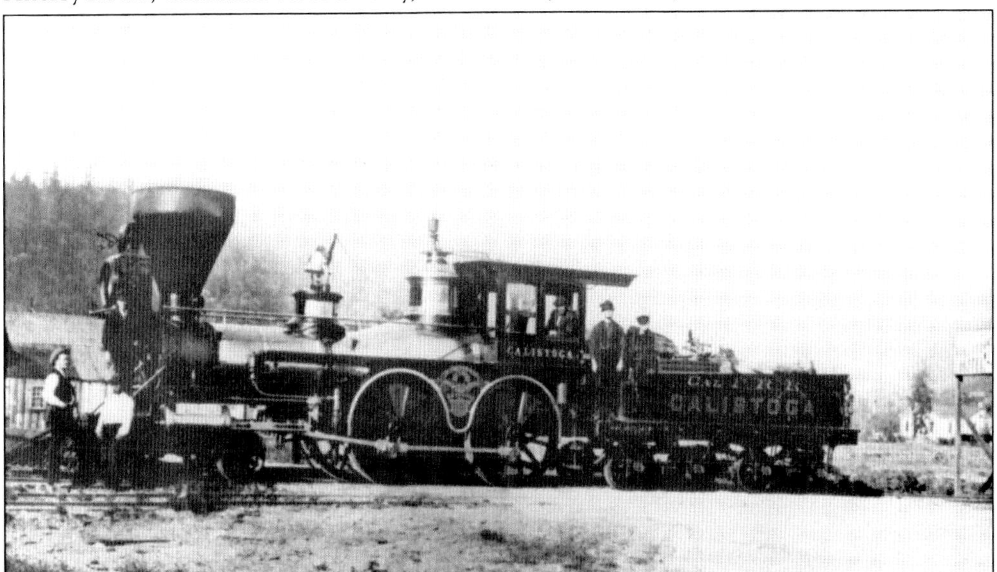

The wharfs and landings in Napa City connected to stagecoach lines and, starting in the 1860s, the railroad. Freight and goods from the interior areas became linked to the river. One of the most important early terminuses was located between just south of the foot of Main Street and Division Street. Just below Main Street, another bridge was built around 1865 for the Napa Valley Railroad Company. On its maiden voyage, a steam locomotive traveled from the hamlet of Suscol in the south, through Napa City, and on to Calistoga. This line, constructed by San Francisco millionaire Samuel Brannon, was used to transport visitors to his spa resort in Calistoga. In 1885, Southern Pacific bought the Napa Valley Railroad. The Napa Valley Wine Train currently uses this line.

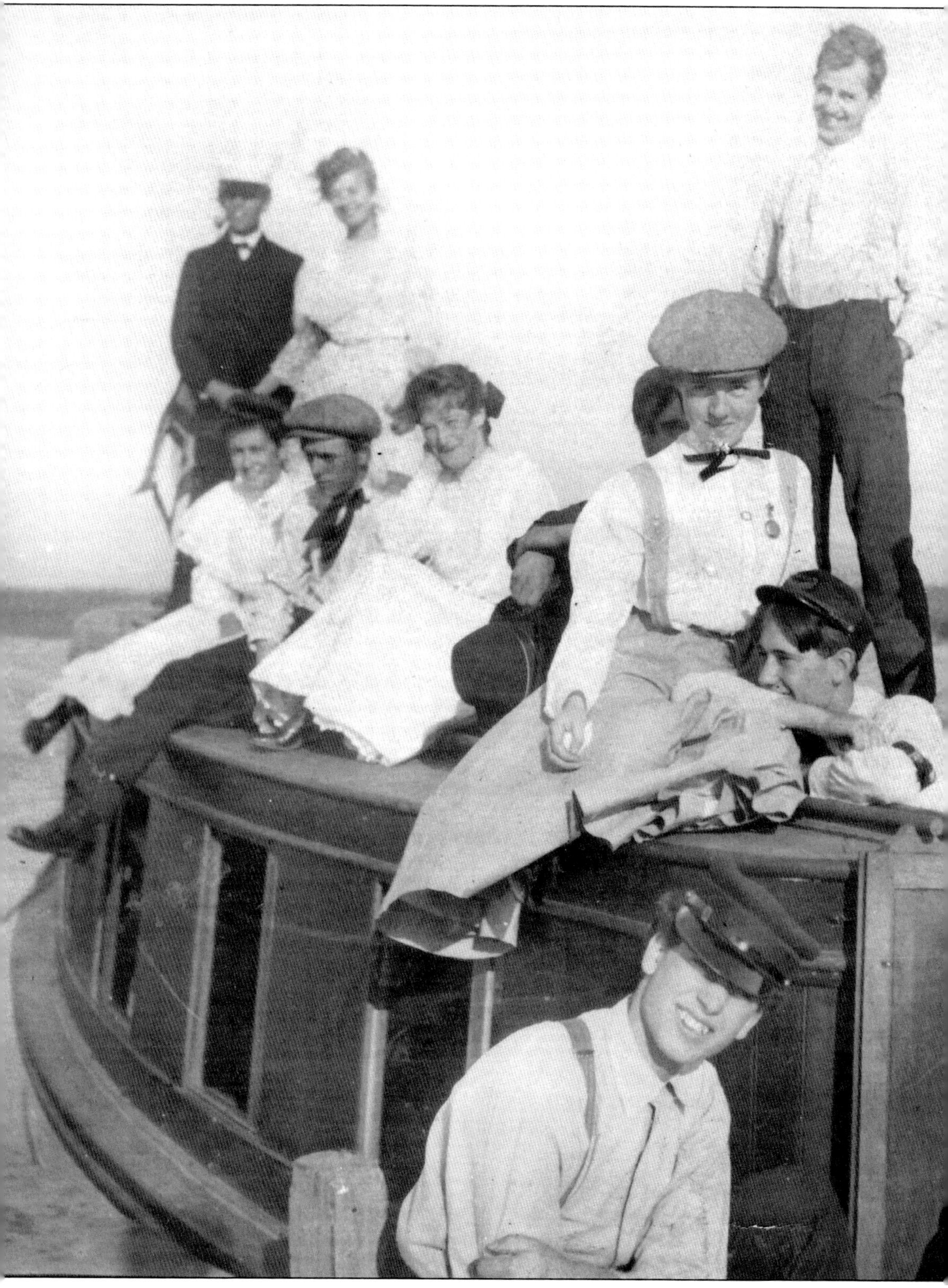

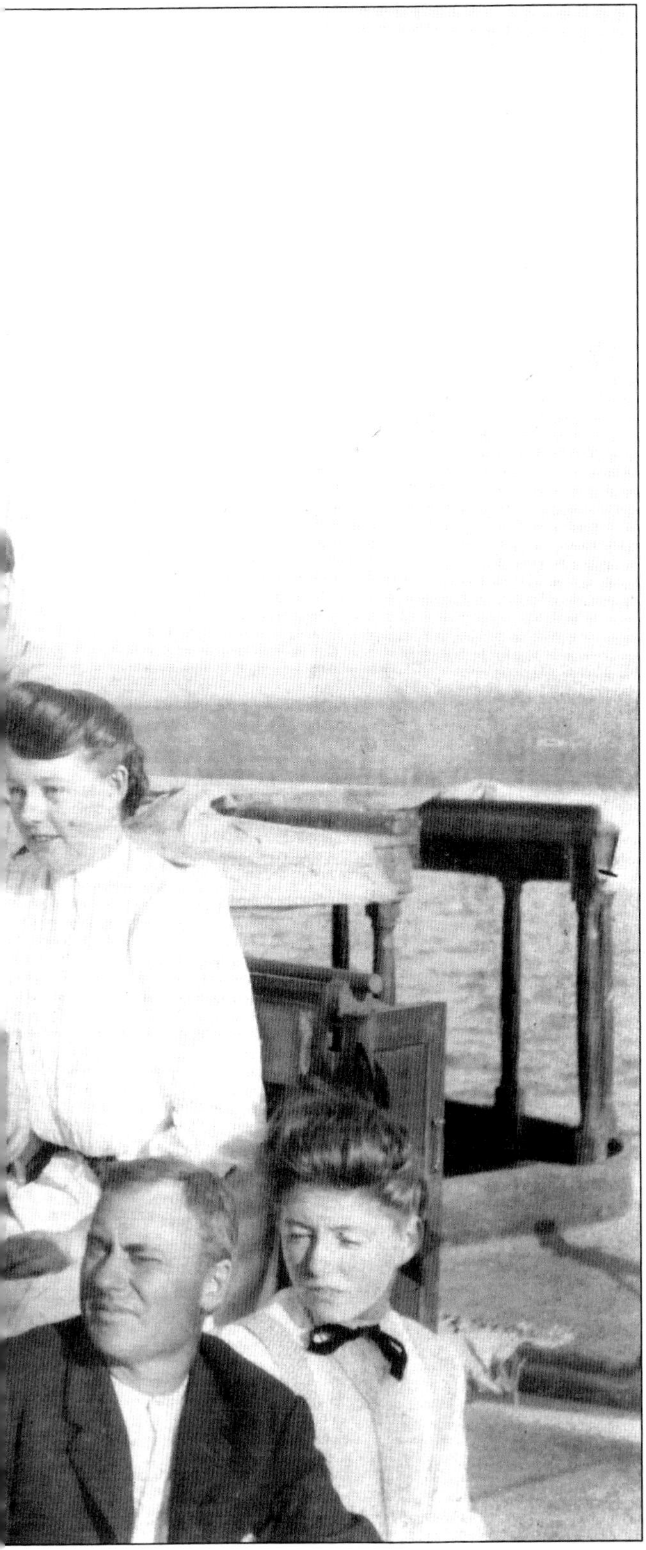

The river provided recreation for locals and visitors. This early-1900s image was likely captured by an unknown photographer in the Carneros area of South Napa where the river widens into San Pablo Bay.

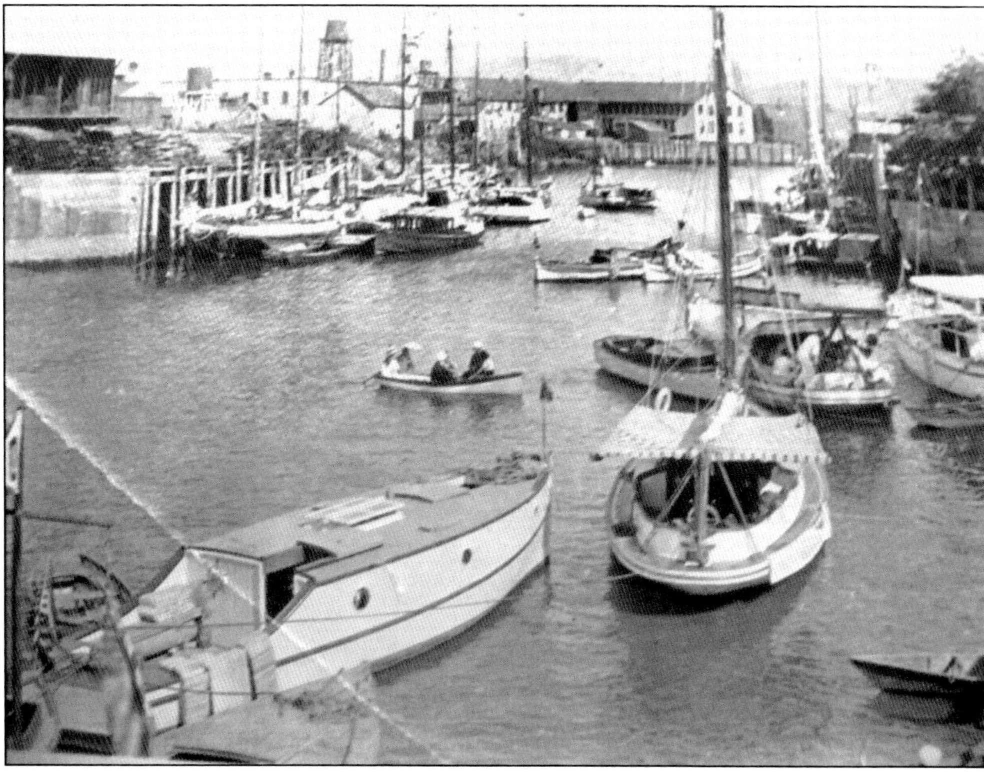

In the early 1900s, commercial and recreational craft crowd the waters downtown.

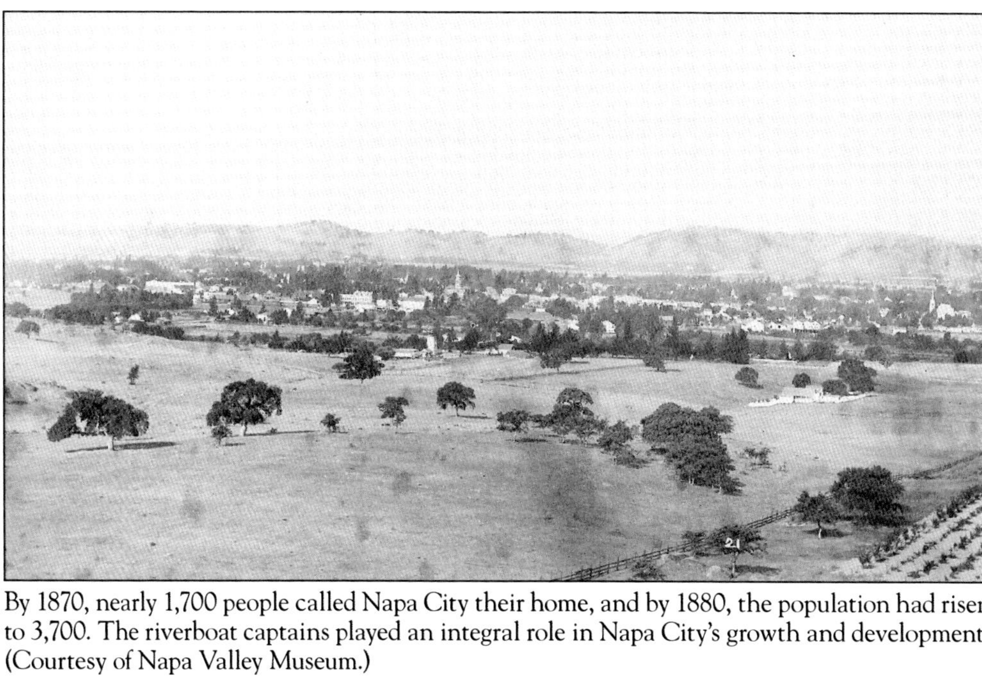

By 1870, nearly 1,700 people called Napa City their home, and by 1880, the population had risen to 3,700. The riverboat captains played an integral role in Napa City's growth and development. (Courtesy of Napa Valley Museum.)

Three

Riverboat Captains and Their Vessels

Steamships, Packets, and Schooners

People came to the Napa Valley from the 1840s to 1900s one of two ways: either by undertaking a rough, overland journey or by embarking upon a sea voyage, which brought them around Cape Horn or to Panama, then overland to the Pacific Coast. Beginning in 1848, rumors of gold for the taking spread around the world. Thousands of people left their homes and loved ones to pursue quick riches. For most of the world, the ocean was the only way to reach California, but for Americans, it was the most expeditious. In 1849 alone, 42,000 Americans headed west over land while 25,000 took to the waves. The riverboat captains, hailing from Maine, New Orleans, New Hampshire, landlocked Missouri, and as far away as Europe, often made circuitous journeys to finally end up in Napa. Many of the Napa riverboat captains were originally from Scandinavia (Denmark, Sweden, and Norway). The majority of these men worked on Redwood Coast lumber schooners. This large fleet of lumber schooners working the west coast were nicknamed the "Scandinavian Navy." Typically, these men were seasoned deepwater sailors who had been around the world on a variety of vessels. What the sailors all have in common is their connection to the Napa River. Like the world-wise captains, the story of the boats they worked on is equally intriguing. Vessels sailed in distant seas, on eastern rivers, and under different names; they were reconditioned, sometimes broken apart, and rebuilt entirely to serve a new purpose on the Napa River and the San Francisco Bay.

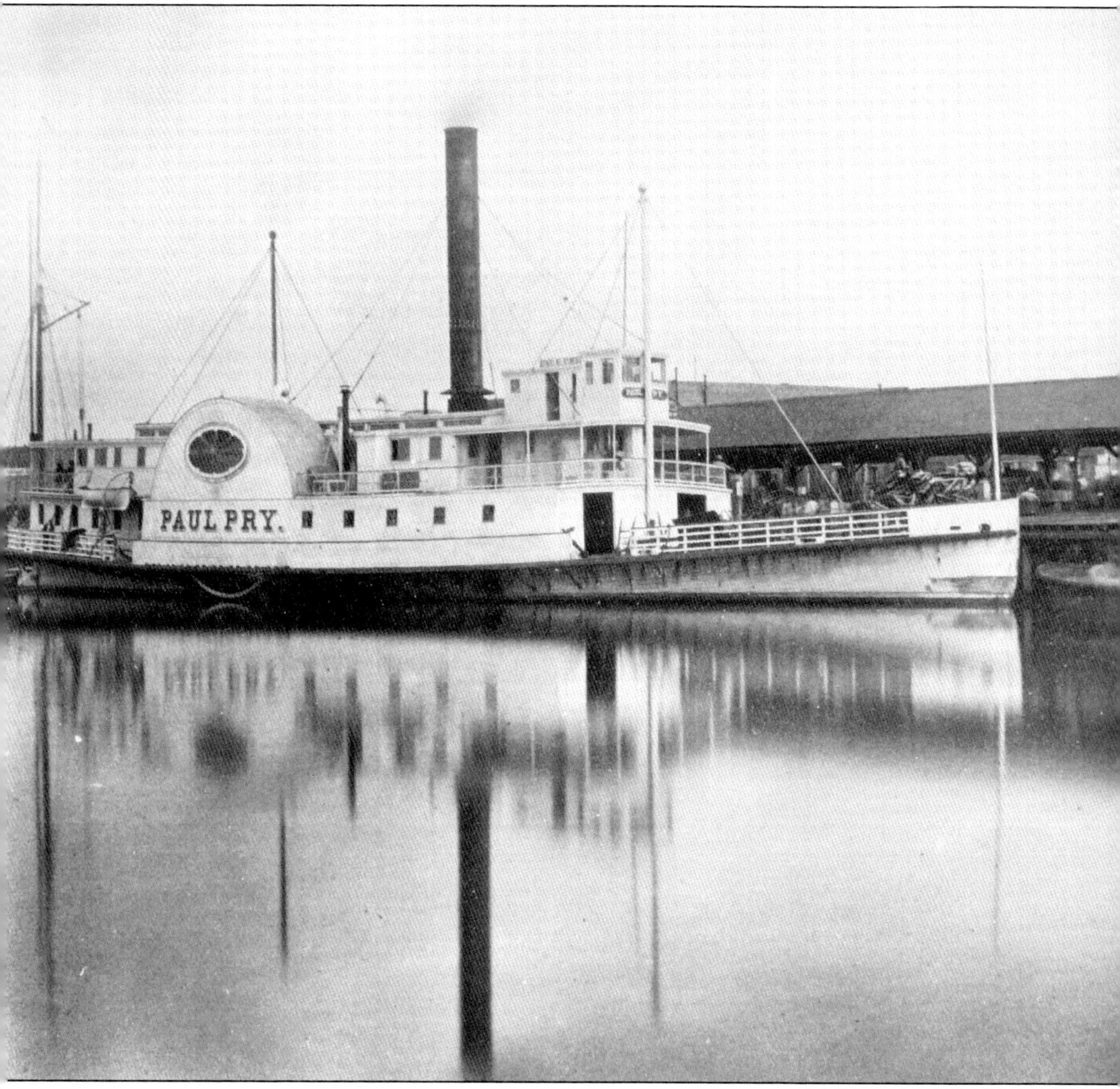

The 157-foot steamship *Paul Pry* was one of the many vessels that Capt. Turner Baxter commanded. Baxter was born in Adair County, Kentucky, on January 10, 1821. At the age of 15, in 1836, he traveled the Sangamon River in Sangamon County, Illinois, on board the small steamer *Talisman*. Later, he traveled to New Salem to learn cabinetry at a mill, where he remained for three years. In 1839, he moved to Jackson County, Missouri, where he had an uncle, and began working as a journeyman. When gold was discovered, Baxter headed west for the California gold fields. He arrived in Sacramento by oxen team and began a trading post. Eight months later, Baxter had settled in Napa City, where he opened a grocery store and saloon. He soon had amassed enough capital to build the Valley House Hotel. He held it for only a short time and sold out with the intention of traveling east, but cholera was very bad at the isthmus, so he reconsidered. In 1850, he purchased the steamer *Dolphin* in San Francisco. This was the first steamer to come up the Napa River. The *Dolphin* is described by C.A. Menefee as "very small, not much larger than a whaleboat, and her engine was similar to that of a locomotive." Because she was so small, passengers had to "trim ship" or move from one side to the other in order to maintain stability and keep the *Dolphin* from capsizing. (Courtesy of the Society of Pioneers.)

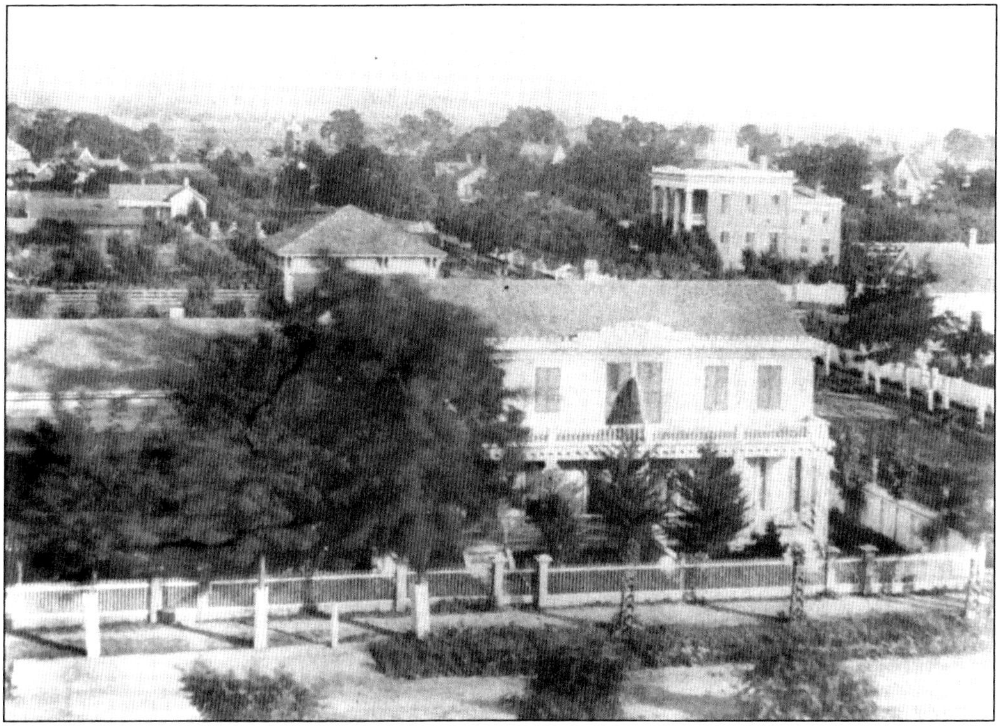

Trees lining the river are seen along the horizon in this view looking south from the courthouse. According to Emory Mount in his 1921 book *Napa as I Saw It in 1854*, it was widely known that Captain Baxter, who was quite tall, came into view long before the *Dolphin*'s smokestack was visible. In the middle of Second Street stood a good-sized oak tree used by Captain Baxter as a snubbing post in 1850 and 1851 to tie the *Dolphin* securely to where she landed. He ran the nose of the little craft into the bank of the creek in order to let the passengers out. The *Dolphin* was the first commercial steamer providing regular service in 1852. (Courtesy of Library of Congress.)

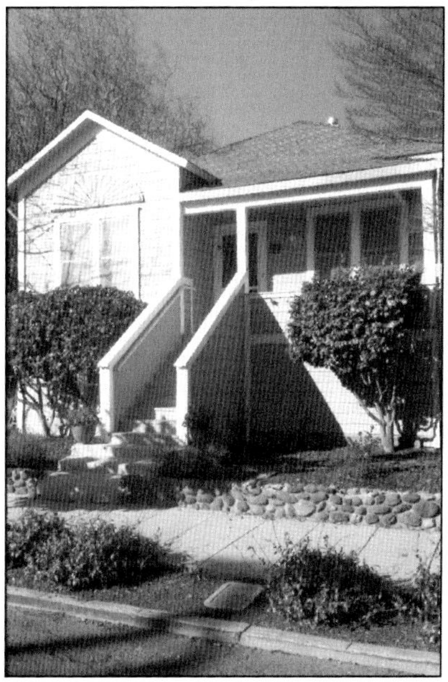

Turner Baxter purchased this modest house at 1532 H Street. After only two years on the river, Baxter returned to the hotel-keeping business. He next captained the *Jack Hayes* but soon sold her. He had purchased several lots in Napa City and erected several buildings, but in 1856, he left Napa for South America to find a place to run a steamboat. At Valparaiso, he obtained the sole right to run a towboat in the harbor for 20 years, but he abandoned the enterprise for unknown reasons. He returned to Napa and opened the Valley House restaurant. In 1860, he began working for the California Steam Navigation Company. By 1864, he was back on the Napa River in command of the *Cleopatra* between Napa and Suscol, in connection with the *Amelia*, which ran from there to San Francisco. By 1877, Baxter had left the company to purchase the steamer *Vaquero*, which he ran for only one summer before selling her. In 1877, he captained the steamer *Princess* for a summer and then returned to the carpenter trade.

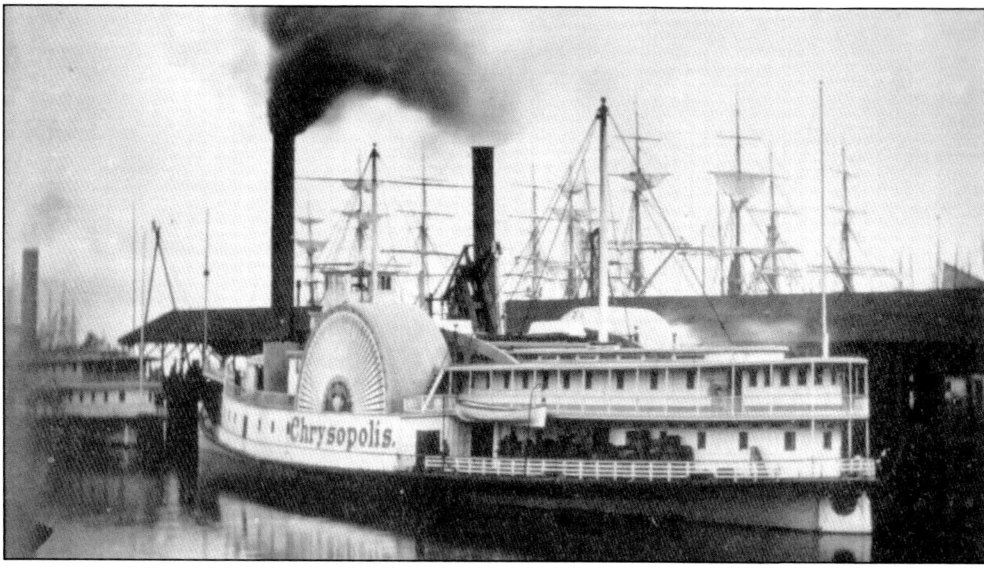

The first steamship to successfully burn coal from the Mount Diablo mines was the *Chrysopolis.* Although coal was in high demand in the 1860s, most of the equipment of that era was designed to burn a different type of coal that could be found only in Washington Territory, British Columbia, as well as England and Australia. After an engineer on the California Steam Navigation Company's riverboat *Chrysopolis* discovered that Mount Diablo coal would burn well if the fireboxes were modified, the demand for local coal increased dramatically. In 1851, Capt. E.C.M. Chadwick was the commander of the bark *Josephine*. Chadwick sailed her up the Napa River to the embarcadero for the lowly sum of $100. There, she was dismantled and used for several years as a wharf boat and storeship east of the First Street Bridge. She was later sold to William Fisher, who rented and relocated the vessel to a steamboat landing. One year later, in 1852, Captain Chadwick was at the helm of the steamer *Reindeer.* She plied between Central Wharf in San Francisco and Napa, leaving San Francisco on Tuesday, Thursday, and Saturday at noon and departing Napa at 9:00 a.m. Monday, Wednesday, and Friday. The journey across the bay took three hours on average, depending upon the tides and wind conditions. In March 1854, Capt. E.C.M. Chadwick took the helm of the steamer *Chrysopolis.* (Courtesy of Society of California Pioneers.)

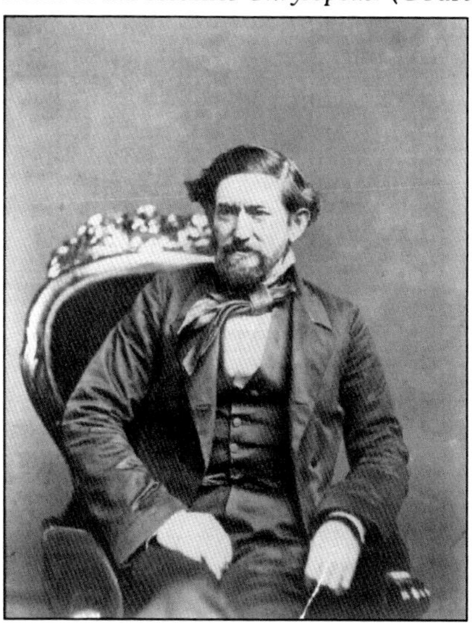

Captain Chadwick also commanded the steamer *Jack Hays*, named after a well-known San Francisco County sheriff and former Texas Ranger John "Jack" Coffee Hayes. This is the same vessel earlier captained by Turner Baxter. In 1849, *Jack Hays* was brought around the horn in pieces aboard the bark *La Grange* and was shipped to Benicia. She was the first steamboat that made the trip from Benicia to Sacramento. Once completed, the vessel was initially called the *Commodore Jones* in honor of Commodore Catsby Jones, but her builders soon had a change of heart and renamed her *Jack Hays.* (Courtesy of Library of Congress.)

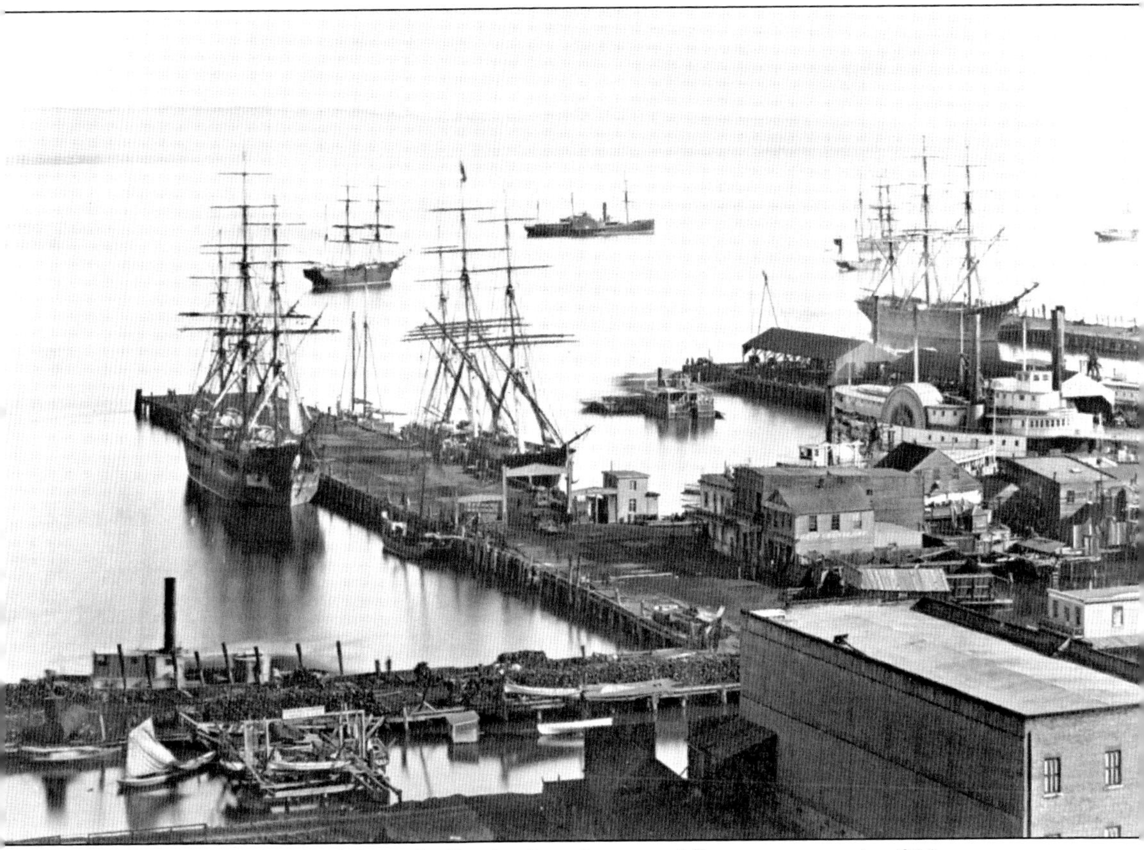

Captain Chadwick lost his life on the *Brother Jonathan*, a paddle steamer carrying 244 passengers that wrecked off the coast of Crescent City in July 1865 en route to Portland and then Vancouver, British Columbia. The ship is seen in the top center of this 1863 San Francisco waterfront scene. At the time, the loss of the *Brother Jonathan* was one of the deadliest shipwrecks on the Pacific Coast. (Courtesy of San Francisco Maritime, NHP.)

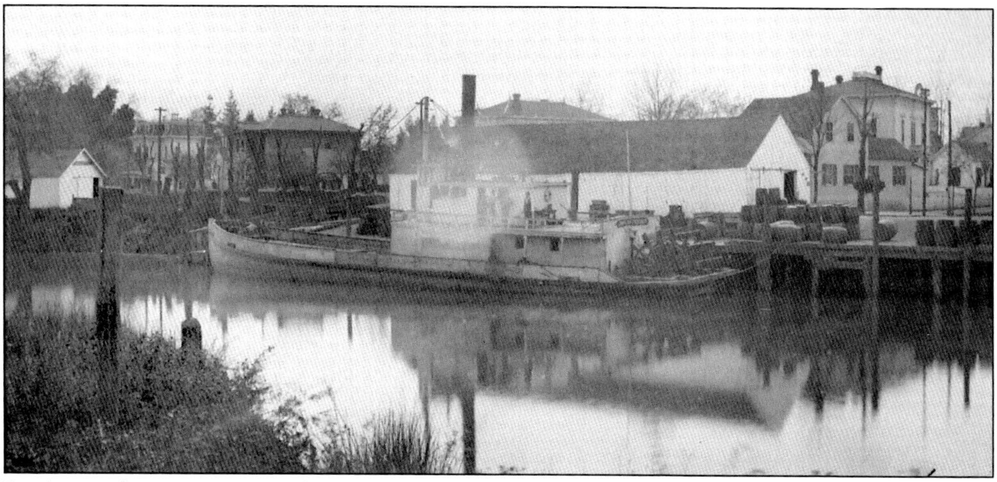

Bank president George Goodman's mansion with the mansard roof at 1120 Oak Street can be seen to the left in this photograph. Wine barrels line the dock at the foot of Oak Street. This type of commercial steamboat would have been familiar to Capt. Robert West. In the same year that the first commercial steamboat service began between Napa and San Francisco, Captain West settled in Napa in 1852 after many years in the European and coastal trade. He was born in Monmouth County, New Jersey, in 1797. After taking his last voyage to Europe in 1847, West arrived in California as captain of the *Pilgrim*, a canal boat of 80 tons that had been used on the circuit between New York and Wilmington, North Carolina. For two years, he sailed the Pacific Coast, alternating between three vessels: the *Aspinwall*, the *Filt*, and the *Pilgrim*. The *Pilgrim* was eventually sold to the California Steam Navigation Company in Vallejo and decommissioned into a barge. By 1855, she was left at the foot of Third Street in Napa City, where she was docked and deserted for several years. She was finally sold, and Capt. Orloff Reed took her apart and used her materials to build the schooner *Zina Reed*, which sank after only a few voyages on the northern coast while carrying lumber. (Courtesy of Napa Valley Museum.)

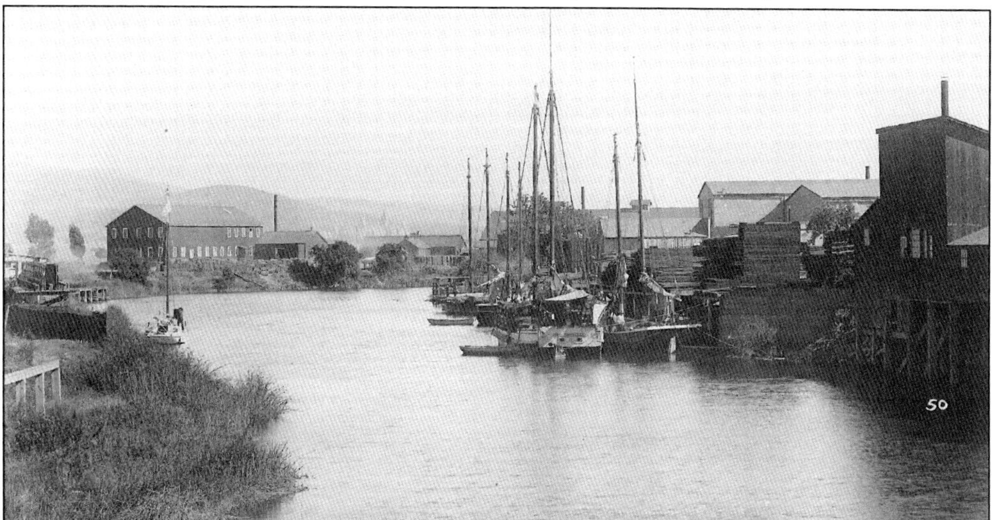

Sailing vessels are docked near Henry Hays Knapp's lumber company, north of the Hatt Building near Third Street. Stacks of lumber can be seen to the right. The Napa State Asylum for the Insane, as it was then called, is in the distance, appearing otherworldly. (Courtesy of Napa Valley Museum.)

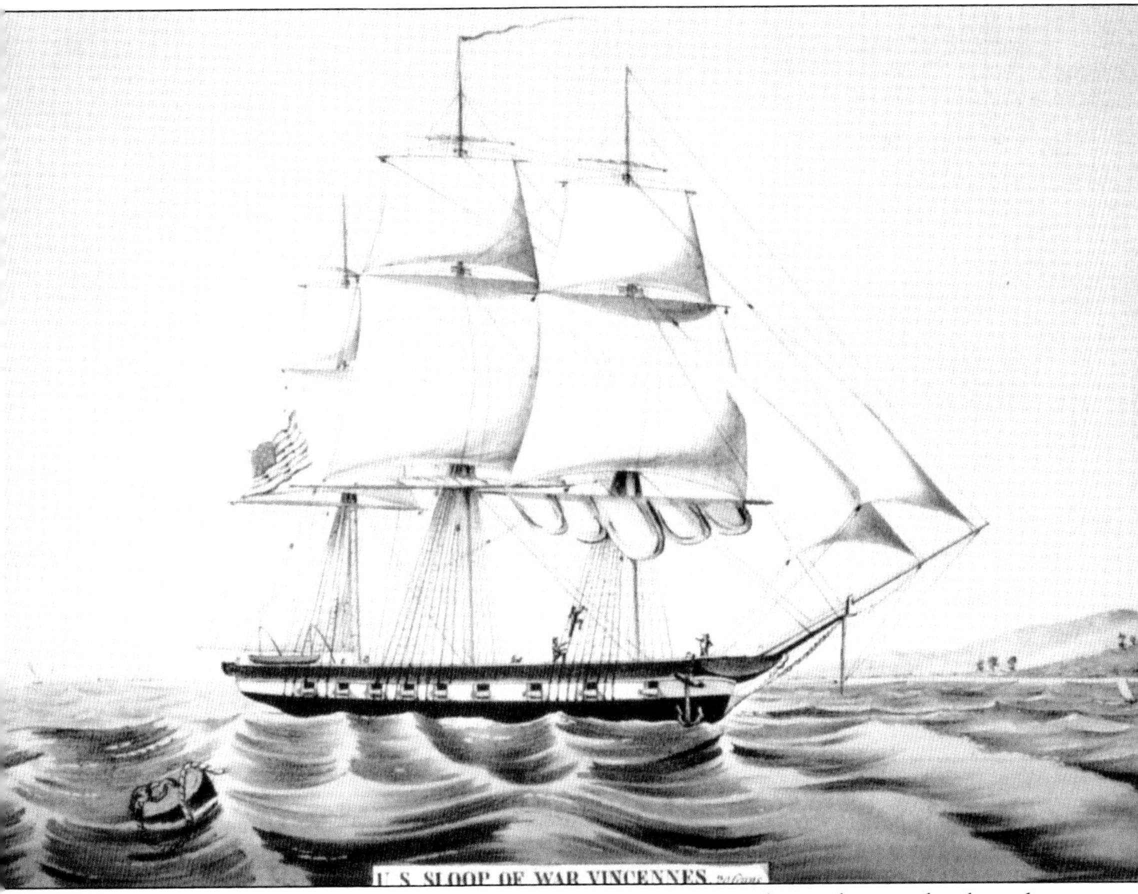

Pictured here around 1845, the US sloop-of-war *Vincennes* was similar to the one that brought Captain Knudsen to Napa. Before coming to Napa, Knudsen survived a shipwreck aboard the *Esmeralda* while traveling between Hong Kong and Singapore. He had the fortune to then work under Captain Appleton aboard the *Serbreyius*. The captain's wife took a special interest in teaching Knudsen English. In 1855, he landed in New York aboard the *Resolute* with a cargo of tea from China. Next, he boarded the *Black Warrior* for San Francisco via Cape Horn. In January 1856, he landed in San Francisco. Following a trip aboard the *Fawn* to the Umpqua River for lumber, he boarded the sloop-of-war *Jilt* bound for Napa, arriving in 1856. After 18 months, he was able to purchase a half interest in the *Jilt* and later became sole owner. Knudsen ran the ship as a freighter for six years until 1866. He then sold it and commissioned the construction of the small schooner *Napa City* in 1872, which he used in the coast lumber trade. (Courtesy of Library of Congress.)

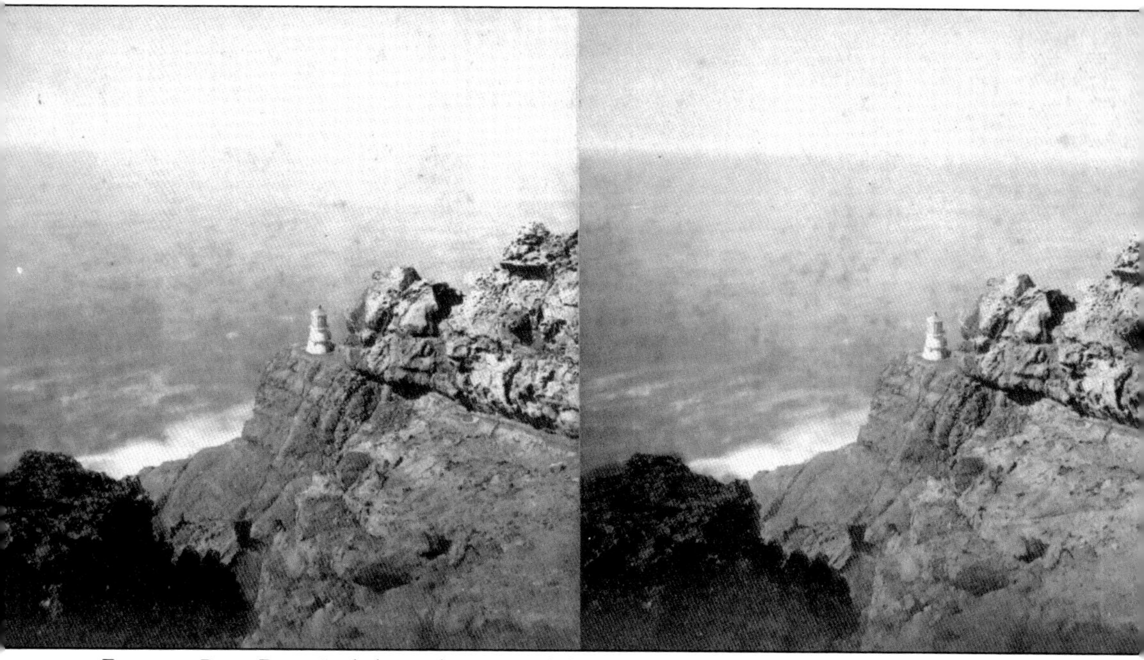

For years, Point Reyes Lighthouse has warned ships of the treacherous coast. According to the Gulf of Farallones National Marine Sanctuary's shipwreck database, the vessel *Napa City* was wrecked off the coast, seven miles northwest of Point Reyes, in 1890. The record shows her as a commercial schooner with four masts and sail propulsion. She was built in Little River, California, in 1872 by Thomas H. Peterson. Two people on board perished on July 7, 1890, as the ship sailed from Point Arena to San Francisco. She carried a cargo of bark and posts on that fateful day. Capt. Andrew Knudsen's bad luck in shipbuilding was not limited to the *Napa City*. Knudsen also commissioned the building of the *H.H. Knapp*, a schooner of 100 tons that he named after Napa's lumberyard owner Henry Hays Knapp. He ran her for three years in the Pacific Coast trade before selling her, and only six months after the sale, in 1887, she was lost off the coast near Westport, California. Undeterred, Knudsen next commissioned the construction of the *City of Napa*, a packet used to ferry people from San Francisco to Napa. (Courtesy of Library of Congress.)

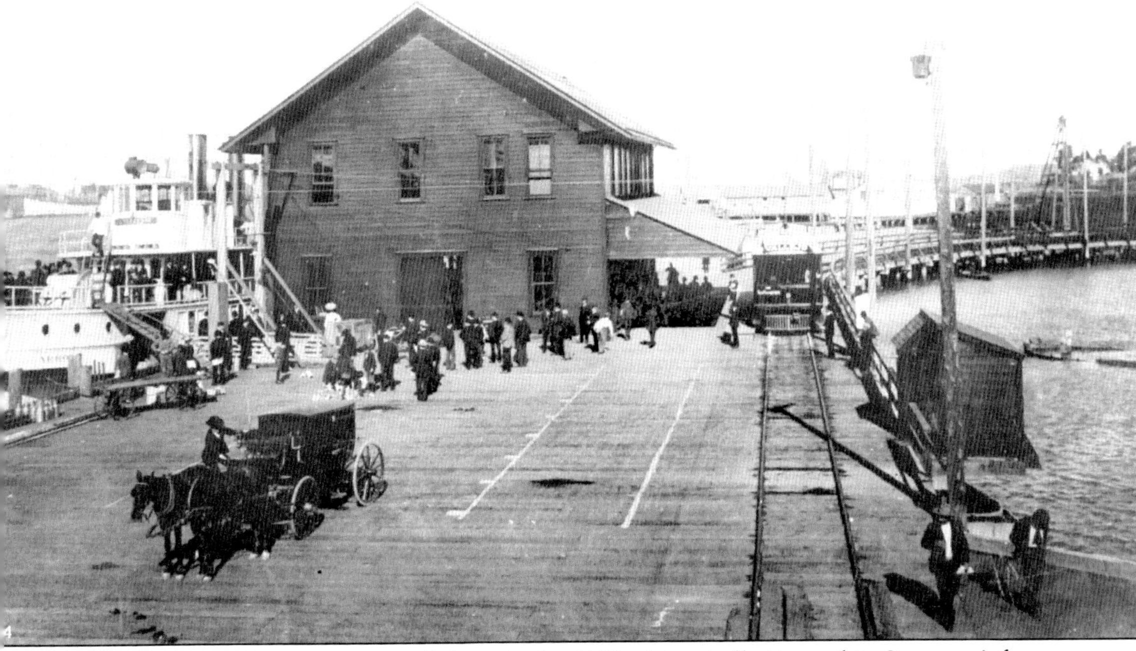

The Vallejo waterfront was extremely busy in the 1900s. Monticello Steamship Company's ferry *Arrow* is docked while electric trains stand ready to bring transferring passengers Upvalley to Napa. (Photograph by Terrill & Miller; courtesy of the Western Railway Museum Archives.)

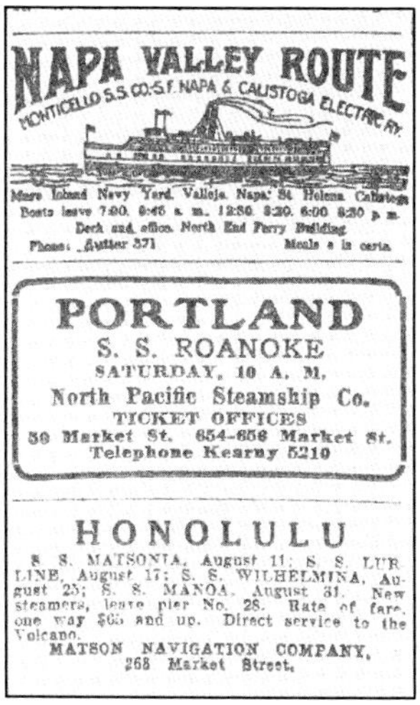

According to this advertisement, the Monticello steamships left six times a day and served meals a la carte.

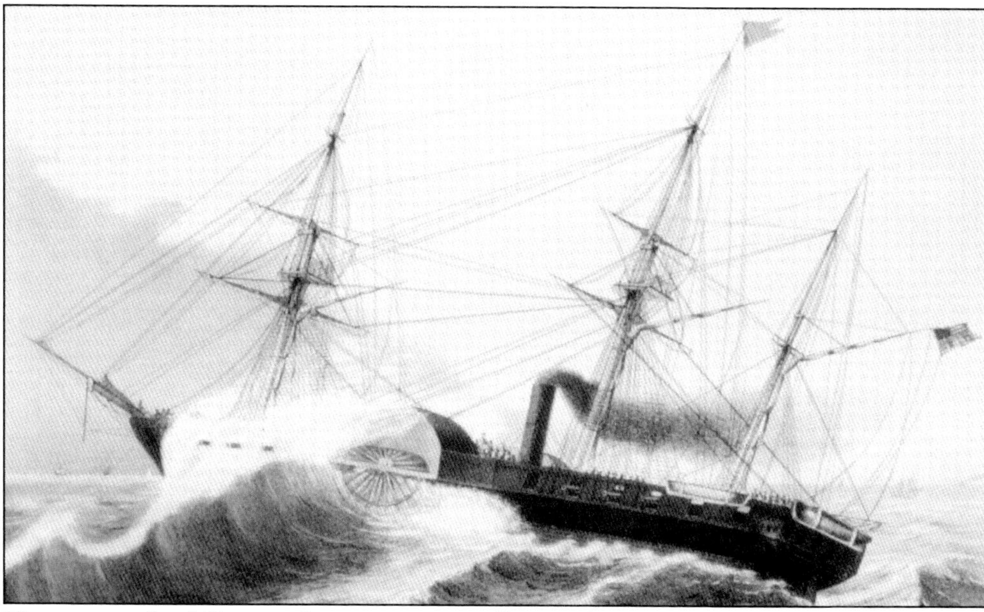

The iron warship US steam frigate *Mississippi*, illustrated here, was similar to the *Guadalupe*, a modern side-wheel steamer from England. Napa riverboat captain P.F. Doling took the helm of the reconditioned packet *Guadalupe*. This infamous boat was said to be in Edwin Ward Moore's expedition to Gila, during which Texas began to separate itself from Mexico in a series of battles. What made the Mexican Army a threat in these naval battles taking place in the spring of 1843 was the purchase of the *Guadalupe* from England. She weighed in at 775 tons at nearly 200 feet long and was armed with 68-pound Paixhan swivel guns. According to Palmer's *History of Napa and Lake Counties*, 13 years later, in 1856, the "elegant and fast steamer *Guadalupe* has been refitted and will leave the Pacific Street Wharf in San Francisco for Napa and way places on Tuesday, Thursday and Saturday." In his 1944 book *Paddle-Wheel Days in California*, Jerry MacMullen notes that the *Guadalupe* took passengers to Napa and Suscol with connections for White Sulphur Springs. The vessel eludes maritime historians in official records of ships on the San Francisco Bay. While it is uncertain that these are one in the same vessels, maritime historians do verify that a ship named the *Guadalupe* was in the 1843 Battle of Campeche during the expedition to the Gila River in the Gulf of California.

Pictured here is Charles Sampson, youngest son of Capt. Andrew Sampson (1865–1926). Andrew, a native of Sweden, became a US citizen in 1858 and worked as a Napa riverboat captain, sometimes hauling wine kegs from the Migliavacca Cellar across the street from his house, which is where the public library is located today. He took an active role in the Napa River trade by running a tugboat line. The boats were drawn down the river to deep water by mules. He also sailed a schooner between Napa and San Francisco and ran a drayage business in which he frequently hauled drayage to St. Helena Sanitarium. He married Capt. Nels Hansen Wulff's daughter Annie and had two boys, James and Charlie. When Annie died in 1868, Andrew remarried Olinda Grover, who hailed from Plymouth, England. Their daughter Laura married Dewitt Treadway, and they continued to live in Captain Sampson's home until Laura's death. Purportedly, during Prohibition when the Migliavacca winery could only produce sacramental wine, it was bottled in the kitchen of the Sampson house. (Courtesy of Nick Sampson Rossi and Gladys [Rossi] Atkinson.)

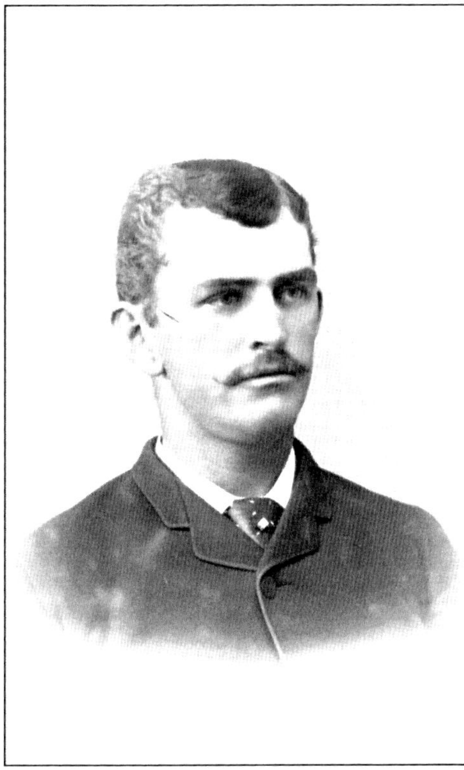

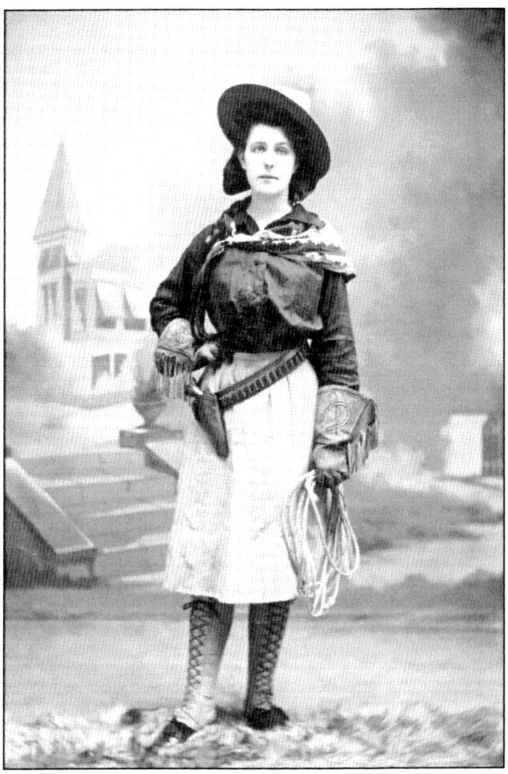

Charles's wife, May Augusta Kather Sampson (1868–1911), noted for her beauty, was said to have had striking violet eyes. Her daughter Bernice (Sampson) Rossi, pictured here, became Napa's Goddess of Liberty in 1911. (Courtesy of Nick Sampson Rossi and Gladys [Rossi] Atkinson.)

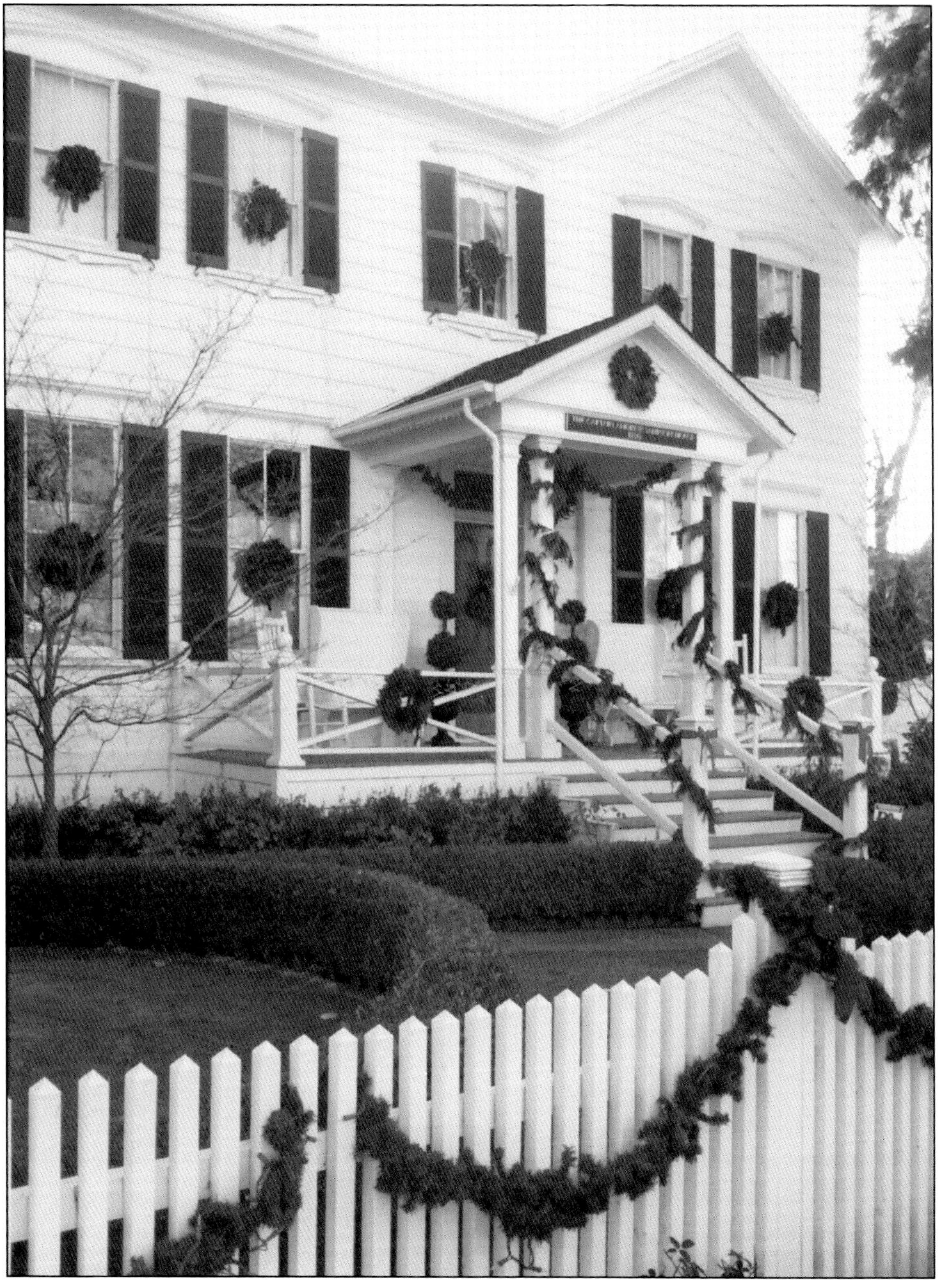

Located one block from the Napa River at the corner of Division and Coombs Streets (1157 Division Avenue) is the two-story house of Captain Sampson. According to the Historic Resources Inventory of the California Department of Parks and Recreation, "It is an excellent example of the 19th century practice in Napa of creating a two story house by raising the original one story cottage and building a new first floor. The original cottage, now the second floor, is believed to have been built in 1850, soon after Stephen Broadhurst bought the land near the Napa River from Joseph P. Thompson, one of Napa's first settlers. The house raising took place in about 1900. The house stands on a fieldstone foundation and is framed with shiplap siding. Two Sequoias in the front yard were planted by Andrew Sampson's wife, Olinda, in the 1870s." (Author's collection.)

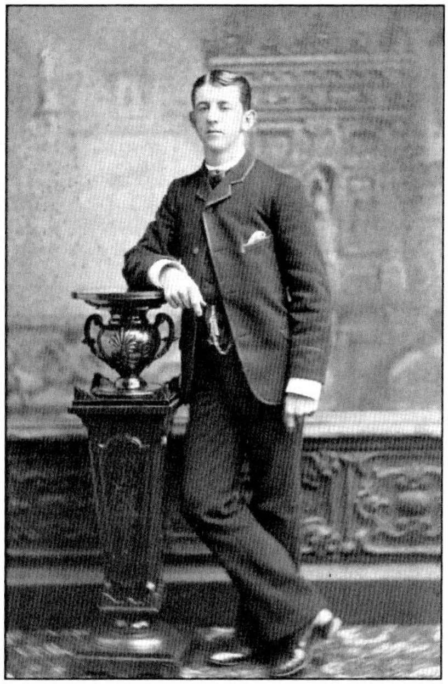

Capt. Nelson "Nels" Hanson came to California in 1850 and settled in Napa in 1859. Born in Denmark in 1830, he was drawn to the sea as a young lad and soon found himself traveling the world, visiting ports of call from China to Europe to South America. His adventures in California began with gold mining on the American River. He made a bit of money and was able to invest in a schooner that he ran on the San Pablo Bay. In 1853, and for three years following, he ballasted ships in Benicia and carried building stone from Benicia to San Francisco. His notoriety came when he transported the first locomotive to operate in California from San Francisco to Sacramento in 1855. In 1859, Captain Wulff was well aware of the bustling flour mill in Napa and the vast amounts of wheat that required transport downstream. Wheat became the main cargo of his shipping business for 11 years. Somewhat of a visionary at the time, Captain Wulff could see that steam would soon replace sails. He divested his interests with sailing vessels in favor of the steamship.

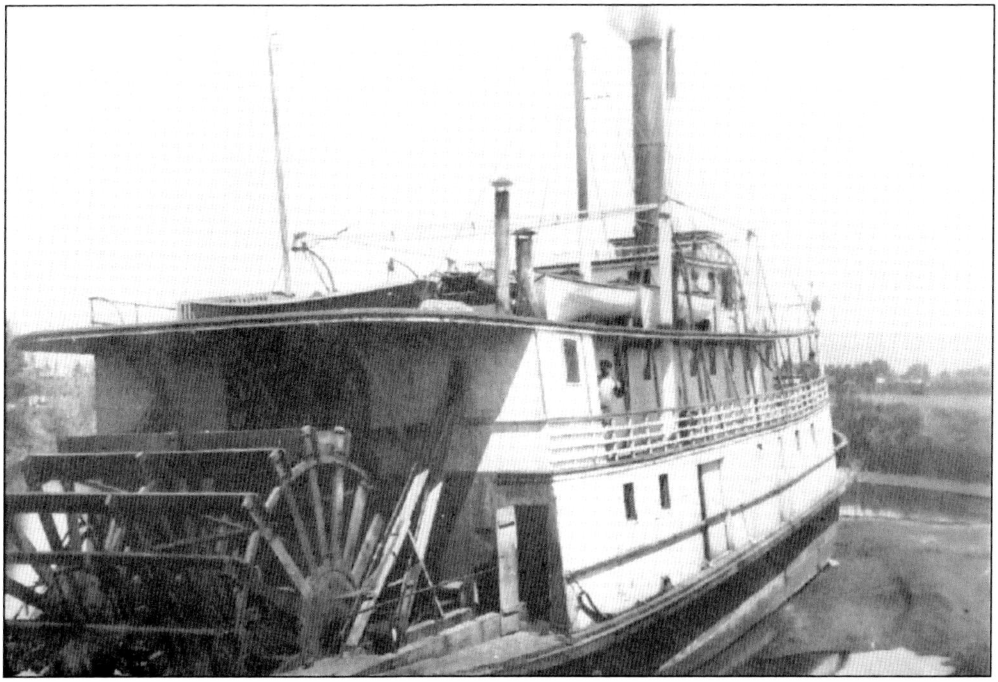

In terms of Napa history, Wulff is perhaps best known as the steamboat captain who commissioned the building of the *Zinfandel* steamer in 1889 by George D. Damon of San Francisco. This was a joint financial venture between Captain Wulff, his son N.H. Wulff Jr., Edward J. Healy, and Charles Carpy from 1889 to 1902. Here, she is stuck in the mud near Suscol. The Napa Navigation Company owned the ship from 1902 to 1907, when she was purchased by Capt. Albert Hatt, who used her from 1907 to 1911 for his wholesale lumber company. Percy S. King and several others owned the vessel from 1917 to 1922. On September 5, 1922, she was lost in Miner Slough in the Sacramento River.

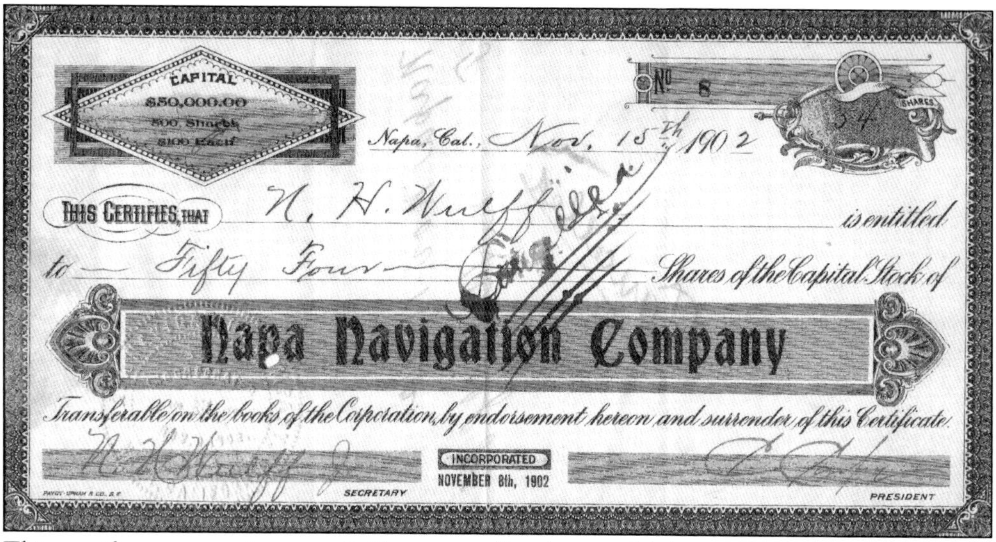
CAPITAL
$50,000.00
500 Shares
$100 Each

No 8

54 SHARES

Napa, Cal., Nov. 15th 1902

THIS CERTIFIES, THAT N. H. Wulff Jr. is entitled to — Fifty Four — Shares of the Capital Stock of

Napa Navigation Company

Transferable on the books of the Corporation, by endorsement hereon and surrender of this Certificate.

INCORPORATED NOVEMBER 8th, 1902

SECRETARY

PRESIDENT

This certificate was written to C. Carpy, entitling him to 54 shares of capital stock in Napa Navigation Company; it is dated November 15, 1902. Henry Brown and N.H. Wulff Jr.'s cancellation is written on the back. So financially successful, Wulff became owner and agent for a fleet of ships: the *Ellen*, *Master Mariner*, *Silver Cloud*, *Cinderella*, and *Caroline*. In addition to these vessels, he owned a waterfront warehouse.

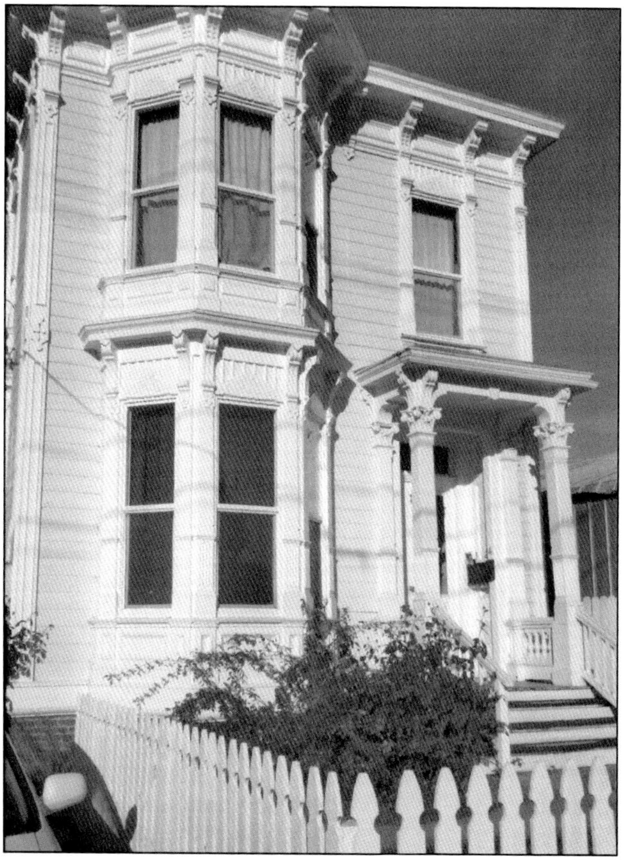

Captain Wulff built an Italianate mansion befitting a man of his stature at 549 Brown Street, complete with a view of the river. Like Capt. Nels Wulff, Pinkham also constructed a house in 1880, just down the street from Wulff at 529 Brown Street.

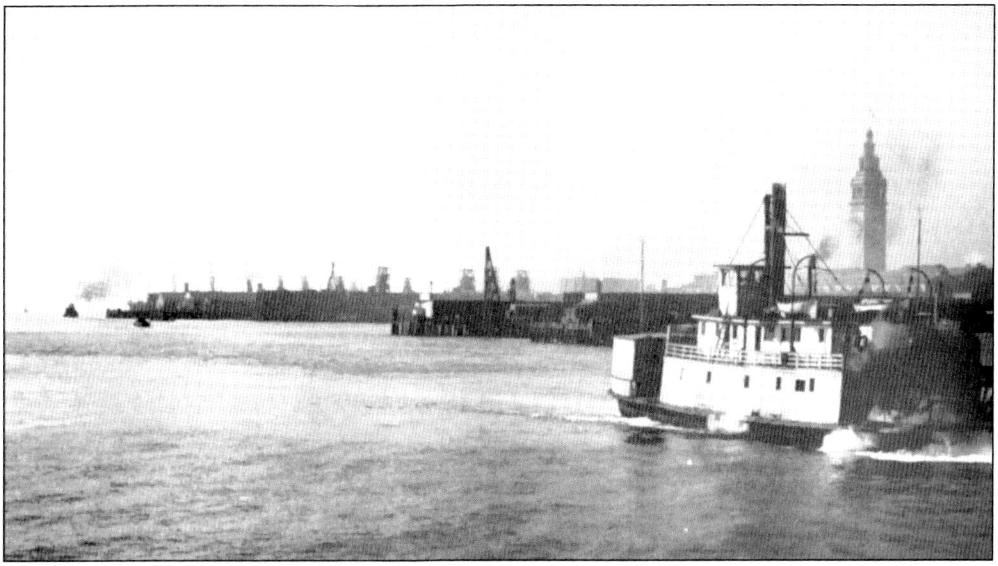

Built in 1891 in Benicia, the packet *Napa City* was a 178-ton vessel overseen by Capt. George Grafton Pinkham. Hailing from the seaport town of Kennebunkport, Maine, George Pinkham was the son of a merchant seaman who was lost at sea when two ships collided in the Bay of Fundy. Like his father, Pinkham was lured to the sea at a young age. He sailed fishing boats on the East Coast trade until 1852, when he became inspired by his readings to head west to the final destination of California. He took passage to Greytown, Nicaragua, and was delayed from going further up the Chagres River by the natives. Taking to land instead, Pinkham walked to Panama and boarded a ship for San Francisco. After landing, he began working on the wharf, bucking 200-pound sacks of wheat. Sadly, Pinkham's employer cheated him out of $2,000 that he had borrowed. Undeterred, Pinkham was able to buy a schooner by the end of the year and sailed from San Francisco to Alviso Bay. The selling of the schooner enabled him to later invest in the steamer *Napa City*. This is not the schooner that was lost off the coast of Point Reyes, but a passenger and freight steamer that made regular trips to San Francisco. So successful was this venture, Pinkham cleared several hundred dollars the first month. (Courtesy of Pentrex.)

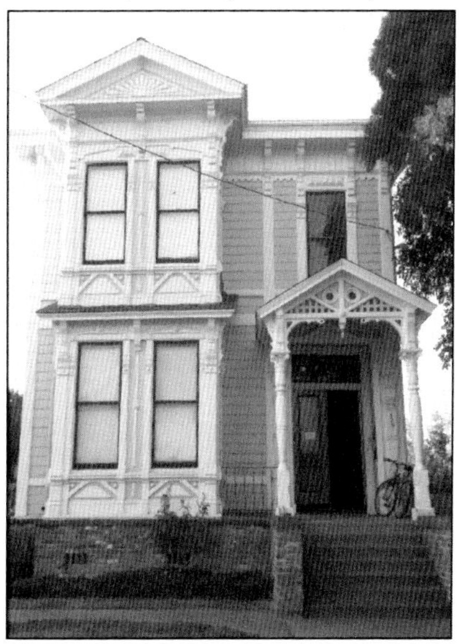

Captain Pinkham's impressive Italianate home was located at 529 Brown Street. He lived just south of Capt. Nels Wulff.

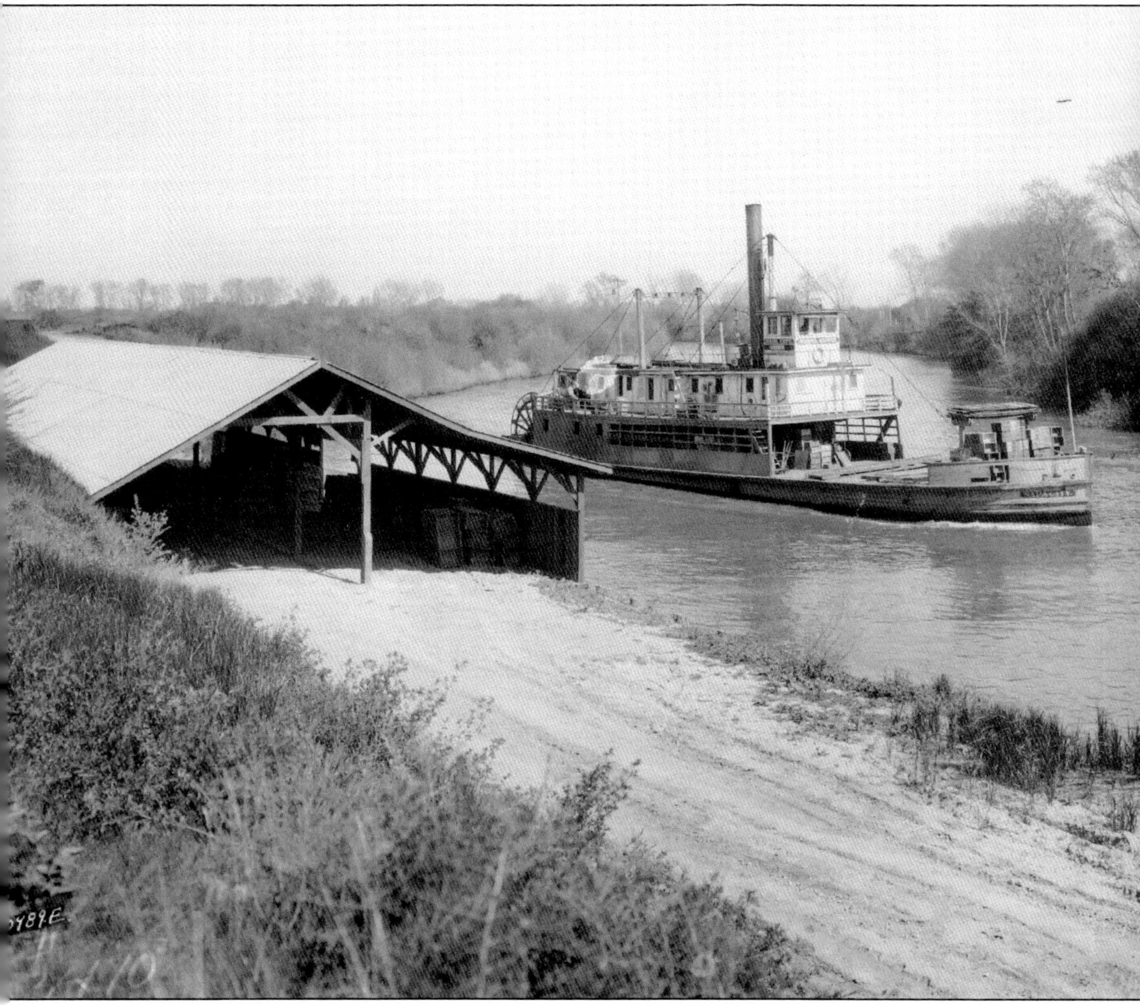

With her hull loaded with goods, the stern-wheeler *Napa City* is likely headed to San Francisco. (Courtesy of California History Room, California State Library, Sacramento, California.)

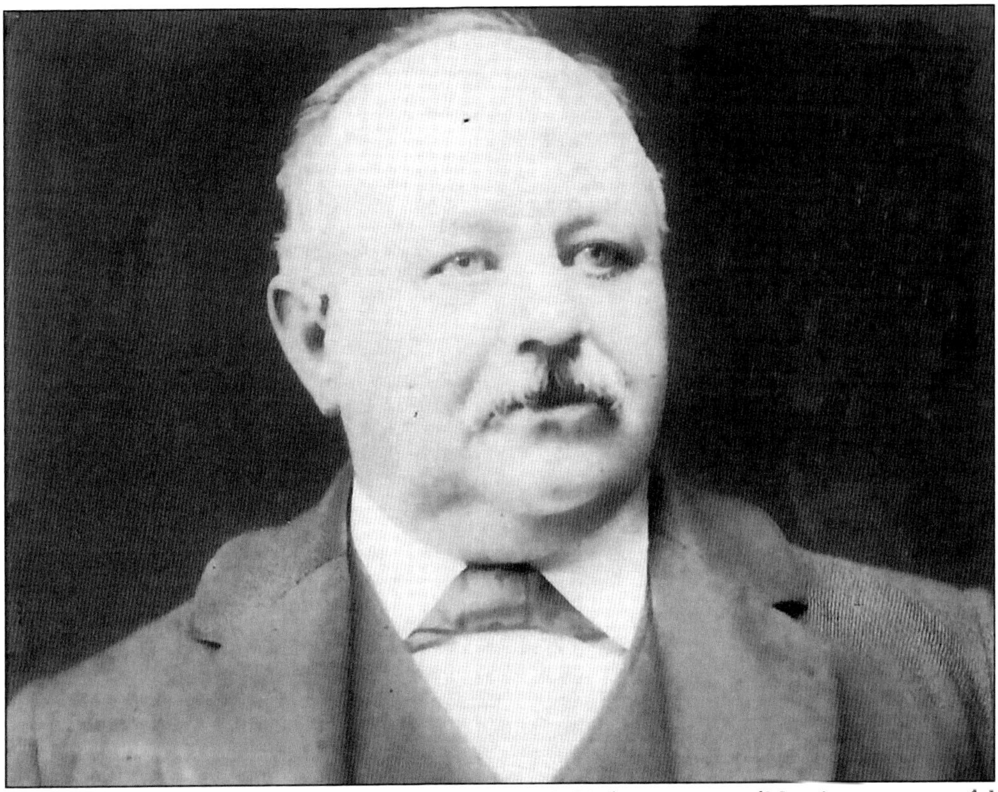

Capt. Albert Hatt was born in Prussia on May 3, 1840. He became one of Napa's most successful and creative merchants for over 40 years and owned the *St. Helena* from 1907 to 1911. He also owned the stern-wheel steamer the *Zinfandel*, pictured below, which he purchased from the Napa Navigation Company in 1907. Captain Hatt sailed around the world before landing in San Francisco in 1859 at 19 years old. Like many seamen of the time, he sailed up and down the Sacramento River and in the Pacific Coast trade for six years. He met an Irish woman named Alma Horgen, married, and had a large family of six children. (Both, courtesy of Napa River Inn.)

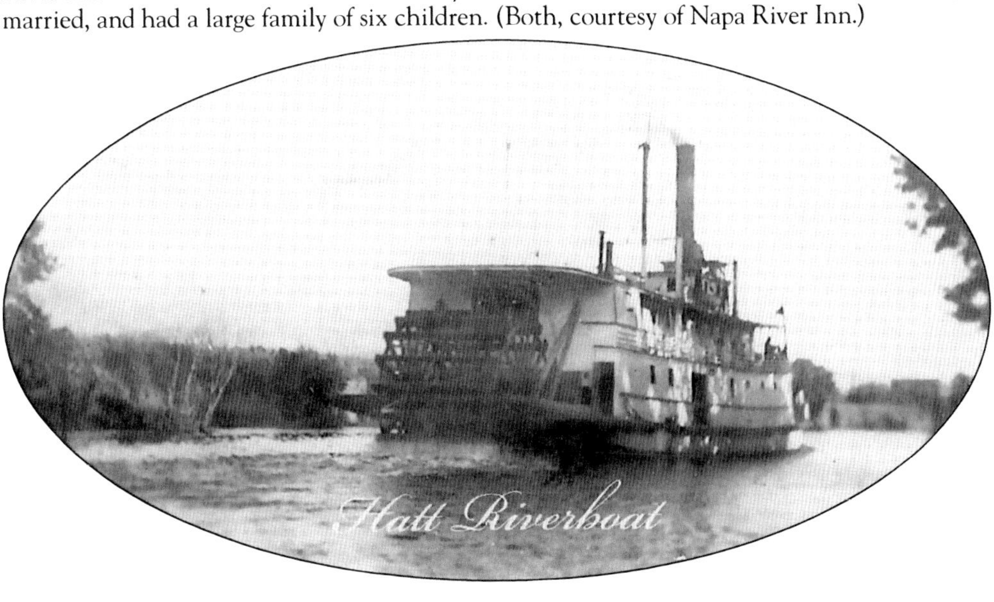

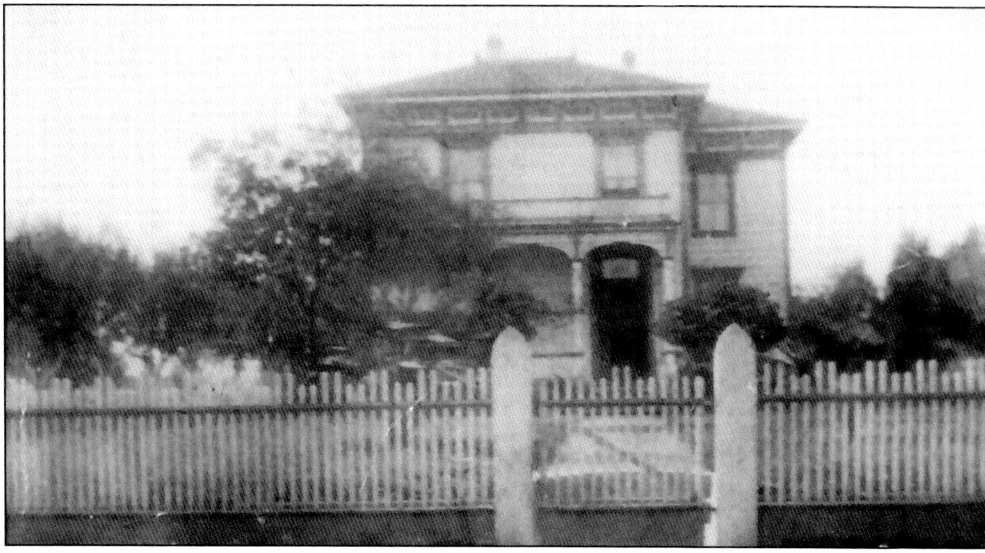

The Hatt family home still stands at 131 Coombs Street; however, the fence is gone. After a brief time running a mercantile shop, Captain Hatt became disenchanted and returned to the river. In 1878, after nearly 11 years on the river, he again went back to the shore. Hatt kept a schooner, the *Amelia* (not the steamer by the same name), named after one of his daughters. With his warehouse business growing, he leased a parcel between Main, Fourth, and Brown Streets and constructed two buildings: a single-story shop for produce and a coal shed. According to Napa historian Rebecca Yerger, as a near neighbor to the new courthouse, Hatt contracted to supply coal at $10.80 a ton. Being quite the entrepreneur, he also sold vegetables from his store. Hatt became involved in flood-control campaigns when the wharfs he owned, which were located near his store, were destroyed in an 1883 flood. Undeterred, he expanded his riverfront property in 1884 and constructed a warehouse with bricks made from Napa River clay and fired onsite. (Courtesy of Napa River Inn.)

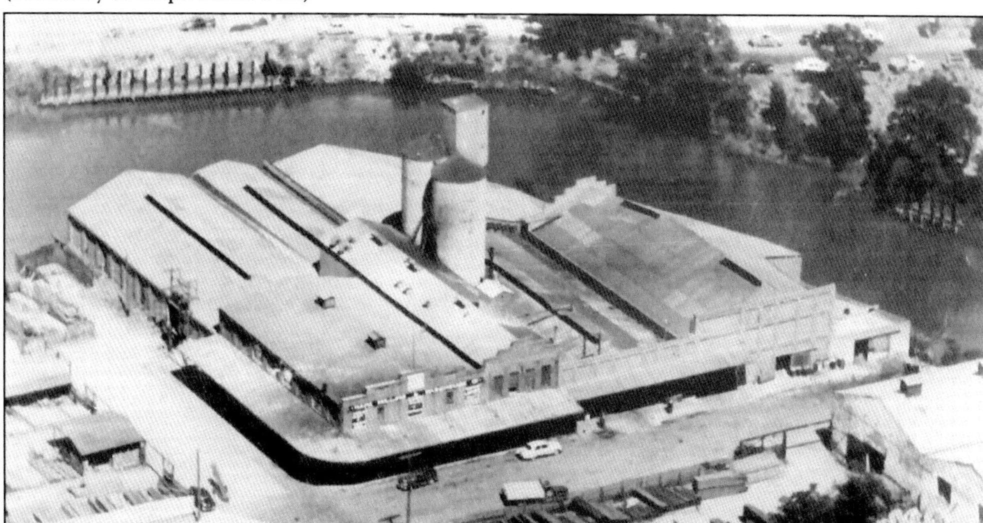

The Hatt Building was also known as the Napa Milling Building. Constructed by Albert Hatt in the early 1880s as a grain warehouse, it once housed a roller rink and basketball court upstairs. The roller rink was in use until 1930. (Courtesy of Napa River Inn.)

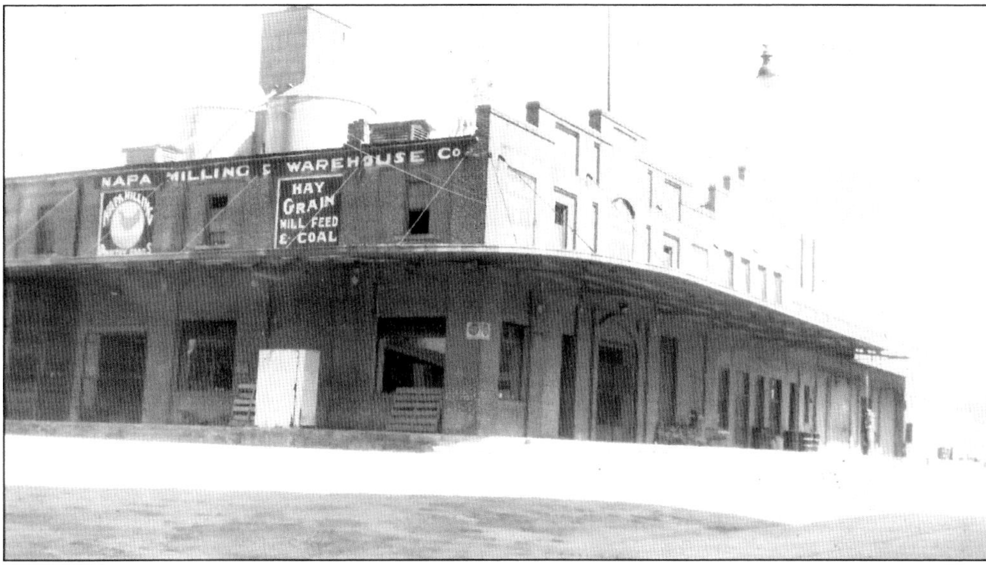

Behind the brick Embarcadero Building at the terminus of Brown and Main Streets, Hatt constructed a wharf in 1887 to load and unload steamships. He also used the wharf to dock his personal schooner *Amelia* and a small fleet of steamships used for shipping. In 1893, Hatt erected a small building out of poured-in-place concrete and rebar with a rolling door that provided access to the wharf. It served as a boathouse. Today, it is a new, high-quality restoration by Harry Price, featuring hotels, restaurants, and shops.

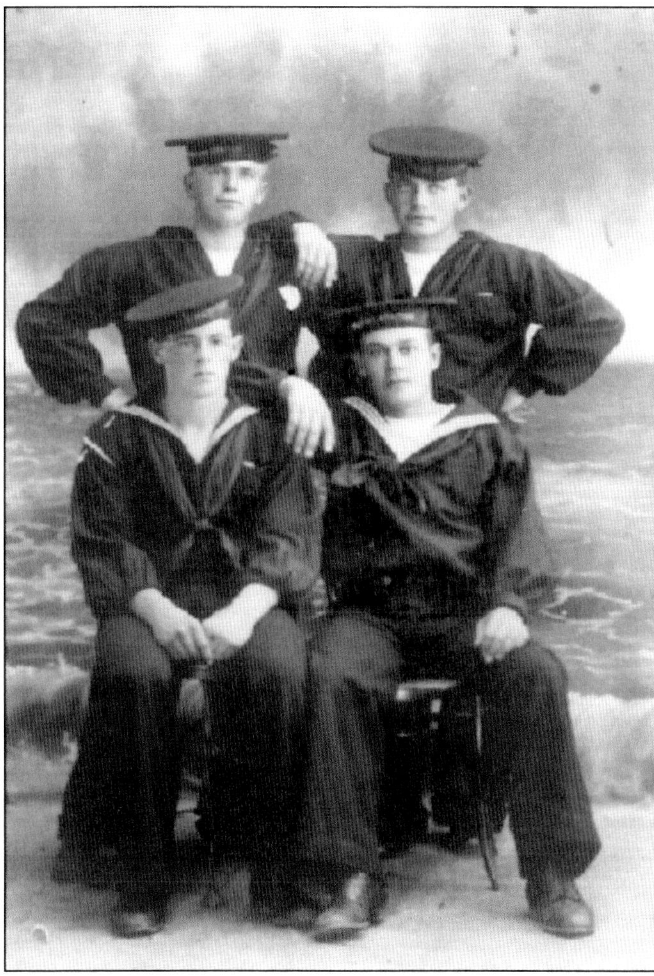

The Hatt's 20-year-old son William Frederick Hatt became a sailor like his father. Here, he poses with his shipmates. Sadly, he was killed in a fall from the main topsail of the vessel *Iroquois* as it rounded Cape Horn bound for New York in late 1887. (Courtesy of Napa River Inn.)

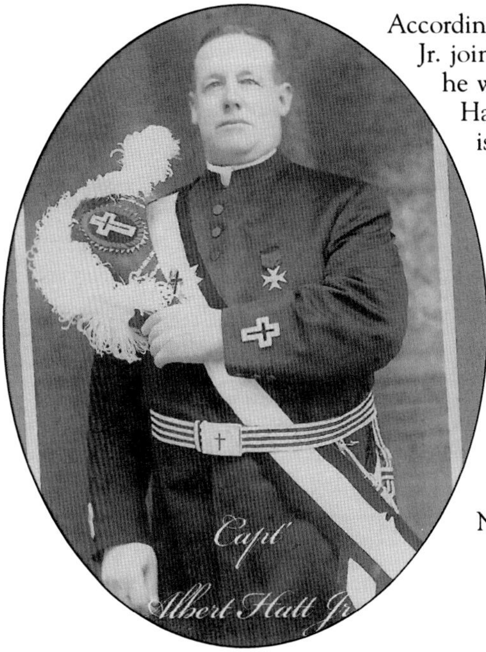

According to Napa historian Rebecca Yerger, Albert Hatt Jr. joined Company H of the National Guard where he was eventually promoted to second lieutenant. Having grown up around riverboats all his life, it is likely he was also a riverboat captain, although there is no other historical evidence to support this hypothesis other than the words "Capt." printed on his photograph. He married Margaret Riley in 1889 and had five children. He took over his father's business following the death of his mother in 1898. Margaret died in 1906 from cancer and left Albert Hatt Jr. a widower with five children. His own health began to fail when he was plagued with business troubles, including the loss of his financial interest in the St. Helena riverboat. Albert Hatt Jr. took his own life in 1912 at the age of 45. (Courtesy of Napa River Inn.)

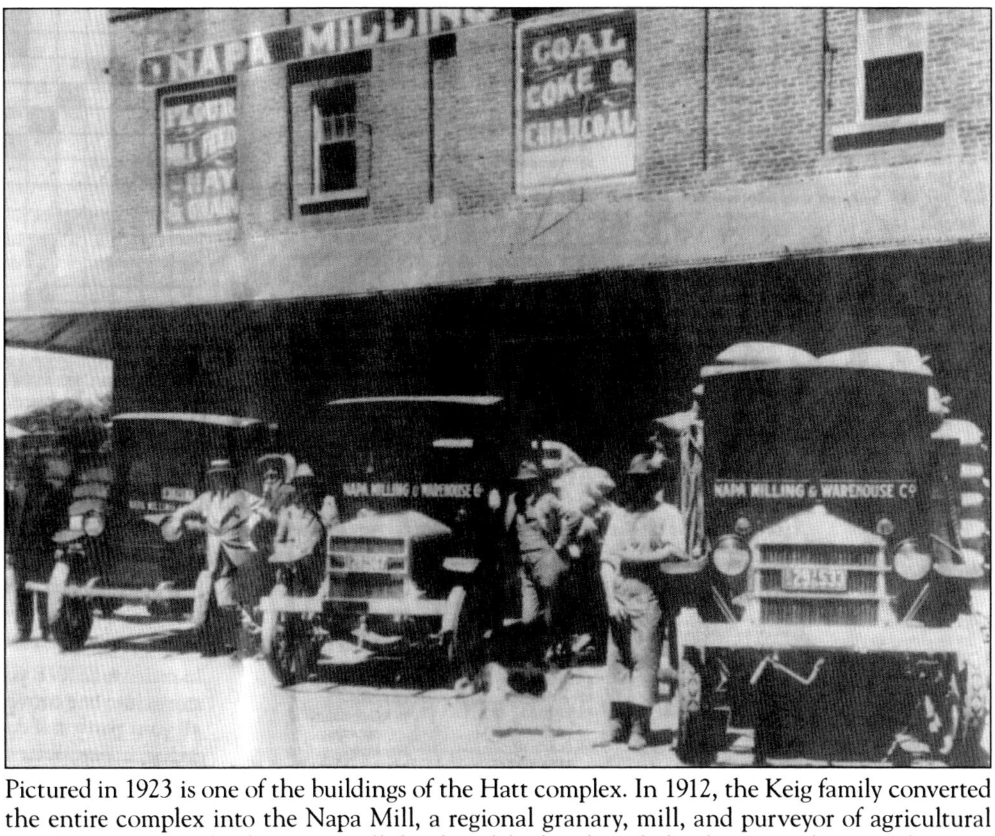

Pictured in 1923 is one of the buildings of the Hatt complex. In 1912, the Keig family converted the entire complex into the Napa Mill, a regional granary, mill, and purveyor of agricultural supplies. Interestingly, the Napa Mill developed feed and mash for the Seventh Day Adventists because they could not use any meat products in the blends. (Courtesy of Roger Knapp.)

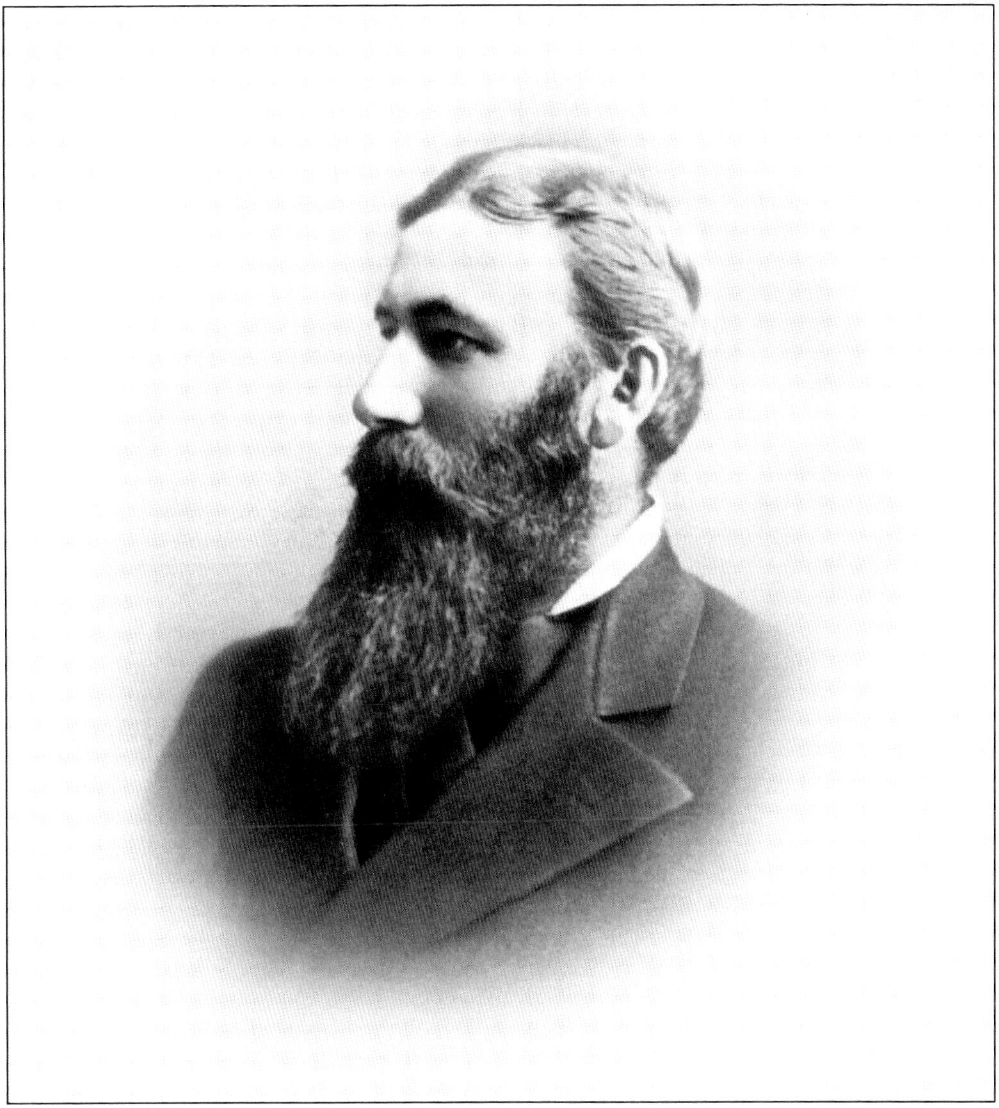

Although not a riverboat captain per se, Gustave Niebaum (originally Gustaf Nybom) deserves special mention in regards to sea captains who settled in Napa. Niebaum was born in Oulu, Finland, in 1842 and was schooled in Helsinki, Finland. At the age of 16, he became a cabin boy aboard one of the ships of the Russian American Company, which had established a fur-trading business throughout all of Alaska. For the next three years, he traveled throughout Alaska and Russia negotiating for furs. He was considered to be an expert on the land, water, animals, and people of the area. By the end of the 1850, Niebaum had become a successful fur trader. He founded the Alaskan Commercial Company in San Francisco and prepared some of the first official maps of the coastline of Alaska. Niebaum became the consul of Russia in the United States in 1867. In this role, he helped explore the Alaska territory and promoted ratification of the Alaska Purchase from Russia. With the sale of Alaska to the United States completed, he journeyed to San Francisco with sealskins valued at $500,000, according K.G. Olin's article "The Cabin Boy Who Became a Multimillionaire," published in the *Swedish Finn Historical Society Quarterly*. In 1868, when he arrived in San Francisco, he was only 26 years old. It was later that he Americanized his name as Gustave Niebaum. (Courtesy of Francis Ford Coppola.)

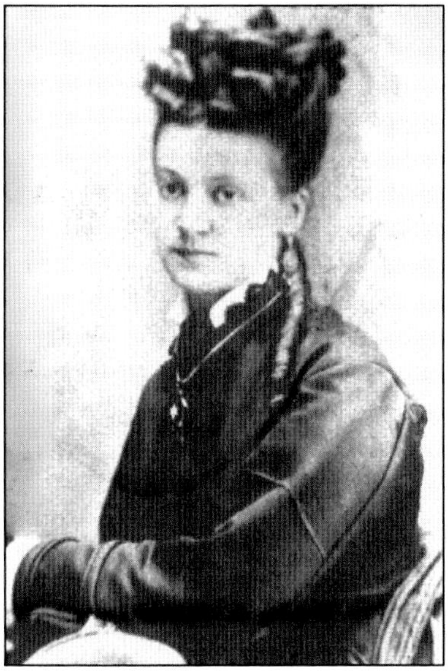

Captain Niebaum married Susan Shingleberger, a German American, in 1873 and planned to build a ship that he and his wife could use to sail around the world. Unfortunately, his wife did not share his strong feelings for the sea. In search of an area of interest they both could share, he looked to the vineyards of Napa Valley. Niebaum was taken with the beauty of the valley and purchased the Inglenook Winery in Rutherford in 1879. Niebaum's wines won gold medals at the Paris World's Fair of 1889, and as his wines gained in notoriety, he shipped wines down the Napa River to customers all around the world. (Courtesy of Francis Ford Coppola.)

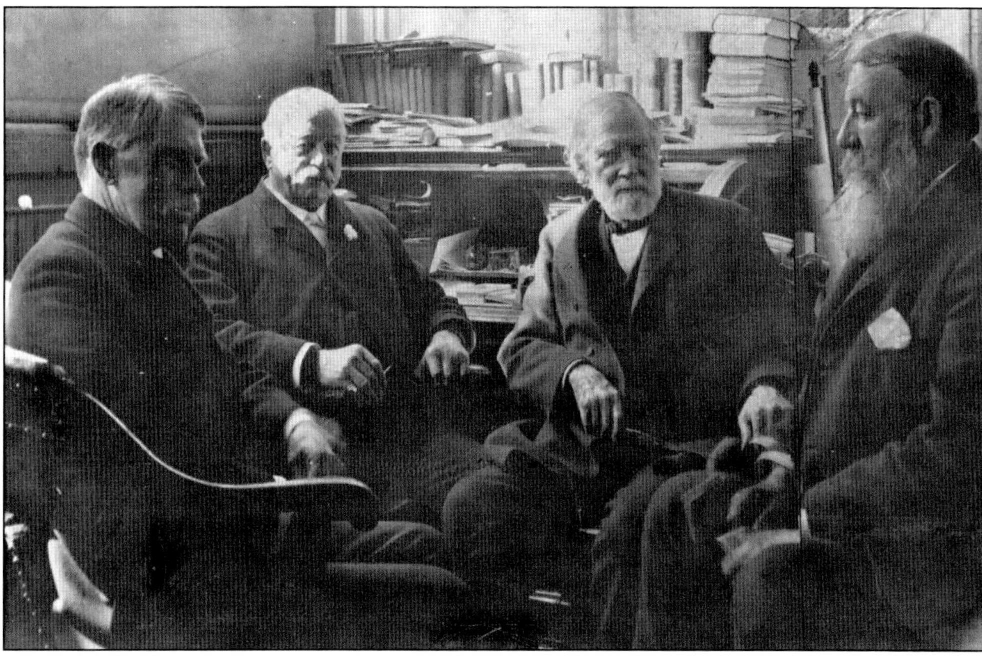

Pictured here from left to right are H.H. McIntyre, Capt. M.C. Erskine, Prof. George Davidson, and Capt. Gustave Niebaum at the San Francisco headquarters of the Alaskan Commercial Company around 1909. Napa mayor John A. Fuller and Gustave Niebaum likely knew each other before either had settled in Napa; both had worked in Alaska, and Fuller had become an agent for the American Russian Commercial Company, directing all of their operations in the fishing and lumber industries. Fuller, born in England in 1828, served as an apprentice in the East India Company in Bombay. One of the first elected councilmen for the town of Sitka, Alaska, he also developed and erected a circular sawmill that lessened the price of manufactured lumber. In 1869, he sawed 10,000 feet of yellow cedar and gave it to Secretary of State William H. Seward to wainscot his library. Fuller settled in Napa in 1872, and in 1899, he was elected mayor. (Courtesy of the Alaska State Library, Historical Collections.)

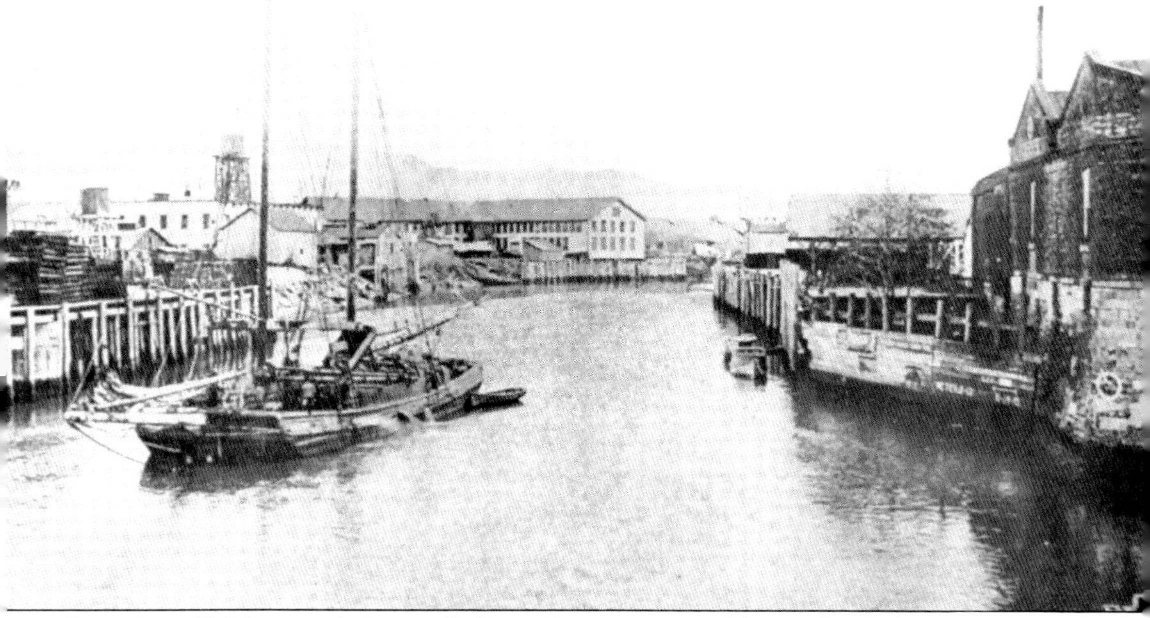

Capt. Harry H. Hammerich (originally Franz Henry Hammerich) owned and commanded the scow schooner *Cinderella.* The vessel could carry 34,000 feet of lumber and often carried hay and other cargo between the Carneros District in southern Napa County and the Sacramento River. Both Hammerich and his son were boatmen. According to the Great Register of Voters 1898, he was born in Germany between 1860 and 1861 and naturalized in San Francisco in 1883. He was 5 feet, 10 inches tall with blue eyes, blond hair, and a light complexion. Hammerich married and had six children: Fritz (likely Americanized as "Fred"), Wilmer, Dorothy, Henry, Harriett, and Alice. He divorced between 1910 and 1920.

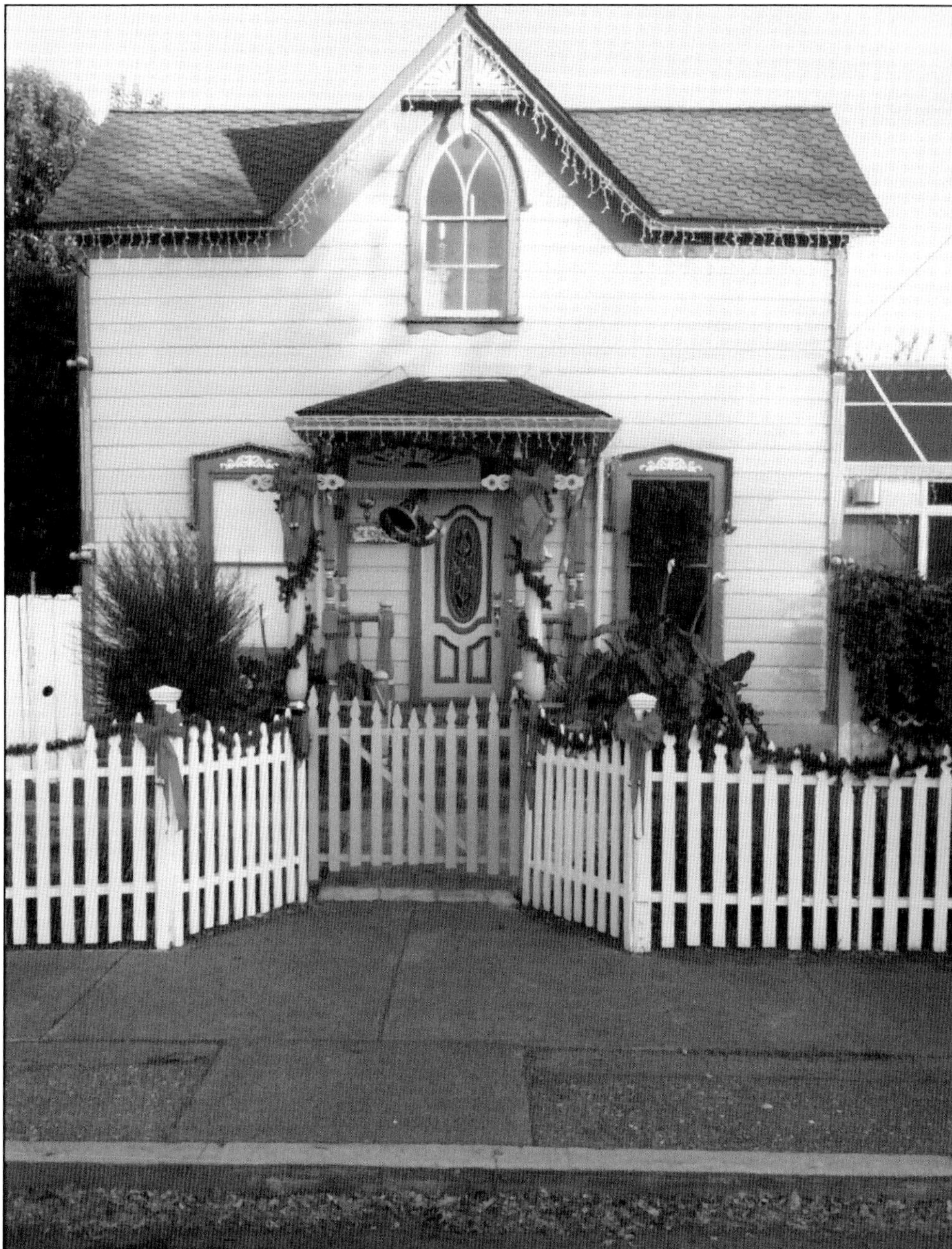

Hammerich purchased one of Napa's finest early Gothic Revival houses in 1883, which then stood on Grant Street (now Brown Street) behind the White House Inn, and had it moved to its present location at 482 Cross Street. It was not unusual to move houses around town in the 19th century. The two-story house has shiplap siding and decorative motifs on the vertical corner boards. According to current owner Steve Robinson, its proximity to the Napa River made it an ideal home for a river man. Hammerich choose the spot because it was on a bit of a higher knoll, and with the knowledge that the river could flood the town, Hammerich made sure that his home would remain high and dry. (Author's collection.)

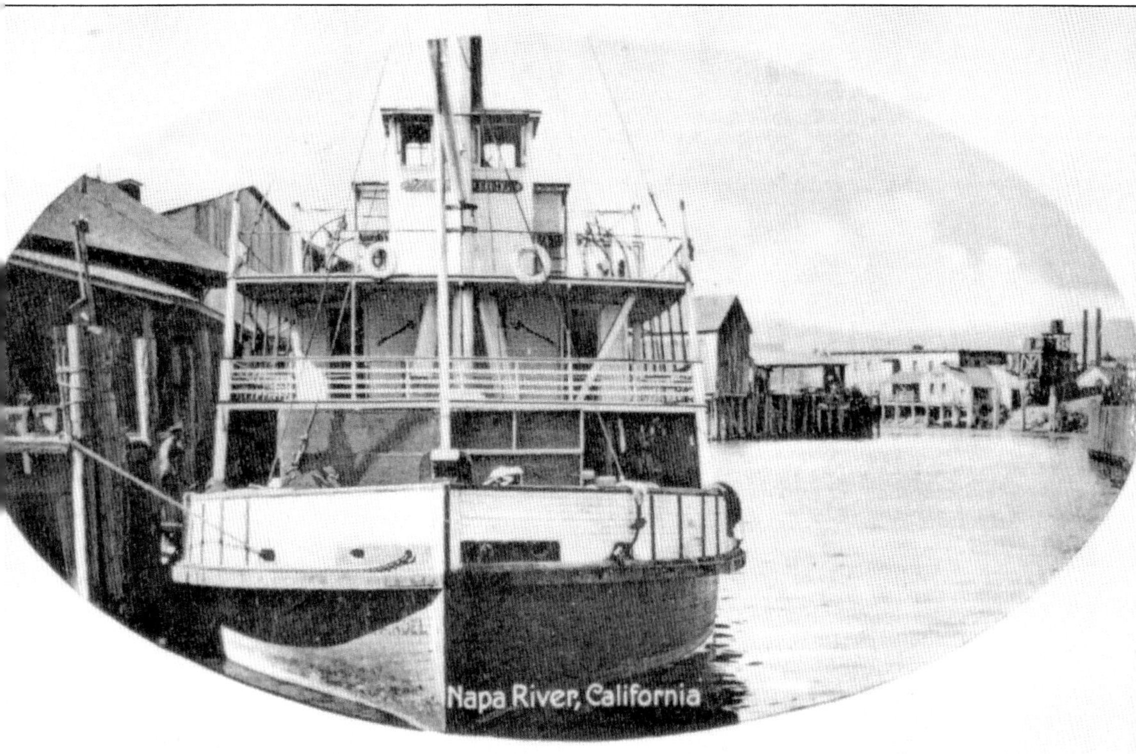

The *Zinfandel* was owned by Capt. N.H. Wulff, but Capt. Horace Greeley Bell piloted her on the Napa River for several years. Bell's family came to California in the 1850s from Boston, Massachusetts. His father worked in San Francisco as a contracting plasterer. His mother, originally from Northern Ireland, settled in Petaluma after her husband died in 1869. Horace attended public school in Petaluma. By age 19, he was working at Haystack Landing in the Lakeville area. By age 20 in 1880, he had secured a place on board the steamer pilot *Captain Graves*. He was aboard her when she blew up on Petaluma Creek above Lakeville in 1883. Eight of the passengers and one of the crewmen were killed, yet Bell miraculously suffered no harm. A new steamer, the *Gold*, took the place of the wrecked *Captain Graves*, and aboard her, Bell became first mate and later pilot. In 1886, Bell moved further east to Napa and became master of the steamer *Zinfandel*. He ran the *Zinfandel* for 11 years before resigning his post. It is not known why he resigned, but he did go on to master several other vessels on the bay. Hired by the DuPont Powder Company, he navigated the *Hercules* between the city of Hercules and San Francisco for three years.

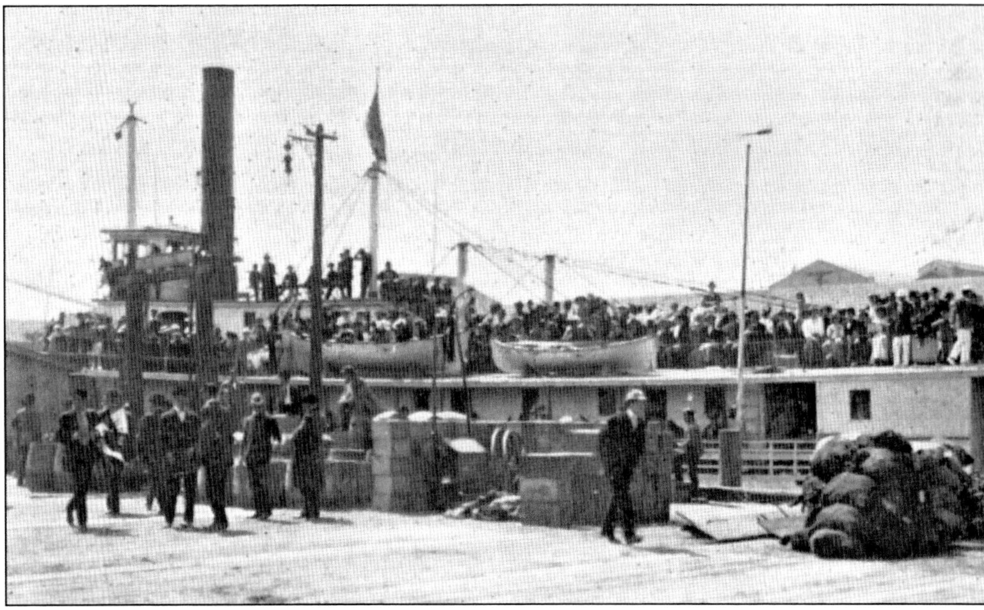

The *St. Helena* is loaded with passengers and ready for an excursion. In 1911, Captain Bell switched his employment to the Napa Transportation Company as master of the *St. Helena* and made regular runs between Napa and San Francisco.

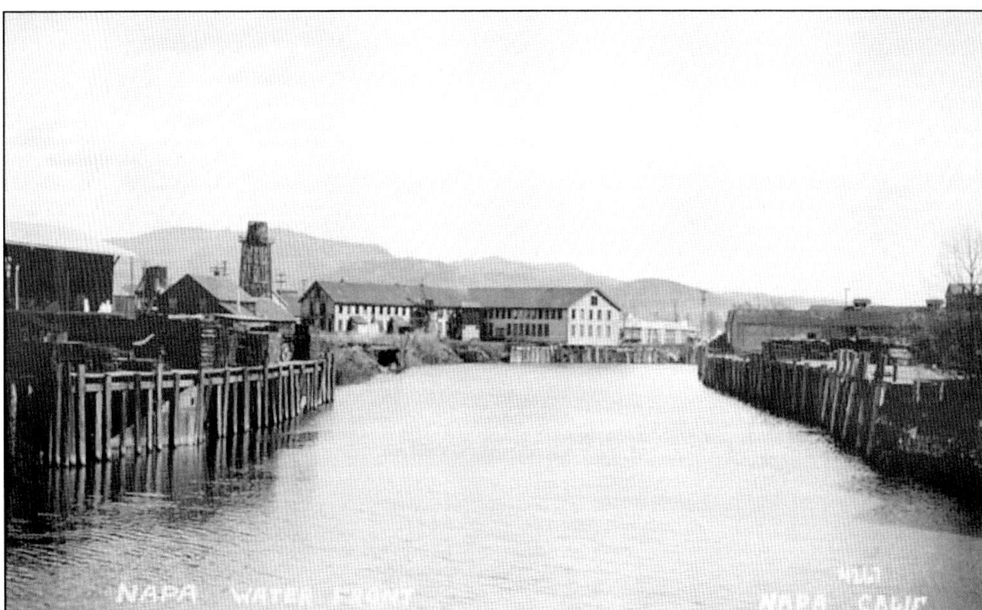

The Napa Woolen Mills is the white building visible in this view taken from the Third Street Bridge.

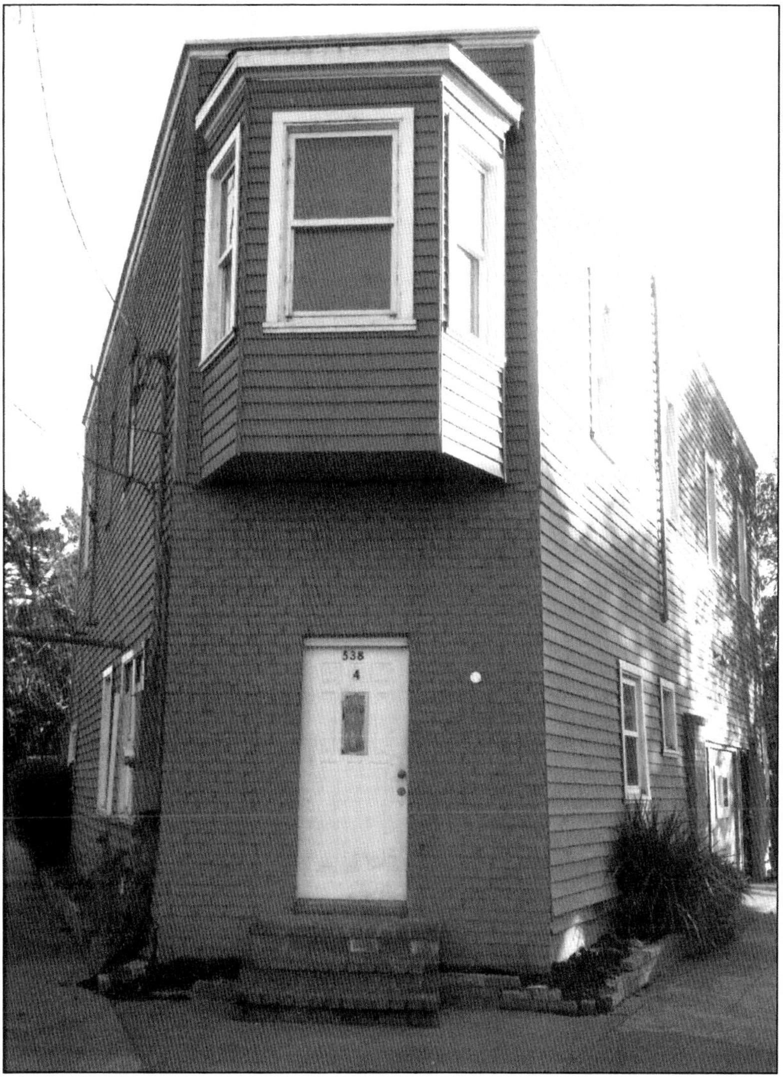

Located at 538 Brown Street, Capt. Otto Walton lived in the Riverboat House in 1910 with his family, directly across the street from Captain Wulff. Purportedly, the Captain Walton kept a riverboat on the first floor and his family lived above. He was born in Lebanon, Laclede County, Missouri, in August 1872. When he was three, his family moved to Kern County, California, where his father found a job on a ranch. His father, Levi, was injured by a mule, and he had to give up his position. The family moved north to Napa, where his father died at the age of 38 from the effects of his injury. Walton's mother moved to Napa to be near her father, Maxwell C. Alexander, who had served the Union cause and relocated to Napa following the Civil War. Otto F. Walton was raised in Napa from the age of three. He worked his grandfather's ranch for four years, and at 17 years old, he became fascinated with the sea. Walton began steam boating on the *Zinfandel*. After serving 11 years as a deckhand under Captain Bell, he was made watchman on the *St. Helena* and later became a mate. In the fall of 1896, he was promoted to pilot of the *St. Helena* until July 1911, when he was offered the position of master of the *Zinfandel*. He worked for the Napa Transportation Company ferrying passengers and freight between Napa and San Francisco. Captain Walton married Marie Nielsen from Rio Vista in a San Francisco ceremony. They had two children: Gladys Irene and Vivian Beryl. (Author's collection.)

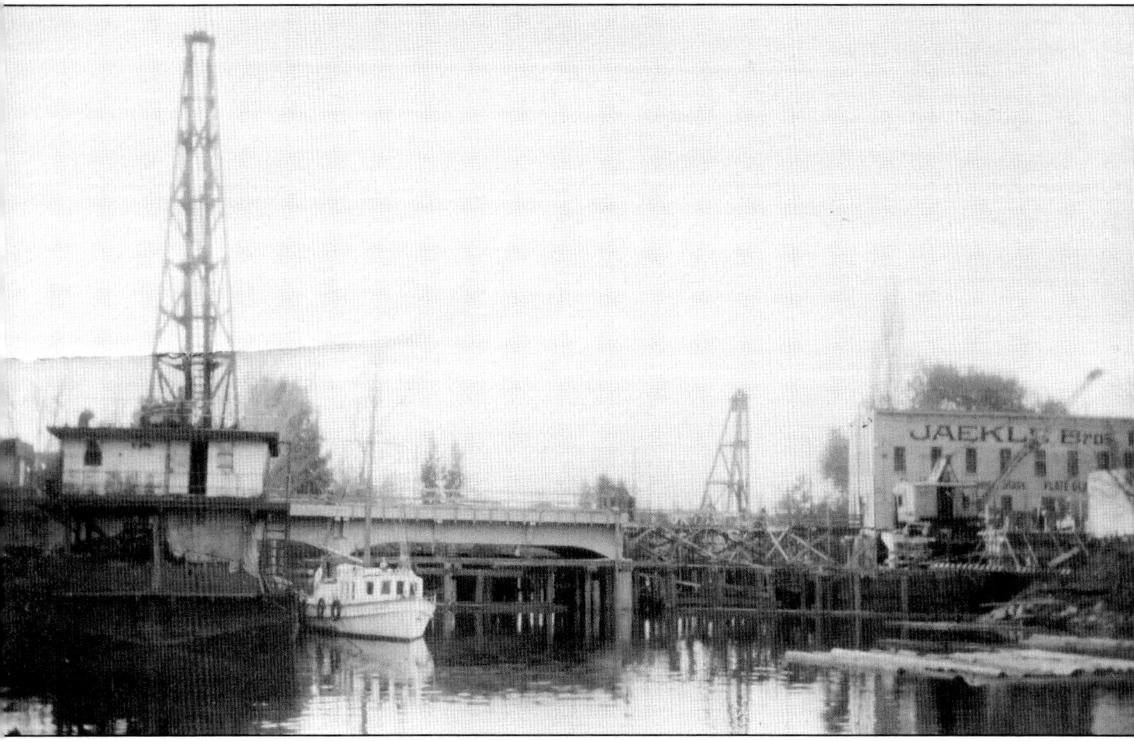

Jaekle Brothers Planing Factory can be seen to the right as the Third Street Bridge is constructed.

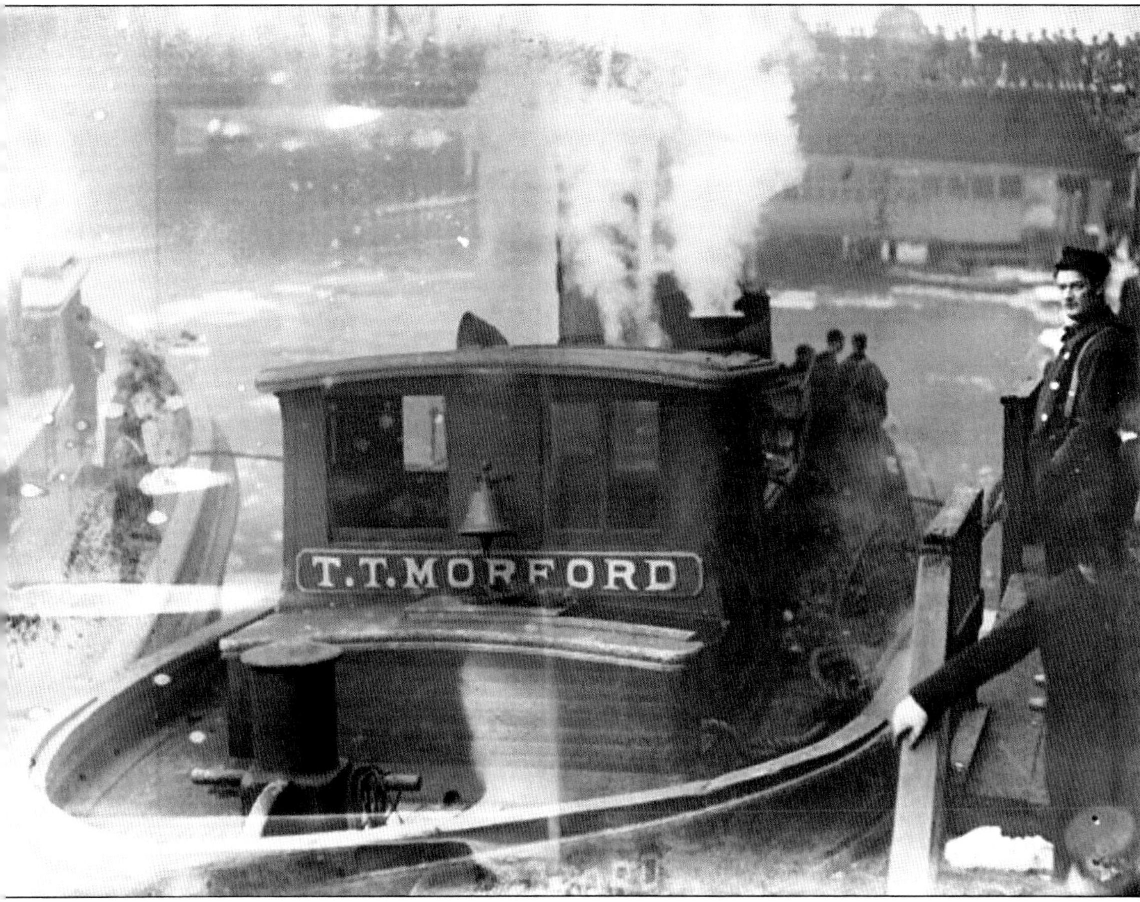

This 1909 tug, the *T.T. Morford*, is similar to the one overseen by Capt. J.H. Edgecumbe. In December 1907, Captain Edgecumbe was injured by an explosion on board the *Fox*, a tugboat originating in San Francisco but anchored in the Napa River opposite Stanley Ranch. He sustained terrible burns while relighting the oil-burning furnace. Fire caused the tank of oil to explode, and the captain jumped into the river to extinguish the flames on his clothing. A passing ship, the *Columbia*, came to his rescue and brought him to Napa City, where he received treatment at St. Michael's Hospital. Sadly, his burns were so severe, they cost him his life. The 14 men briefly described in these pages provide a glimpse into the story of the Napa River and its pivotal role as a transportation engine. There were many other captains who sailed vessels through the San Pablo Bay up the Napa River from 1844 to 1890.

Vessels Documented on the Napa River	**Year**	**Captain**
Amelia, schooner		Hatt
Amelia, steamer	1864	Curry; Jones
Anna Abernethy, steamer	1856	Folger
Antelope, steamer	1864	
Aqua Caliente, schooner	1871	
Aspinwall		West
Calistoga, schooner	1867	
Caroline, schooner	1889	Wulff
Chrysopolis	1854	Chadwick
Cinderella, scow schooner	1871-1910	Wulff; Hammerich
City of Napa, schooner	1884	Knudsen
City of Napa, steamer/packet	1892	Knudsen; Pinkham
Cleopatra, steamer	1864	Baxter
Columbia	1907	
Commodore Jones, steamer (renamed *Jack Hayes)*	1859	Baxter; Chadwick
Crawford, steamer	1871	
Dolphin, steamer	1850	Baxter
Ellen, schooner	1871	Wulff
Emily Dale, schooner	1871	
Emma	1889	Pinkham
Express, steamer	1878	J.G. White, Owner
Fairfield	1871	
Fannie, steamer	1871	
Filt		West
Fox	1907	Edgecumbe
Georgie Woods, steamer	1868	
Greenwood, schooner	1871	
Guadalupe, steamer	1856	Doling
H. H. Knapp, schooner	1884	Knudsen
Hamlet, schooner	1864	
Harriett, steamer	1879	
Heckle, schooner	1889	
Hercules, schooner	1890	Jensen
Hope, steamer	1889	
Ide of Brooklyn, schooner	1889	
Jack Hays (previously *Commodore Jones)*		Baxter; Chadwick
Jesse Fremont, scow schooner	1878	

While not all captains are known, a vast array of ships brought goods and passengers to Napa during the years of 1844 to 1890.

Jilt, sloop	1856-1866	Knudsen
John Frederick, schooner	1878	
John McCullough, Schooner	1873	
Josephine, bark	1851	Chadwick
Katie Me, schooner	1890	
Kiturah, sloop	1856	John Strikland
Lizzie Williams, schooner	1889	
Malek Adhel	1848	
Master Mariner, schooner	1878	Wulff
Napa City, schooner	1872	Knudsen
Napa City, steamer/packet	1910	Pinkham
Paul Pry, steamer	1859	Baxter
P.R. No. 7, scow schooner	1878	
Pilgrim	1855	West
Princess	1877	Baxter
Reindeer, steamer	1852	Chadwick
Rosselle, schooner	1889	
Sacramento, schooner	1844	Sutter
Salina, schooner	1871	
San Francisco, paddleboat	1880	
San Jose, scow schooner	1887	
Silver Cloud, schooner	1870	
Sophia, steamer	1857	
St. Helena, steamer	1886-1911	Hatt; Bell; Walton
Susana, schooner	1841	Davis
Susan Owens, schooner	1855	
Taccao, schooner	1863	
T. C. Walker, steamer	1871	
Traveller, schooner	1884	Caubriel
Two Brothers, schooner	1891	
Vaquero, steamer	1877	Baxter
Violante, sloop	1878	
Witch of the Bay, sloop	1889	
Zina Reed, schooner	1858	Reed
Zinfandel, steamer	1889-1911	Wulff; Bell; Walton,Hatt
Chart based upon the work of Jack R. Greig,		
The Vessels of the Napa River 1844-1890.		

Examining newspaper records, historian Jack R. Greig offers a glimpse into the robust trade and traffic along the river.

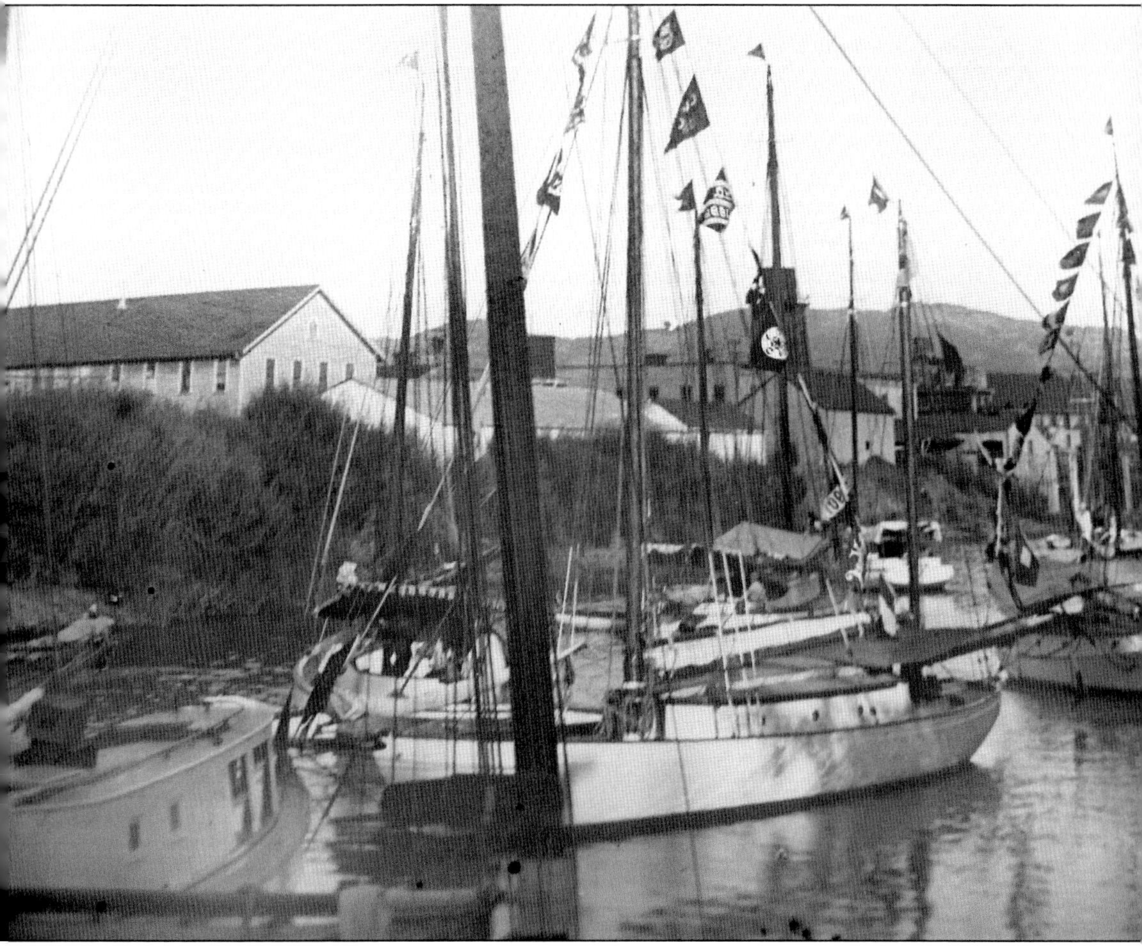

Sailing vessels display flags on their rigging as they prepare for a race.

Four

River of Plenty
Industry Profits Napa, Poisons the River

Napa was well situated with both rail and river traffic, and there was business to be done, unrestrained by environmental concerns. Almost all manufacturing operations were located on the river, lining the waterfront by 1898. The area between Division and Third Streets became the industrial center. There were four tanneries that made glove, shoe, harness, and sole leather; a woolen mill; glove factory; shoe factory; cannery; cream of tartar works; a lumberyard; planing mill; flour mill; fruit driers; distilleries; wineries; and warehouses. As Earl Dietz, longtime owner of the Napa Glove Company and Hide House, explained, "Napa was a leather community and you need water to make leather." The river and industry went hand in hand. So many businesses resulted from the Sawyer Tannery, Dietz referred to Napa as a "leather colony." The tannery was famous for their sheepskin coats. Belt factories, shoe factories, and hide houses sprung up. Every industry that was dependent upon leather products became part of this colony. According to a March 13, 1898, *San Francisco Call* article, "Napa's commercial advantages are great; in fact, superior to those of most California towns for Napa has water as well as rail communication with the outside." By 1898, the freight and passenger steamer *Zinfandel* journeyed from Napa to San Francisco three times per week. According to Richard Dillon in *Napa Valley Heyday*, the ship left in time to catch the night's high tide and made it into the city in three hours. If she met strong tides or wind, it could take twice as long to make the journey. In addition to passengers, the boat's hull was loaded with grain and, later, wine that would be shipped to the East Coast. She had the capacity for 600 fifty-gallon barrels. The *Napa City* sailed the same route as the *Zinfandel*.

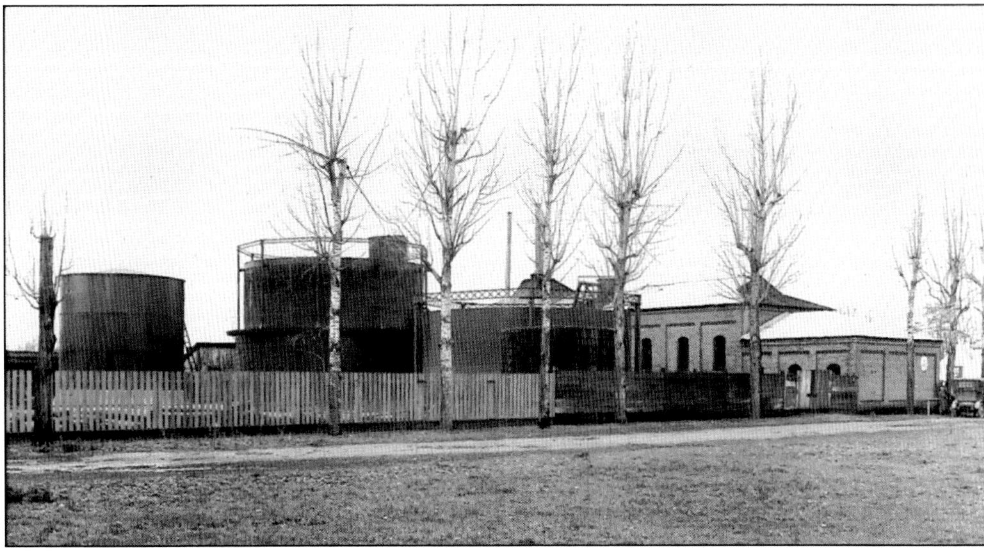

In the 1800s and early 1900s, before natural gas was available, manufactured gas plants used coal and oil to produce gas for lighting, heating, and cooking. In 1867, city supervisors approved the Napa City Gas Light Company to lay gas pipes in the streets. The gasworks was located in a brick building on Fifth Street between Main and Brown Streets, and the gas was produced from coal shipped to San Francisco all the way from Australia and Scotland. The coal was then transported via barge and wagon to Napa. Coal that was gasified in coal ovens gave off a noxious mixture of sulfur, ammonia, and heavy hydrocarbons. Notoriously, residues produced from distilled coal were usually either disposed into rivers or stocked in basins that polluted the soil. In 1888, a new manufactured gas plant was built on Riverside Street. (Courtesy of Pacific Gas & Electric.)

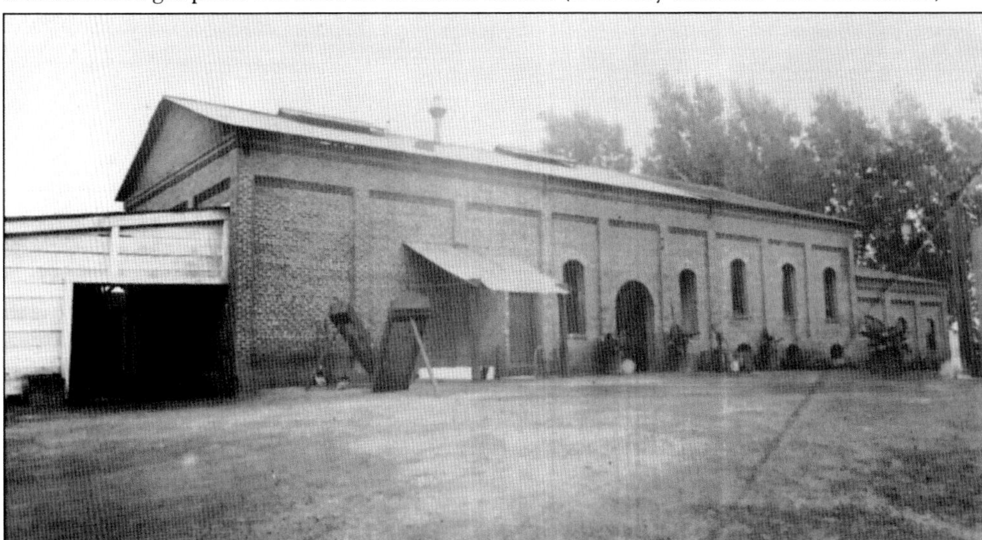

From 1888 to 1905, Napa City Gas Light and Heat and Napa Gas & Electric operated a manufactured gas plant on Riverside Avenue between Elm and Pine Streets along the river. Gas lighting was one of the most hotly debated technologies of the first industrial revolution. The development of high-pressure gas mains and compressors in the 1900s made the transportation of gas over long distances possible, but the nuisance and hazards associated with these plants in residential areas were cause for concern. (Courtesy of Pacific Gas & Electric.)

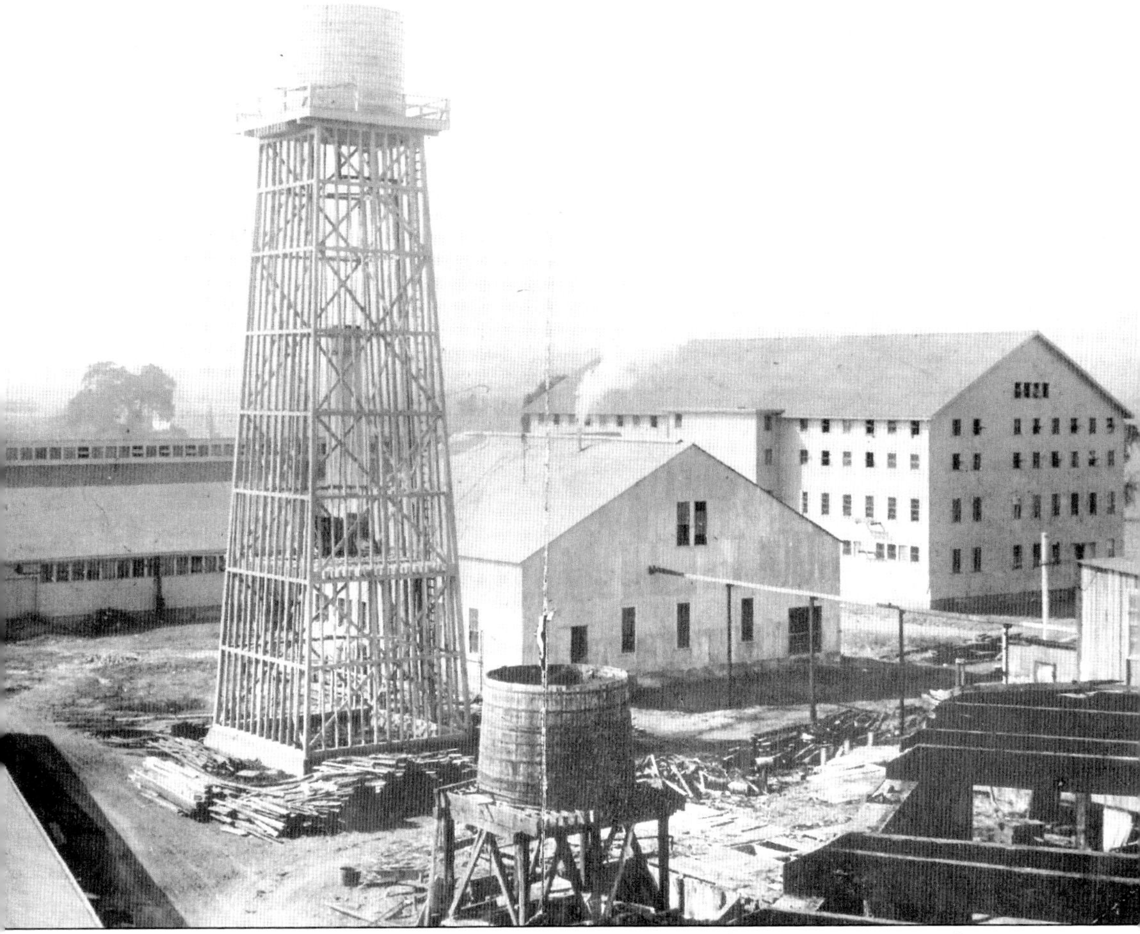

At the south end of town, the Sawyer Tannery was the largest and most extensive manufacturing plant in Napa County. In 1939, it was the largest tannery west of the Mississippi. Men processed about 1,500 hides per day. Over one million pounds of wool were pulled from sheep pelts per year and shipped to Boston commercial houses. The new buildings of Sawyer Tannery stand in the background, while the old buildings are situated in the foreground.

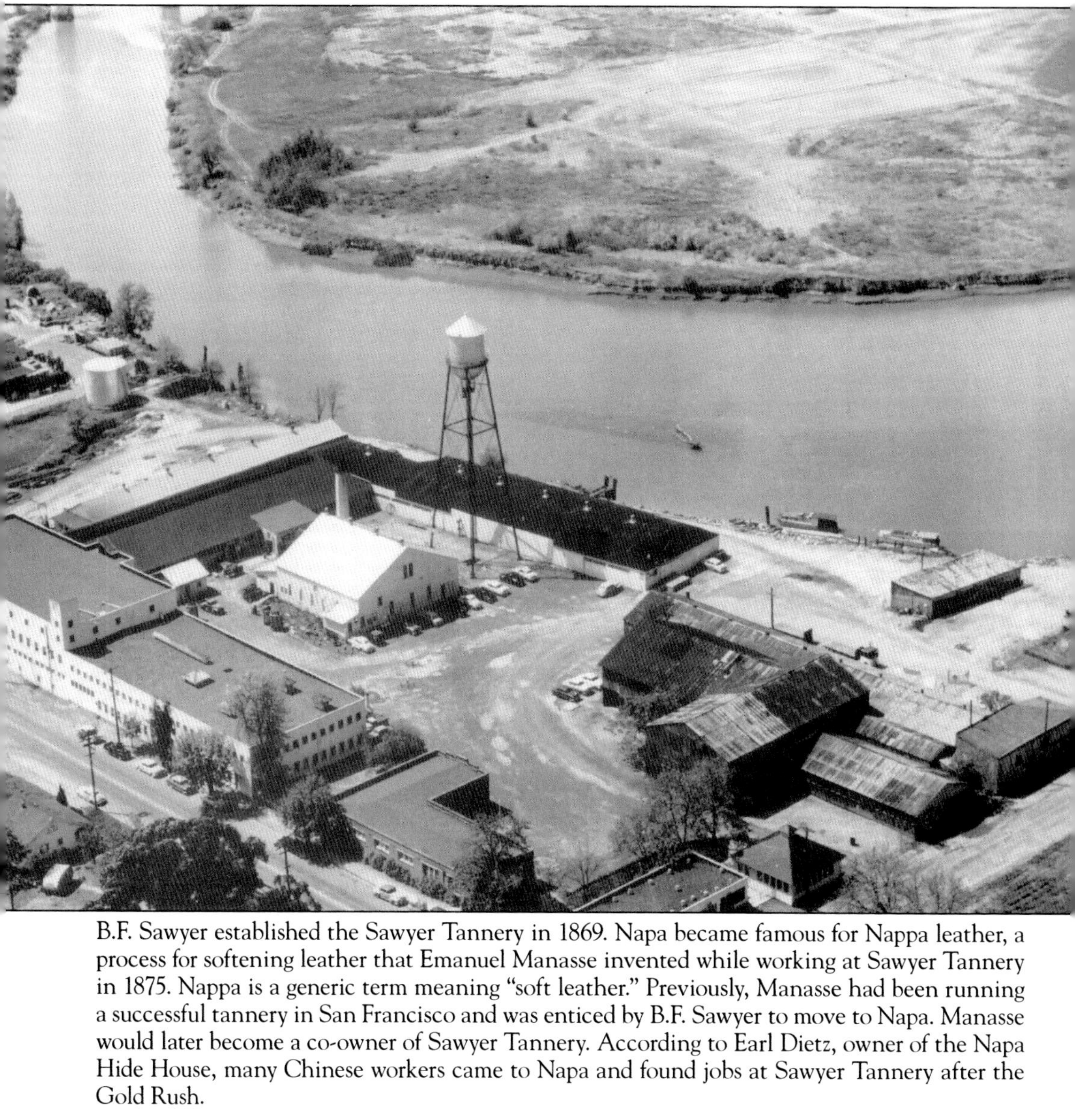

B.F. Sawyer established the Sawyer Tannery in 1869. Napa became famous for Nappa leather, a process for softening leather that Emanuel Manasse invented while working at Sawyer Tannery in 1875. Nappa is a generic term meaning "soft leather." Previously, Manasse had been running a successful tannery in San Francisco and was enticed by B.F. Sawyer to move to Napa. Manasse would later become a co-owner of Sawyer Tannery. According to Earl Dietz, owner of the Napa Hide House, many Chinese workers came to Napa and found jobs at Sawyer Tannery after the Gold Rush.

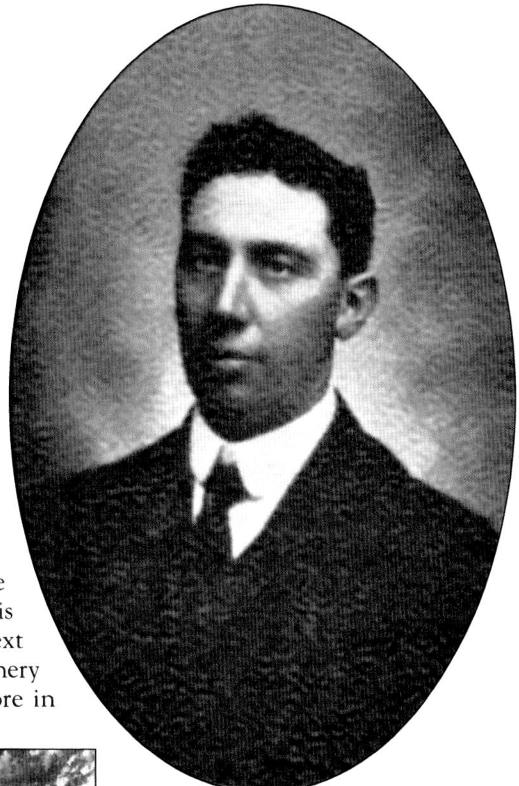

Thriving from the tannery trade, Edward Manasse and his three brothers—August, Irving, and Henry—lived in a beautiful mansion with their father, Emanual Manasse, at 433 Brown Street. It is now the White House Inn. Edward, pictured here, remained with Sawyer Tannery for the duration of his working life. According to Napa historian Lauren Coodley, August founded the Manasse Block Tannery in Berkeley, California, and his brother Irving later created his own tannery next door to Sawyer's tannery called CalNap Tannery in 1945. Henry Manasse opened a shoe store in downtown Napa. (Below, author's collection.)

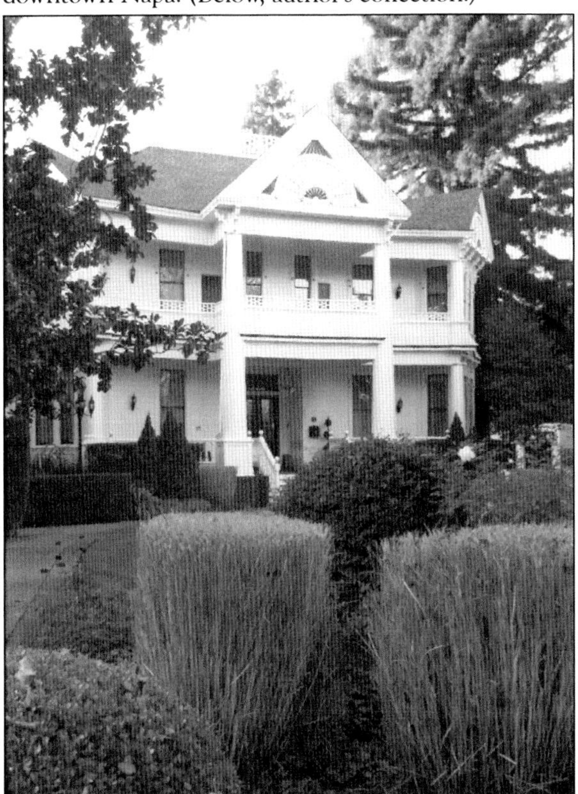

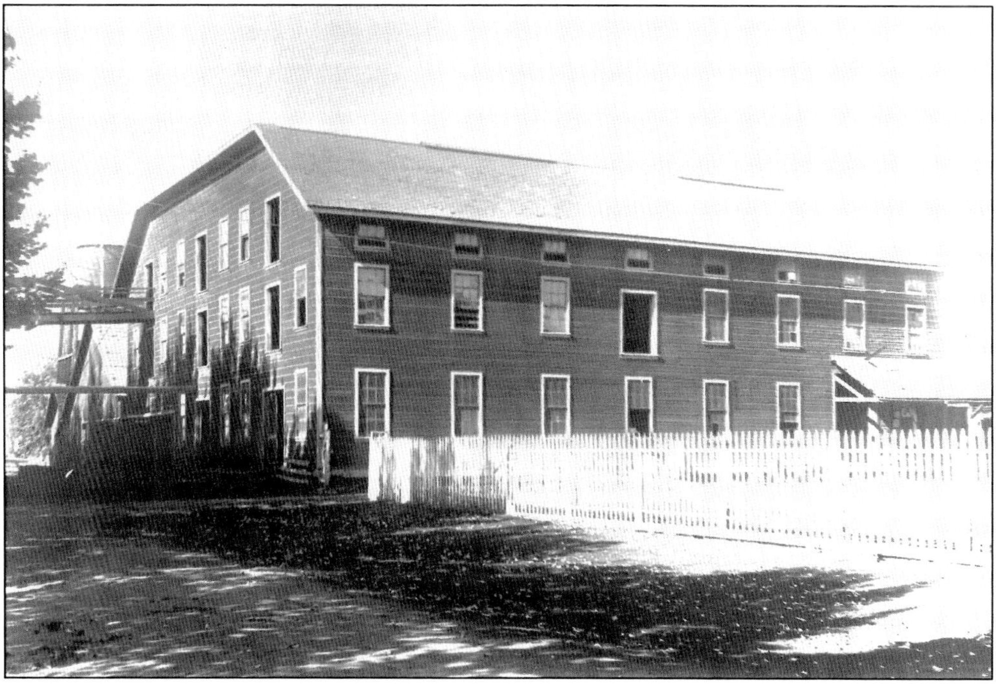

In the northern part of town beyond where the Napa River is navigable, Thomas McBain owned and managed the McBain & Company Tannery. He employed 18 men who processed 1,200 to 1,300 hides monthly. This smaller operation focused on harness, skirting, and sole leather. (Courtesy of Napa Valley Museum.)

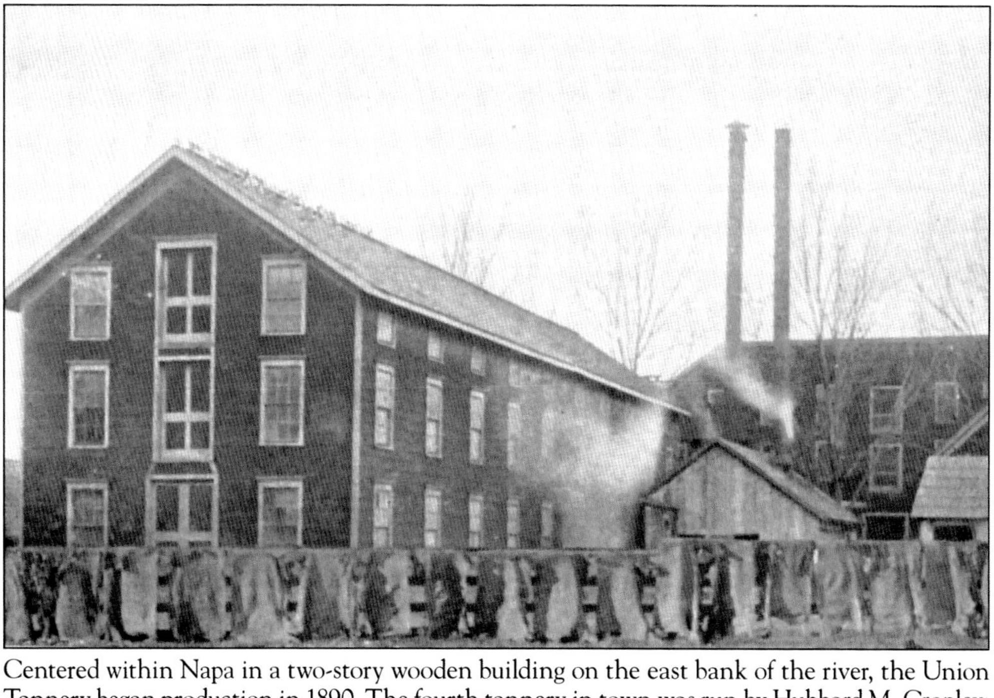

Centered within Napa in a two-story wooden building on the east bank of the river, the Union Tannery began production in 1890. The fourth tannery in town was run by Hubbard M. Cropley; the Sawyer Tanning Company owned the building.

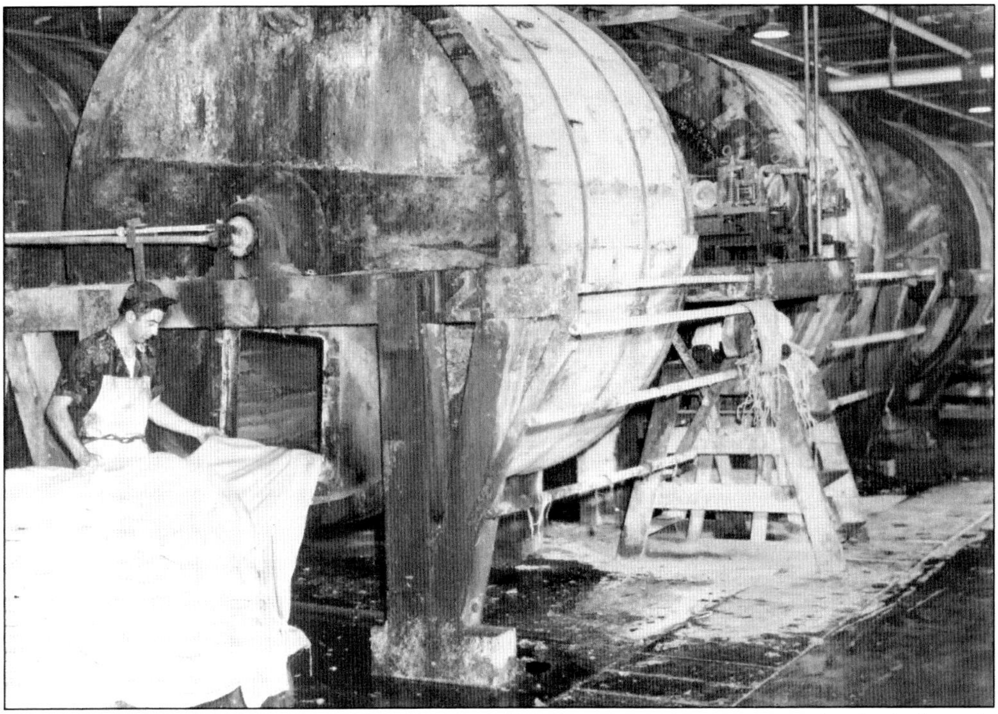

Salts of chromium or aluminum sulfate were used in the tanning process to make the hides soft. The Napa River suffered greatly from all four tanneries; during the production process, dyes, soaps, and tallow, along with animal carcasses, were dumped into the river. At the time, it was a common practice, as the concept of pollution was not understood. In an interview with Napa historian Lauren Coodley, Peter Manasse, a fourth-generation tanner and great-grandson of Emanuel Manasse, remembers the chemicals and dissolved hair being tossed into the Napa River, while the fleshings went to a tallow company. He described barges coming up the river, bringing diesel fuel for their boiler, and the hides arriving by freight train.

At Sawyer Tannery, animal hides were run through large scrapers (dehairing machines) that pulled and shaved the hair off the hides. According to a 1995 report prepared by the US Fish and Wildlife Service, "In the Napa River and San Francisco Bay, anecdotal information indicates pollution by tannery, chemical company and garage discharges may have resulted in substantial mortality of aquatic life as early as 1924."

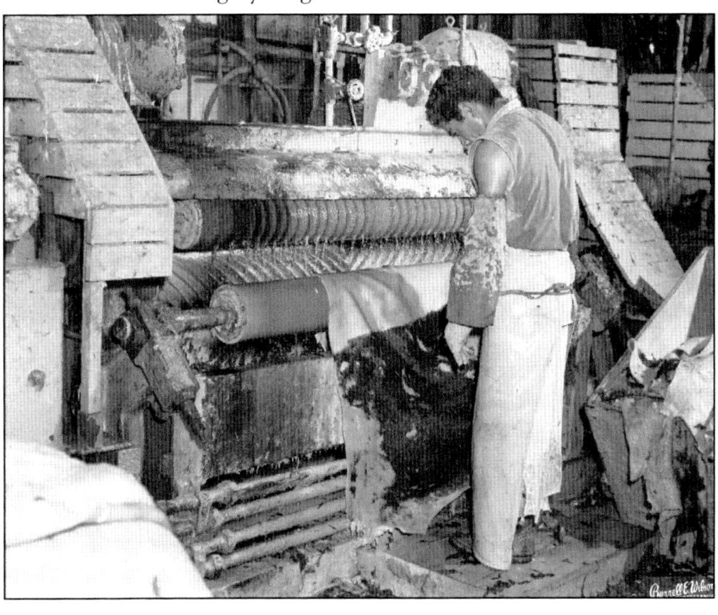

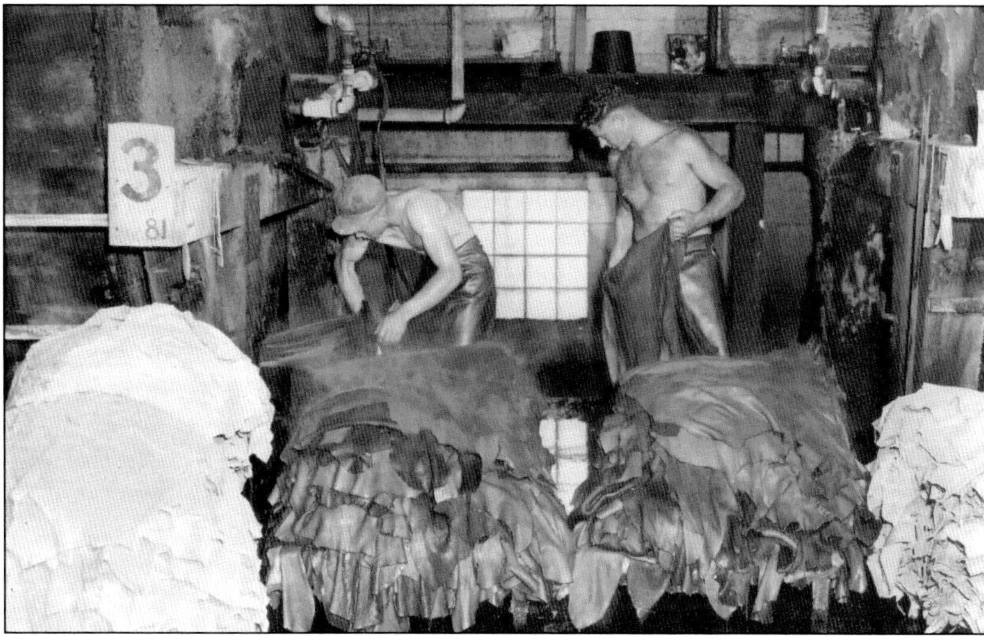

Layering piles of tanned hides was likely a hot and dirty job, which explains why the workers have removed their shirts.

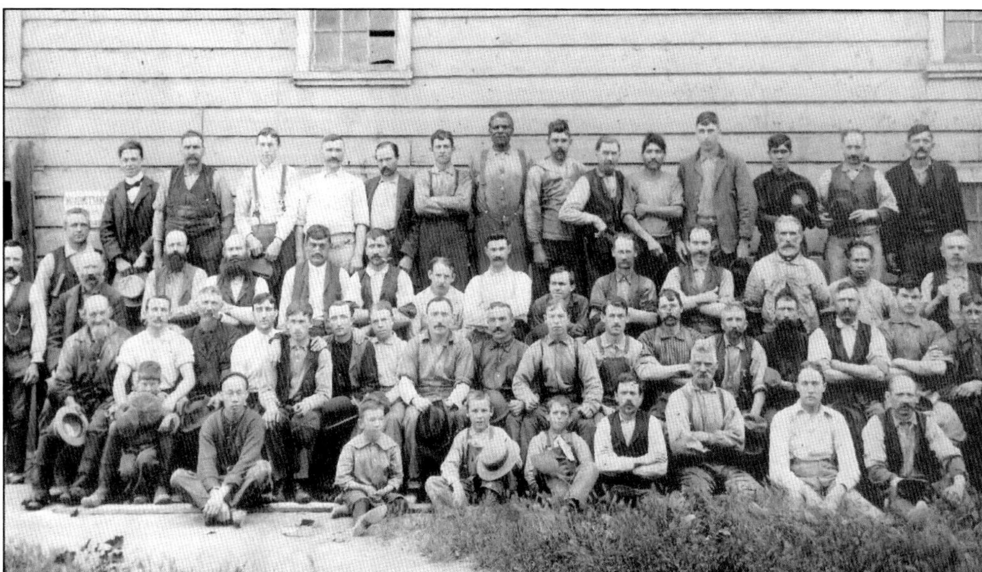

Note the young boys in the front row of this late-18th-century group photograph of tannery employees. Just north of McBain & Company's Tannery, a glue works factory was opened by C.N. Souther in 1877. The three-story building contained an eight-horsepower engine to help process more than 1,500 pounds of glue per week. Glue was linked to the existence of the tanneries. Bones, hides, skin, sinew, and other connective tissues from animals were processed to remove collagen, the protein in these tissues. The sticky collagen was useful for holding things together. Milk solids (casein) and blood (albumin) could also be used as a basis for glue. Dried serum from cows' blood results in albumin, which coagulates when it is heated and becomes insoluble in water.

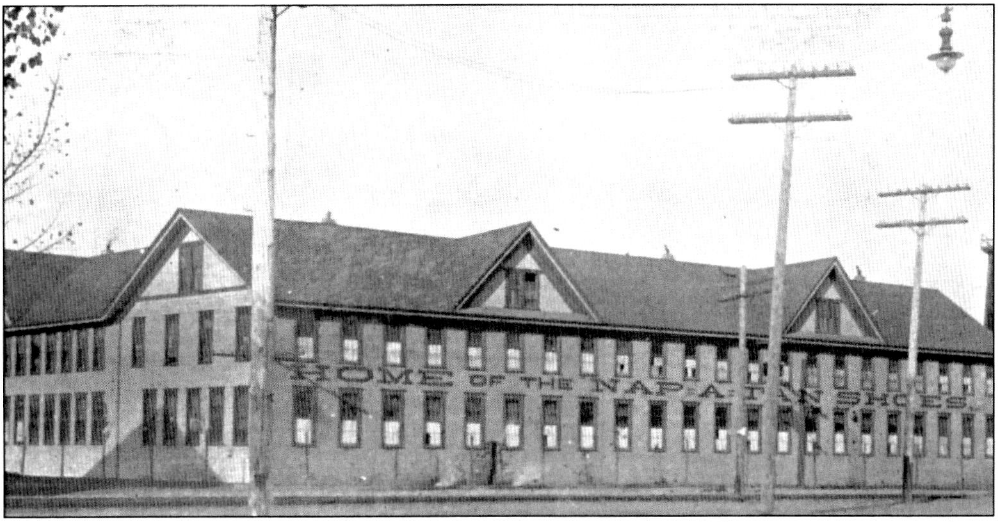

With a ready supply of leather products, shoes, boots, and belts could be manufactured nearby at the Napa Shoe Factory, whose slogan was "Home of the Nap-a-tan Shoes."

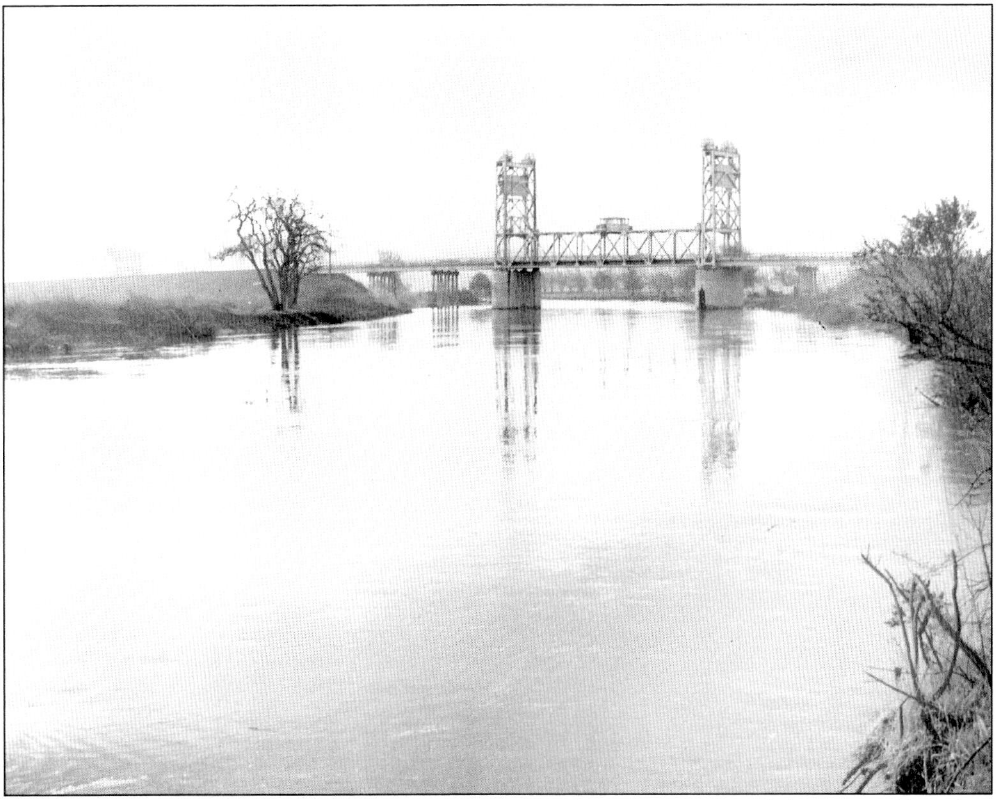

East and West Napa were united downstream with the construction of the Maxwell Bridge, making it easier to transport goods by truck. The old iron bridge was removed in 2006 to allow sailboats through.

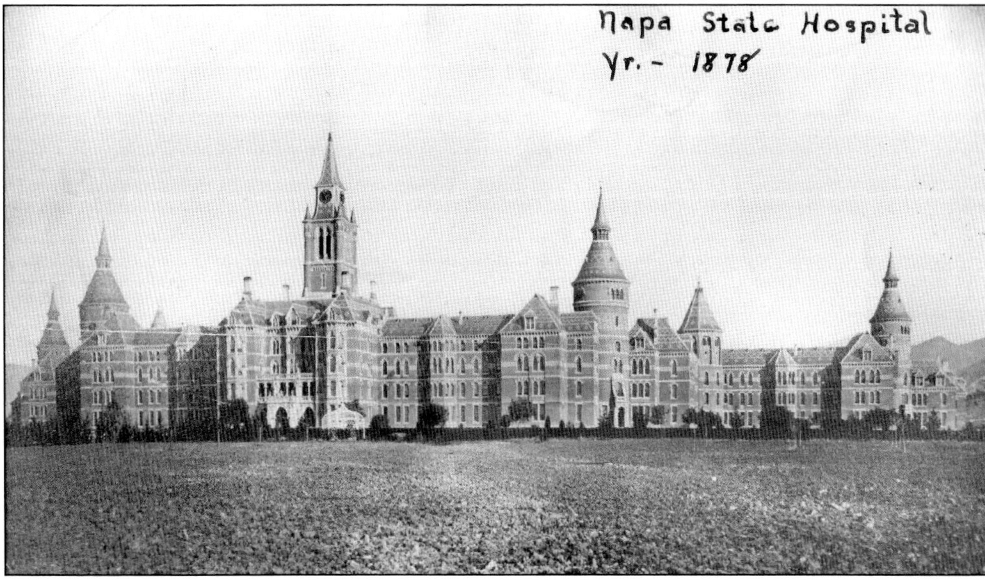

Eerily Gothic in architecture, the Napa State Asylum for the Insane, also known as the Napa State Hospital, was located in South Napa on over 192 acres. It is pictured above in 1878 and below in 1920. It also was home to the Asylum Slough, where products made by patients were shipped via the river to San Francisco and elsewhere from its own wharf. Produce grew on site, and cattle were raised for food.

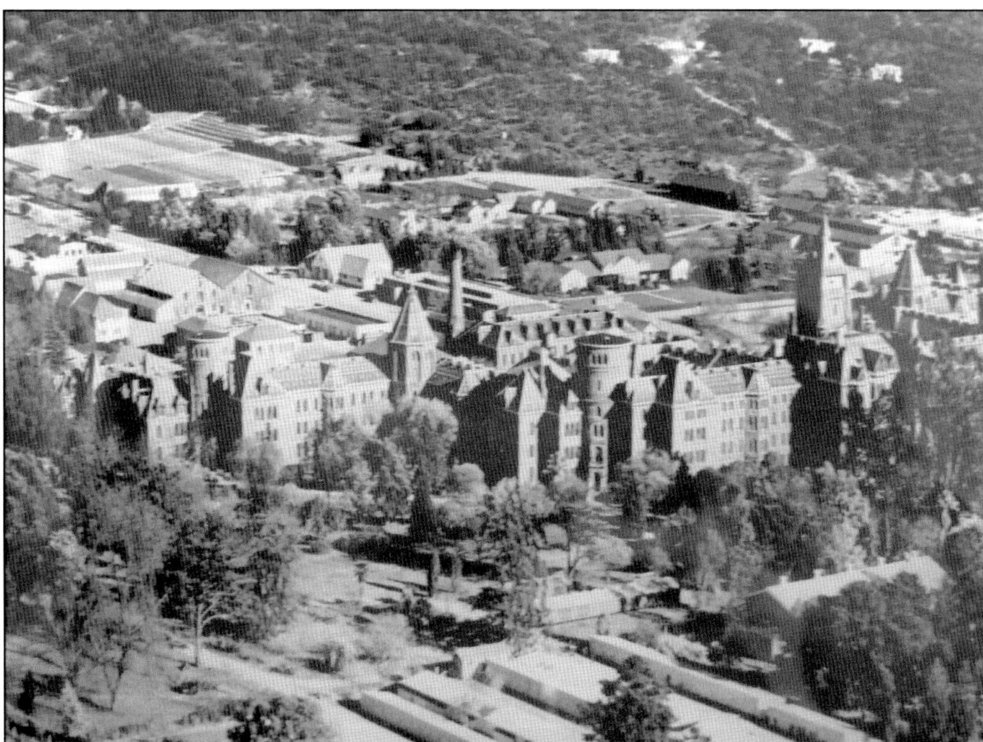

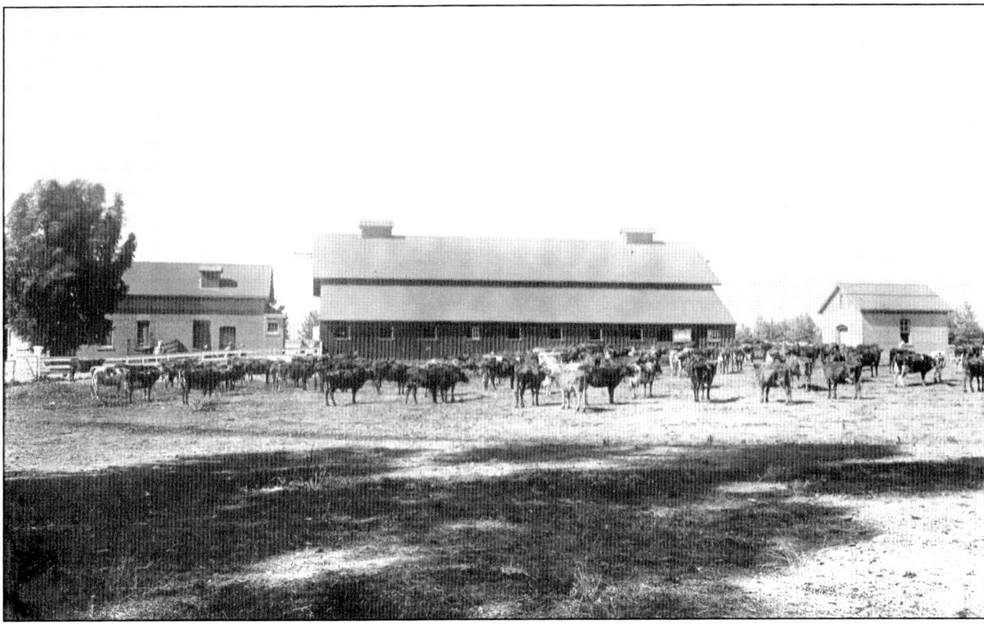

Cattle were raised at the Napa State Hospital Farm, located just northeast of Yountville. These animals provided beef for the asylum, veteran's home, and San Quentin Penitentiary.

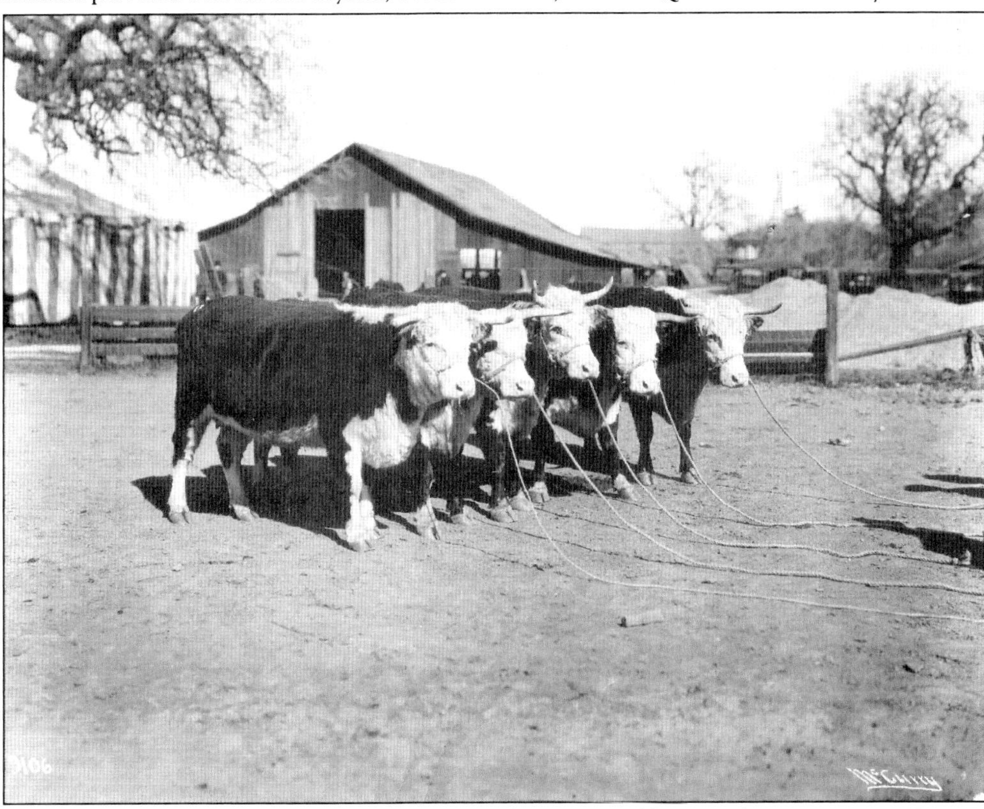

The foundation herd of purebred Hereford stock is pictured here at the Napa State Hospital Farm in 1900.

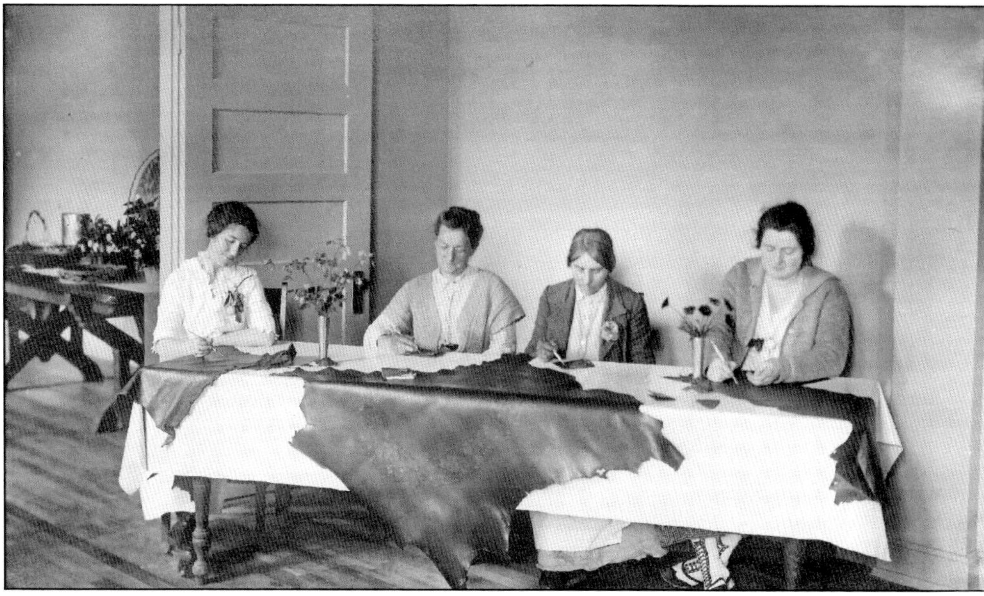

Napa State Hospital patients participated in tooled leatherwork and basket weaving. Several other therapeutic activities were available, including needlepoint, rug looms, and clay work.

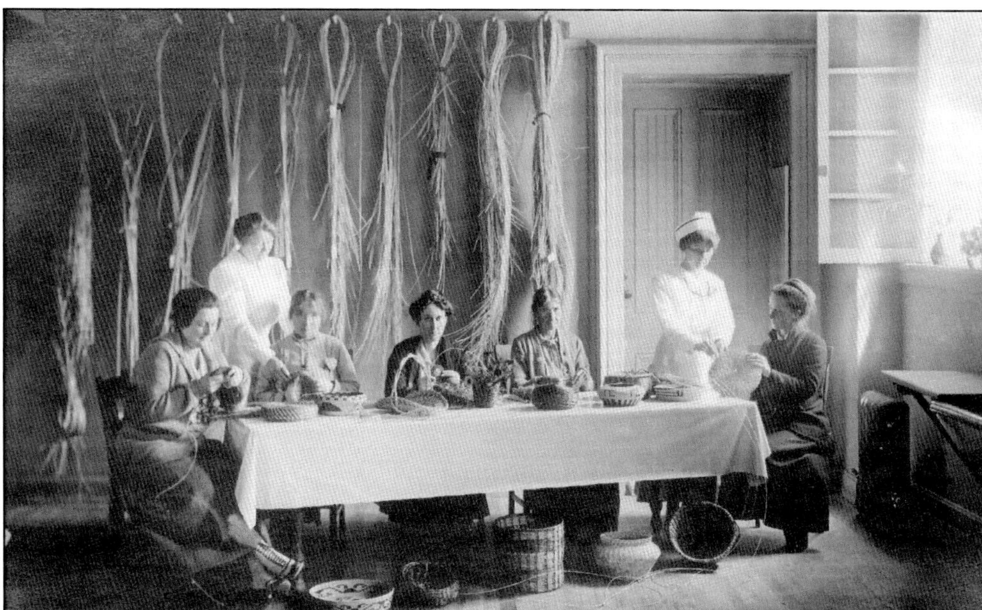

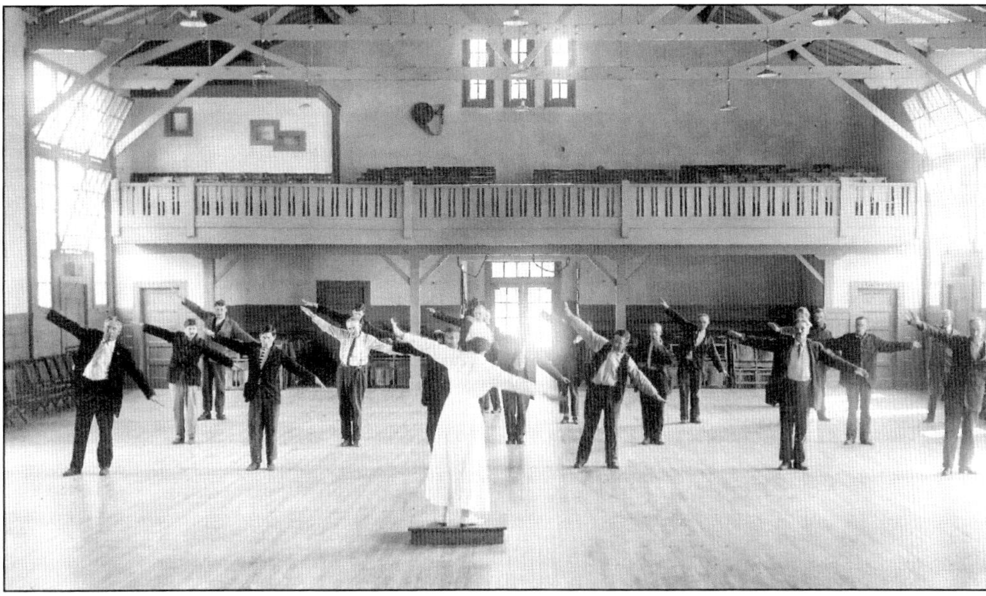

Napa State Hospital patients participated in exercises led by a nurse. The asylum was fairly self-sufficient and offered a dairy, bakery, piggery, car shop, coffin shop, and farm.

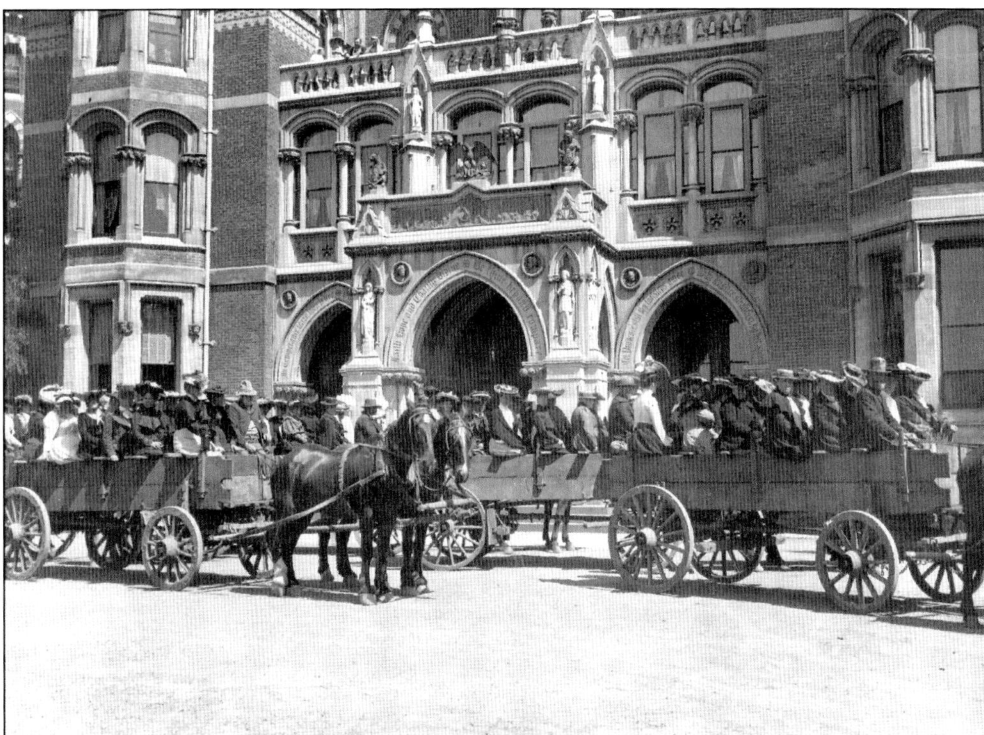

Staff accompanies Napa State Hospital patients aboard wagons in front of the main building as they prepare for an outing.

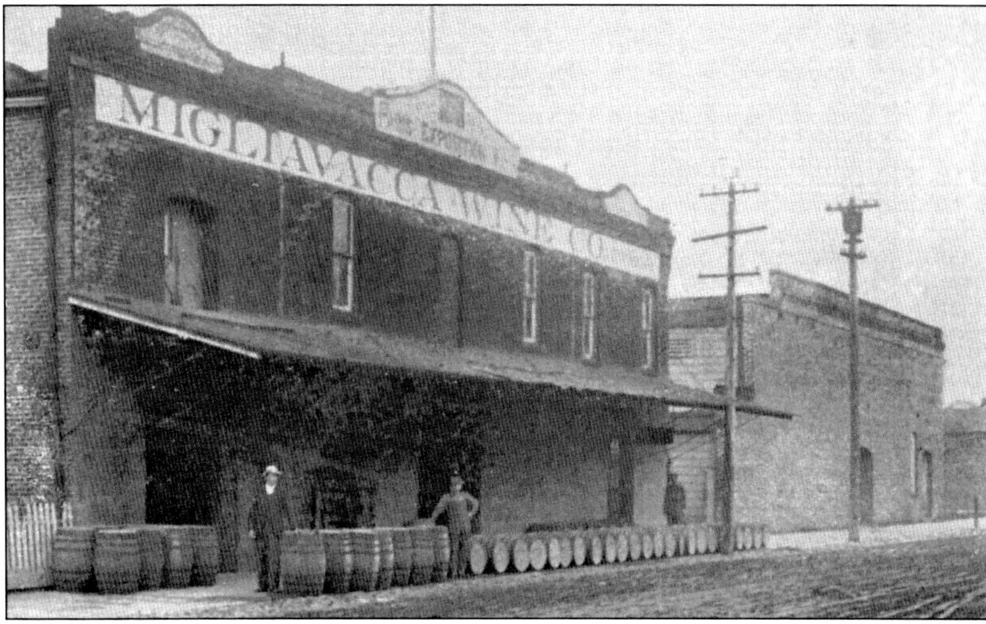

Napa had three great wine cellars, all belonging to the California Wine Association and located near the river. In 1898, the capacity of these cellars was over one million gallons, according to the *San Francisco Call*. The Migliavacca Wine Company was established in 1866. Its brick building, erected in 1874, was located west of the Hatt Building where the Napa Public Library now stands.

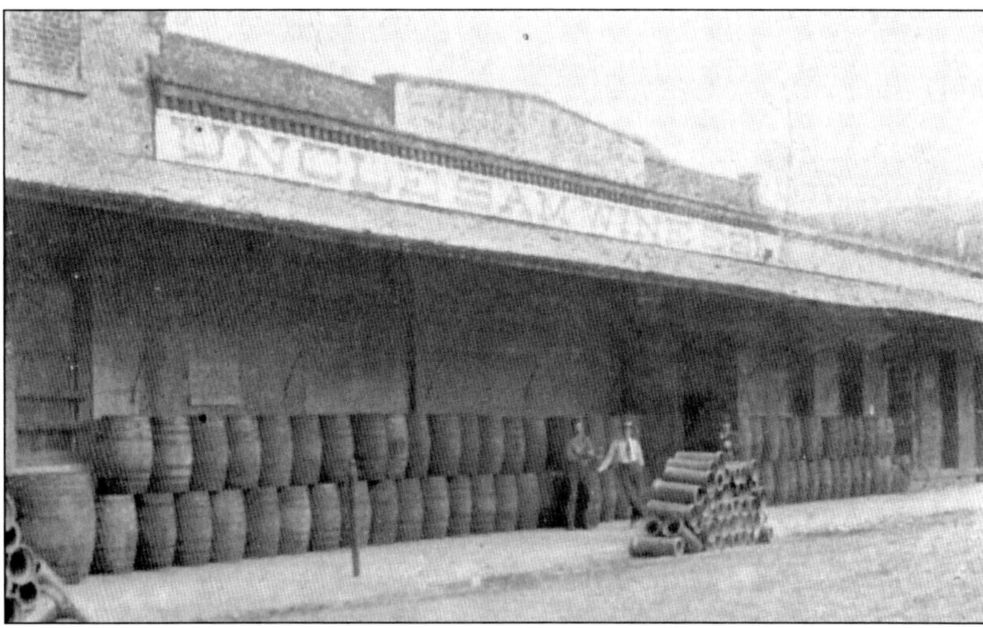

Uncle Sam's Wine Cellar was located north of the Hatt Building on Main Street between Third and Fourth Streets. Historian Rebecca Yerger notes that both of these wineries produced nearly 500,000 gallons per year. They also made vinegar, sherry, and brandy. Uncle Sam's was later sold to Charles Carpy. Today, the county courthouse and the complex of shops and restaurants comprising the riverfront development are located here.

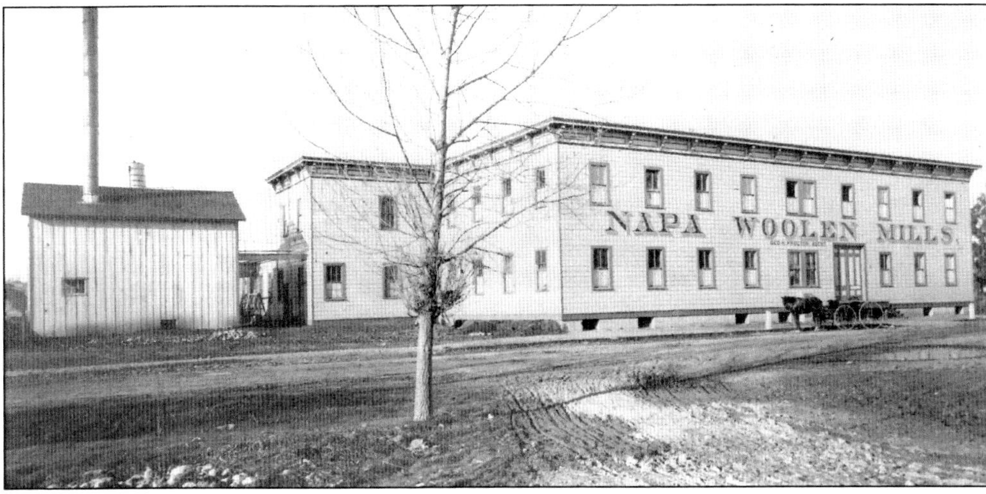

One of the most prominent businesses in Napa in the late 1800s was the Napa Woolen Mill. Constructed in 1885, it was situated along the banks of the east side of the river across from the Hatt complex, where sorting, carding, spinning, finishing, and weaving of the wool took place. Wool drying occurred on the roof. Later, a brick warehouse was added to the plant. An 1866 map depicts numerous buildings, including a dye house, scouring and washing buildings, and a boiler house adjacent to the main buildings. A plank wharf extended into the river. Workers processed about 1,200 pounds of scoured wool daily. In 1898, the plant produced a large number of blankets for the Klondike trade. These 10-, 12-, and 14-pound blankets kept Napa's 65 woolen workers on overtime. The plant was owned by 20 stockholders, including president S.E. Holden, vice president Manuel Manasse, and secretary and treasurer B.F. Holden.

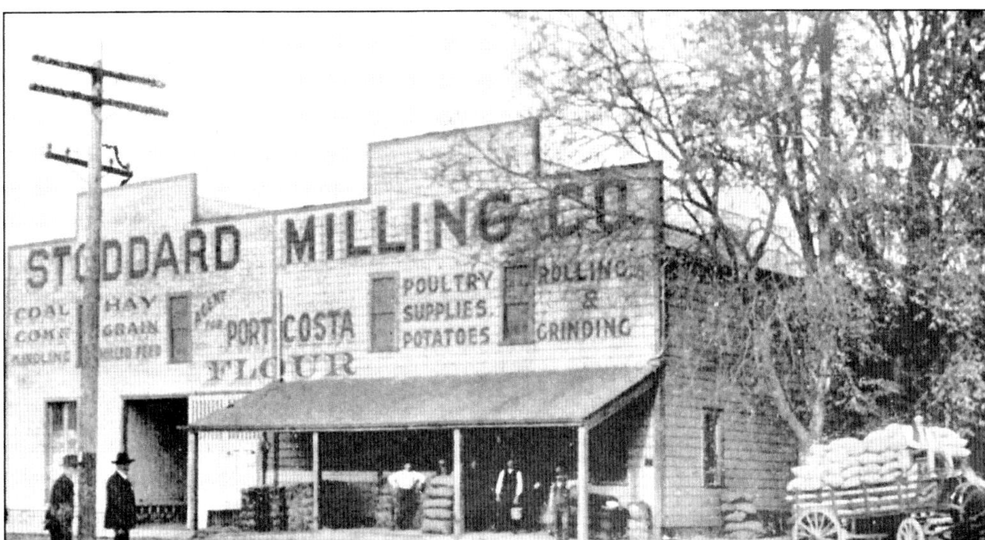

At the foot of Brown Street, adjacent to a warehouse, William Stoddard established a flour mill enterprise in 1878. Napa City mills could turn out 120 barrels of flour in 24 hours, and Stoddard relied upon a 50-horsepower engine to drive four stones to grind the flour. Wheat from Napa traveled around the world to European ports. Sacked wheat was regularly shipped downriver from Napa's granaries via Vallejo, where the only grain elevator capable of loading wheat in bulk was found.

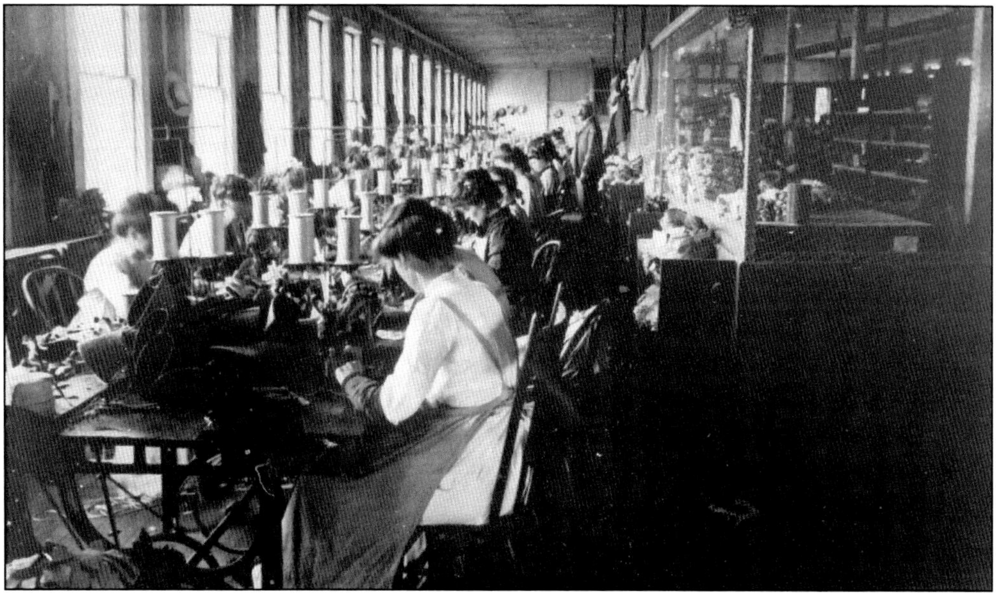

One electric motor drove all the machines in this second-floor sewing room of the Napa Glove Company. Sewing and shipping was done upstairs, and the office and leather rooms were located on the first floor. The first buildings of the Napa Glove Company were situated on the river in Napa, but in 1910, they relocated to a two-story concrete building designed by famous architect Luther Turton at 597 Monroe Street. In 1888, the Napa Glove Company bought leather from Sawyer Tannery and shipped goods to San Francisco, as well as around the world.

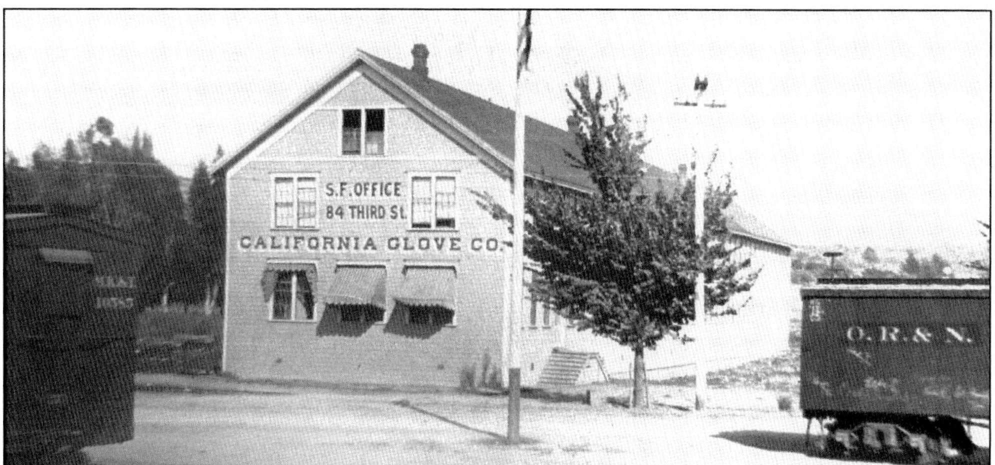

In 1885, San Francisco native F.W. Williams and Englishman Reuben Raymond, partners in the glove business in San Francisco, were enticed to relocate to Napa. Several Napa citizens raised funds to purchase a site and build a structure to house their glove factory on the condition that 35 people were to be hired for a minimum of five years. Three years later, in 1888, the Napa Glove Factory grew to employ 110 people. After Reuben Raymond's death, his sons Ralph and Earl carried on the business. During World War I, the company expanded and opened up branch factories Upvalley in St. Helena and also in Sonoma. According to Rob Dietz, manager of the Napa Hide House, US Army Air Corps flight jackets were made in Napa for World War I before an official US Air Force came into being. When American World War I airmen were asked by their British allies where they got such soft leather jackets, they replied, "From Napa."

Five

Dredging and Straightening the River

The Rise of Levees

The Napa River has a long history of dredging. As it became a river of commerce, its channel had to be deepened to allow larger vessels upriver to reach the factories. The focus on the river had begun to shift from simply using the river to manipulating the river itself. As early as April 10, 1855, an act of legislation was approved, stating that "the people of Napa County may levy a tax not to exceed one half of one percent, half of which is to be applied to the removal of snags from the Napa River, and the other half to the construction of a wagon road from Napa Valley to Clear Lake via Pope and Coyote Valleys." In February 1871, the *Napa County Register* described the river as not maintained and supported building a levee at the Third Street Bridge, not just to control floodwaters, but to stabilize the riverbank. According to an October 2, 1895, *San Francisco Call* article, Napa turned to the National River and Harbor Congress in Washington, DC, to obtain appropriations for channeling and other improvements in 1883 ($800 for a river fork survey), 1888 ($7,500), 1890 ($10,000), and 1894 ($4,000). The goal was to create a channel 75 feet wide from the river's mouth in the San Pablo Bay to Napa City and 55 feet wide further upstream at Vernon Mills, yet only four feet deep at low tide. In 1889, the Army Corps of Engineers figured the undertaking would cost $21,000. The corps used a 50-foot-by-30-foot scow near Jacks Point in April 1889 and pulled out a large oak tree from the riverbed near the gas-manufacturing plant. This was not enough to keep schooners and steamboats from snagging on logjams and mud. According to historian Richard Dillon, people called for a dredger and snag boat to be stationed on the river permanently. During the late 19th century, a rock and gravel company contracted to dredge out stones from the Napa River's bed to sell as street paving in San Francisco, which affected the river's condition in the saltwater section according to a report by JRP Historical Consulting. Barges and scows in the bay dumped rubble from the 1906 San Francisco earthquake, creating an artificial landfill. Gravel mining also led to disposal of solid wastes in landfills. A map detailing the San Francisco North Bay along the Napa River indicates substantial landfill between 1900 and 1915.

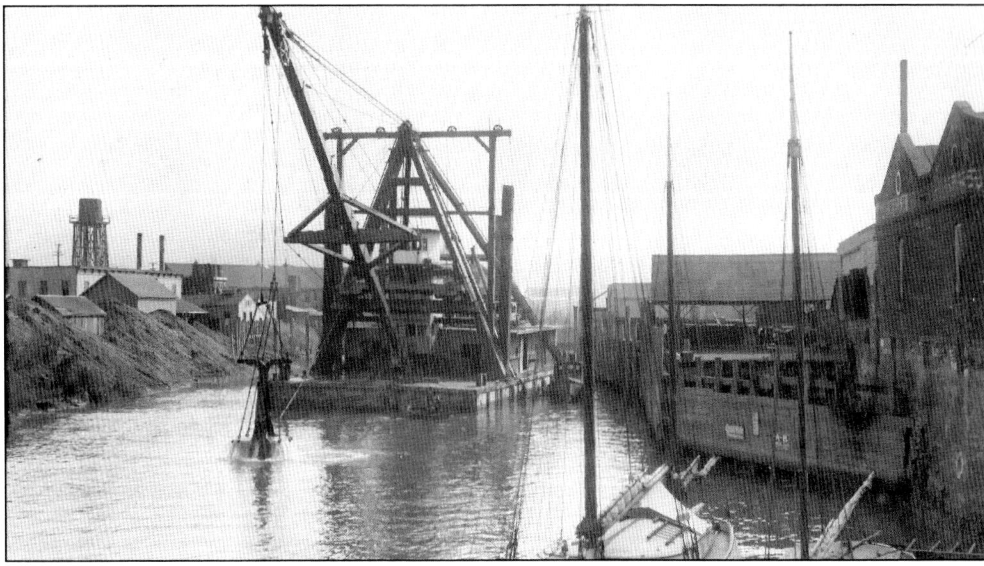

In 1906, deepening the channel of the Napa River through dredging was proposed again. In October 1907, an important meeting addressing the straightening of the Napa River was held at the Napa Chamber of Commerce. Members decided to send statistics on the freight carried by steamers on the Napa River to the National River and Harbor Congress. The chamber members sought an appropriation for dredging and straightening the river. According to a November 17, 1907, article in the *San Francisco Call*, Congress had appropriated $5,000, and a large dredger soon arrived on the river.

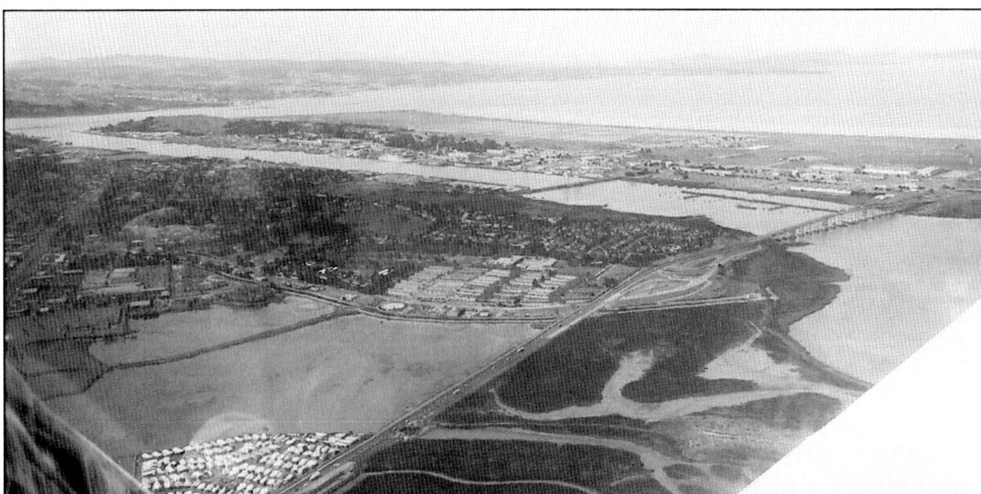

In the south, a delta formed by the Napa River, and the Sonoma and Tolay Creeks created a vast area of tidal marshland. The river widens and meets the San Pablo Bay. Here, tidal and seasonally flooded wetlands, sloughs, rivers, salt ponds, and diked agricultural fields can be found. In the 1850s, Chinese work crews began constructing some of the first levees in the marsh. Mud was hand-dredged by the workers. By the 1870s and early 1880s, more than 12,000 acres downriver and west of Napa City were dredged by tule breakers, a term given to the first mechanical dredgers that had a winch system with a ladder of buckets to pull the dredge forward. By 1949, a channel was dredged to 12.5 feet to handle barge traffic. The river was seen as a branch of commerce, not as a living thing. (Courtesy of Bernhard Krevet, FONR.)

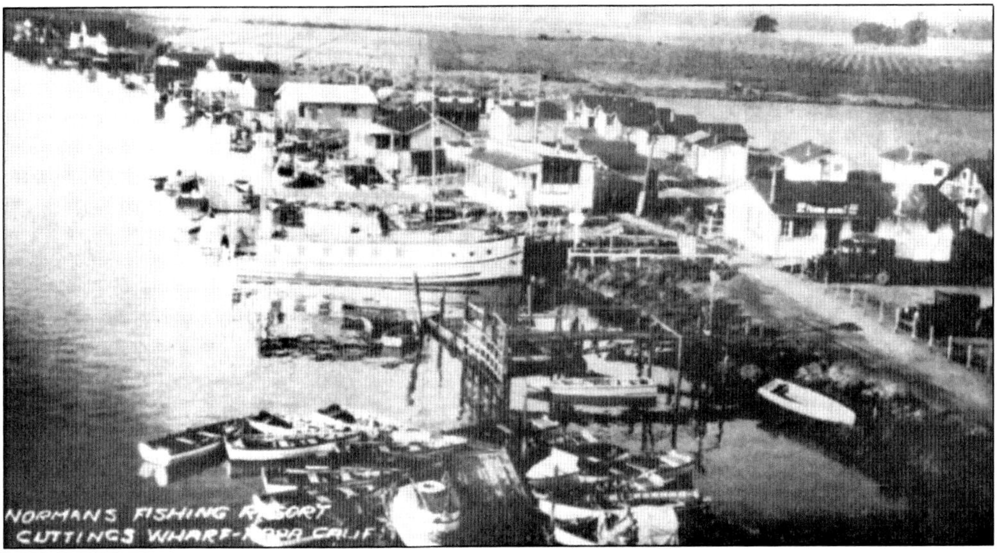

In the 1950s, a more sophisticated mechanical dredge converted agricultural lands, producing grain into shallow, solar, evaporative ponds for the salt industry. In the 1970s and 1980s, much of the land that was occupied by hay farmers and dairymen gradually shifted to wine production. The area's soils are considered excellent for chardonnay and pinot noir grapes. According to biologist Tom Huffman, "Until 1915, the bay shrimp fishery flourished in nearby waters of San Pablo Bay and many Chinese shrimp 'camps' were set up in the area. The Napa River served as an important nursery area for juvenile steelhead as well as a favorite location for striped bass fishing." Norman's Fishing Resort on Cuttings Wharf Road was a popular boating, hunting, and fishing location from the 1890s to 1962. The facilities included a wharf and rental cabins. At its height, more than 200 sportsmen gathered there over a weekend. (Courtesy of the California History Room, California State Library, Sacramento, California.)

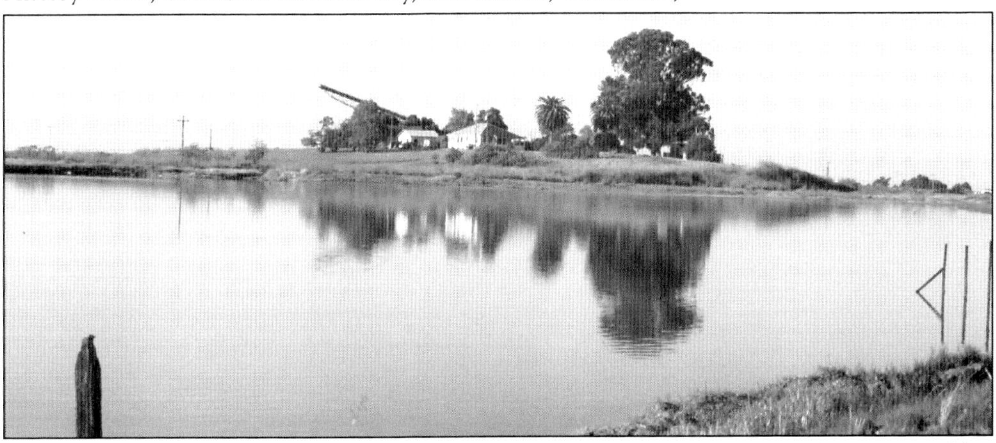

Leslie Salt Refining Company purchased property from the estate of Holland Dutton and his former wife, Diane, on Green Island, located on the east side of the river in the Carneros region. The couple was once known for holding lavish gatherings on their little knoll. Dutton was institutionalized in 1940 after experiencing an emotional episode and excitedly warned officials at the Napa County Courthouse that Japan was going to attack the United States. Later that day, he was found directing traffic dressed in a Navy commander's uniform. Dutton died the same year at Napa State Hospital at the age of 44. Dutton's Landing was dismantled in 1962. The only remnants of the landing at the site today are a few pilings. (Courtesy of JRP Historical Consulting.)

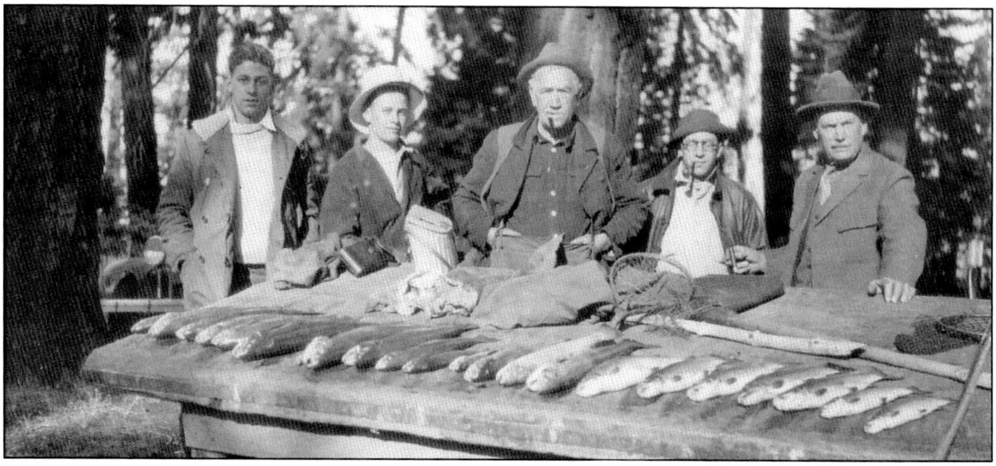

Fishing was good in the 1920s, as demonstrated by these men displaying their catch. In the mid-1960s, the California Department of Fish and Game estimated there to be 94,000 steelhead spawning in rivers and tributaries leading to San Francisco Bay. By 1991, only 30 years later, the Department of Fish and Game became concerned about potential extinction of steelhead in the Napa River and its tributaries. A combination of dredging (which made the waters too muddy for fish gills to siphon), raw sewage, and runoff from agricultural fertilizers and top soil was to blame. Striped bass were also negatively affected. The US Department of Fish and Wildlife estimated that between 1860 and 1959, nearly half of the estimated 570 square miles of marsh and tidal habitat were drained and separated from the river by dikes and levees.

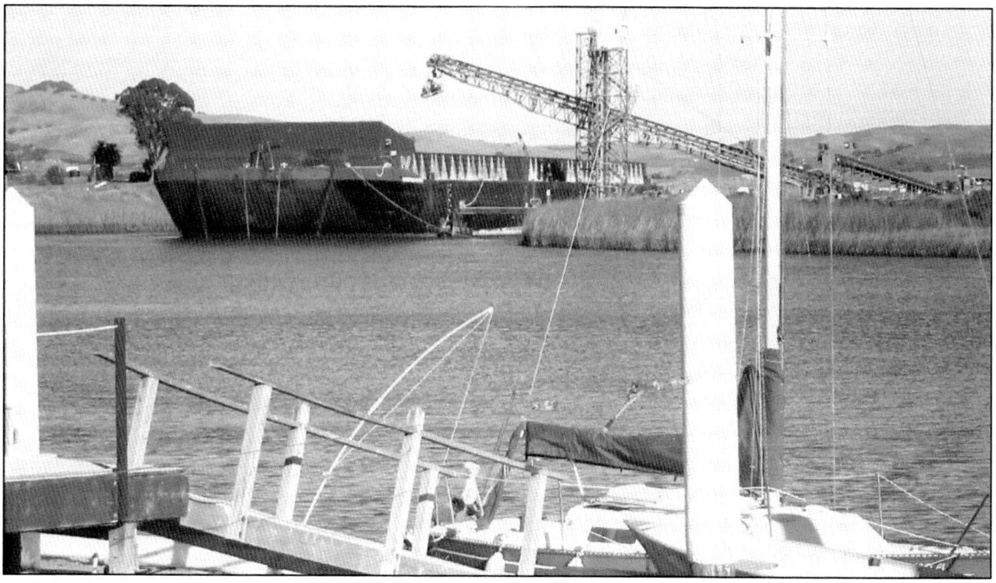

California's salt industry started in 1856 when the demand for salt increased after the discovery of silver ore. Leslie Salt Refining Company, established in 1901, was one of the first to operate on the west side of San Francisco Bay. Before setting up its salt ponds on the Napa River and plant on Green Island, salt had not been produced in the San Pablo Bay. By 1961, the company operated ponds around the bay that covered over 40,000 acres and produced one million tons of salt a year. Leslie Salt continued operations until 1979, when Cargill, an agricultural products corporation, acquired the company. The California Department of Fish and Game acquired the entire property in 2003. Here, a salt barge is filled by conveyer belt at Cargill. (Author's collection.)

Six

The Coming of the Railroads and Electric Trains

An Interurban for Napa

The development of railroads played a major role in the growth of Napa City during the Victorian era (1860–1899). Enthusiasm for a railroad project first gained momentum in 1863, when there was talk of building a railroad from Vallejo to Calistoga. According to a City of Napa Historic Preservation report on Spencer's Addition, a collection of parcels of land owned by Spencer and added to the city of Napa, the county secured funding for the project, and a steam railroad line was built from the town of Suscol (south of the city) north 4.5 miles to Napa City for an estimated cost of $100,000 in 1864. Named the Napa Valley Railroad, the new line was completed in July 1865. In Napa City, the tracks initially ran along Main Street to Fourth Street, then along Division Street to Jefferson Street. The route of the tracks through the city was completed in 1877. The tracks ran north from Vallejo along the east side of the river, crossed the Napa River just east of Soscol Avenue to bypass downtown, ran along Lawrence Street, paralleled Soscol Avenue on the east, and continued northwest from Lincoln Avenue. The Napa Valley Railroad was extended north to Calistoga in 1868 and stretched south to Napa Junction, a tiny town near present-day American Canyon the following year, where it met up with other local rail lines. The completion of the first transcontinental railroad in 1869 caused fierce competition over transportation and shipping nationwide, and the steam railroad and ferry service linked Napa City with the rest of the country, providing the primary mode of transportation until electric trains were introduced in the early 1900s.

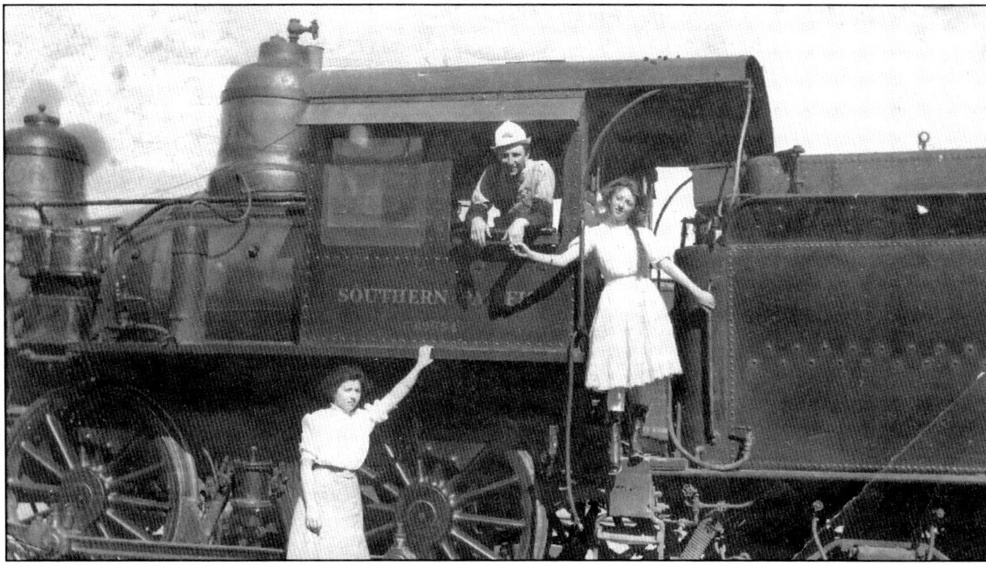

By 1875, the Napa Valley Railroad had been acquired by the Southern Pacific Railroad, with passenger depots constructed in East Napa at Fourth and Soscol Streets and in West Napa along what is now California Boulevard at Stockton Street. Southern Pacific stopped passenger service in 1929.

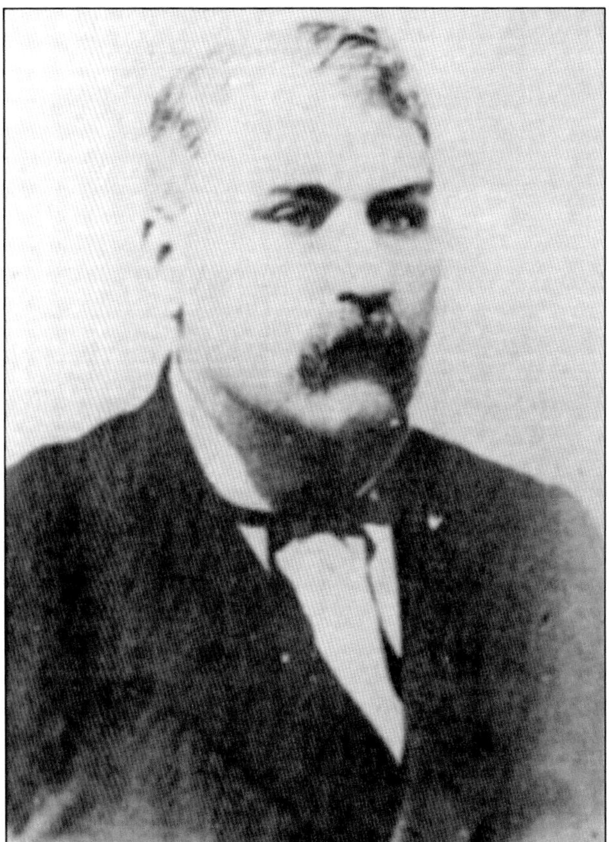

In their 1975 book *Napa Valley Route*, Ira L. Swett and Harry C. Aitken Jr. tell the story of the rise of the electric railroad in Napa. Col. J.W. Hartzell and his brother came to California in 1889 to build an interurban line from San Francisco to San Mateo. They invested in tracts of land in Vallejo with the intention of running electric cars south from Napa through Vallejo to Benicia, where connections would be made to the ferry en route to San Francisco. They also envisioned lines extending northeast of Napa to Lakeport in Lake County and on to Jackson's Soda Springs.

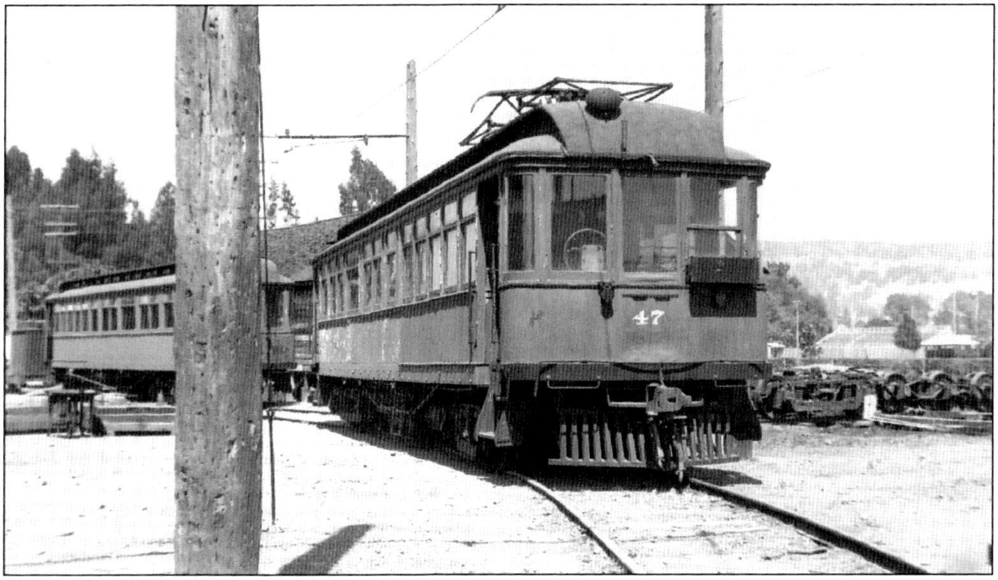

Interurban (electric) train No. 47 makes its way to the station around 1931. The Napa Valley Interurban operated from 1903 to 1910 as the Vallejo, Benicia & Napa Valley Railroad Company (VB&NV). By 1908, the interurbans followed the Southern Pacific tracks to Rutherford and north to St. Helena. A rival company, the San Francisco, Vallejo & Napa Valley Railroad, gained franchise rights and became the successor to VB&NV for a sum of $50,000. By 1911, a third company, the San Francisco, Napa & Calistoga Railway Company, operated from 1911 to 1935. By 1912, interurbans ran as far north as Calistoga.

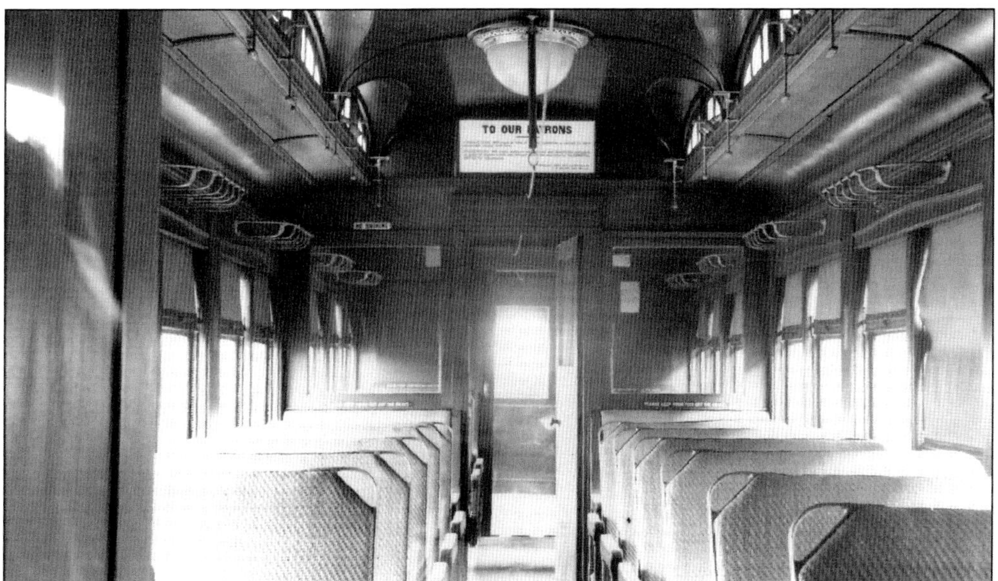

Passengers enjoyed a good view through numerous window seats.

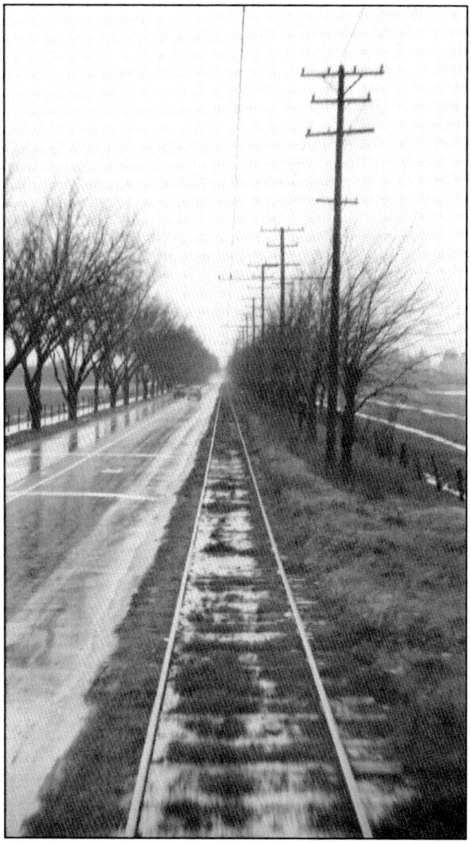

In 1901, six routes throughout the city were proposed, including this one down Soscol that provided Napa with a network of streetcar lines. The Hartzell brothers partnered with Capt. John Cross, a Los Angeles investor. On April 24, 1902, the Vallejo, Benicia & Napa Valley Railroad Company incorporated with Cross as president. After delays and financial difficulties beset the project, the decision was made to abandon the streetcar routes in favor of a line extending only to the southern terminus of Vallejo and only to Napa at its northernmost terminus. Finally, the first steamer load of ties (71,000 feet of lumber) arrived in Vallejo on October 20, 1903.

By November 1904, tracks reached Napa on Jefferson Street and Calistoga Avenue. Tracks would be stretched out to Lincoln Avenue by December.

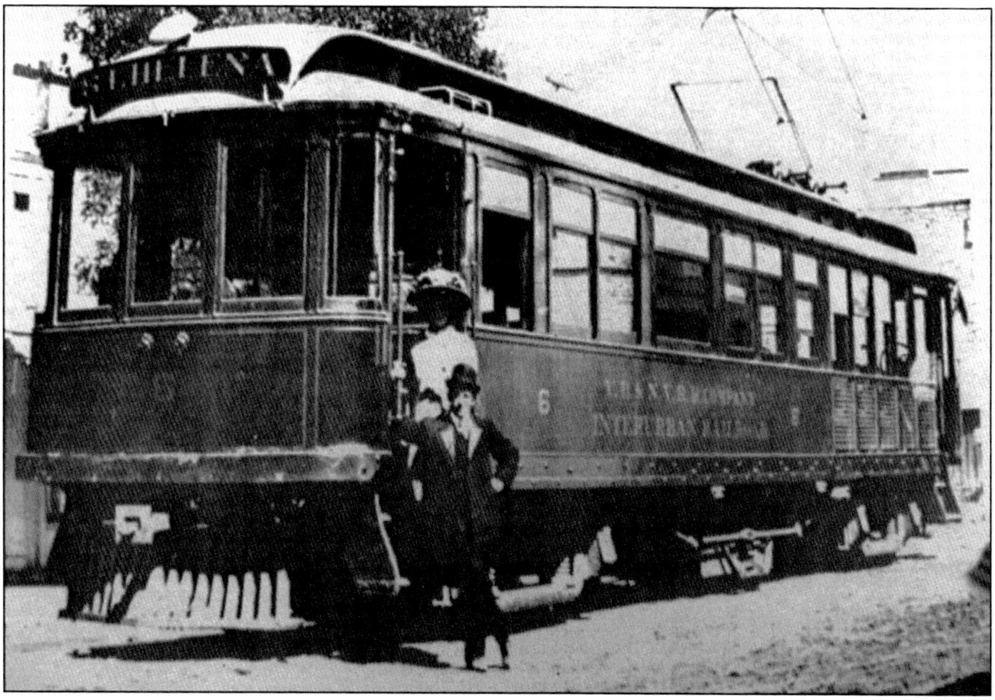

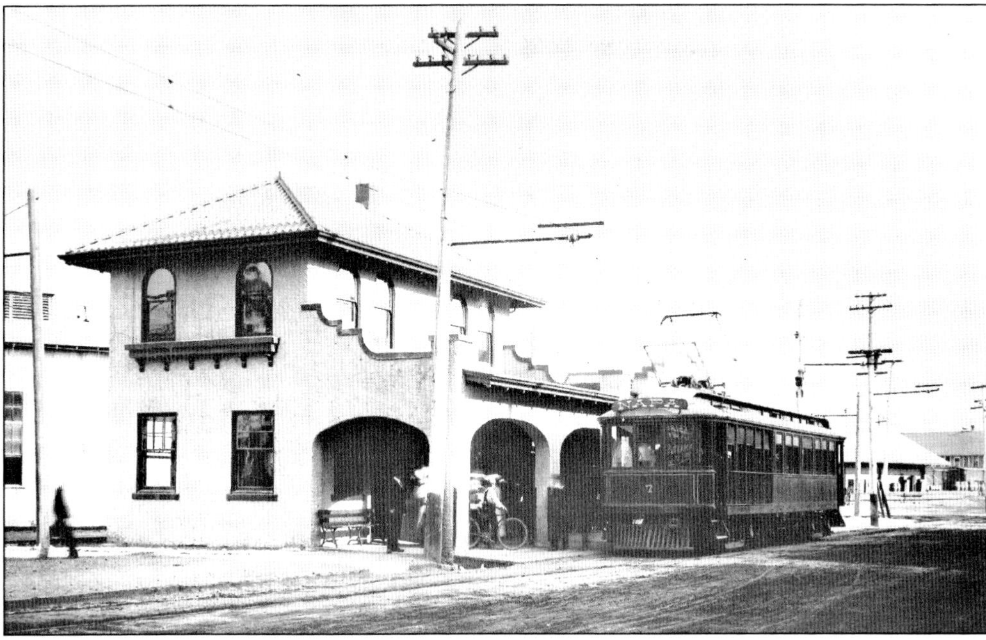

By May 1905, Captain Cross, along with fellow Los Angeles capitalist W.H. Hollibard, purchased the Migliavacca property and planned to build a depot and baggage room in the California Mission style. It was erected at the corner of Soscol and Third Streets. The power to run the new interurban railway was supplied by the Napa Gas & Electric Company.

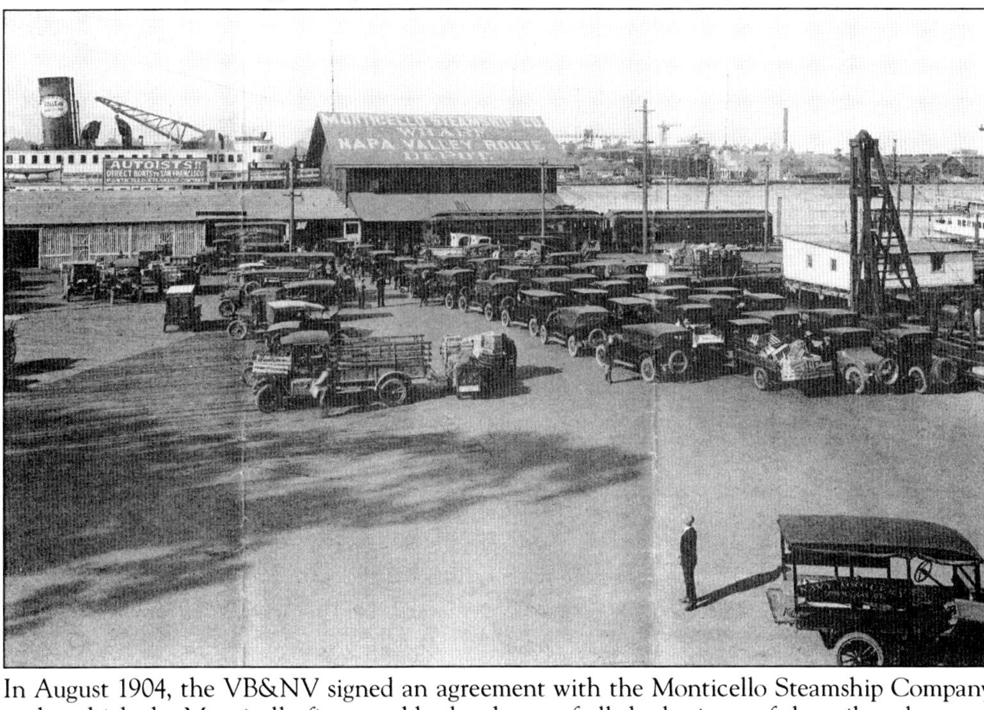

In August 1904, the VB&NV signed an agreement with the Monticello Steamship Company under which the Monticello firm would take charge of all the business of the railway between Vallejo and San Francisco. Note that motorists were referred to as "autoists" in the photograph. (Courtesy of the Vallejo Naval and Historical Museum.)

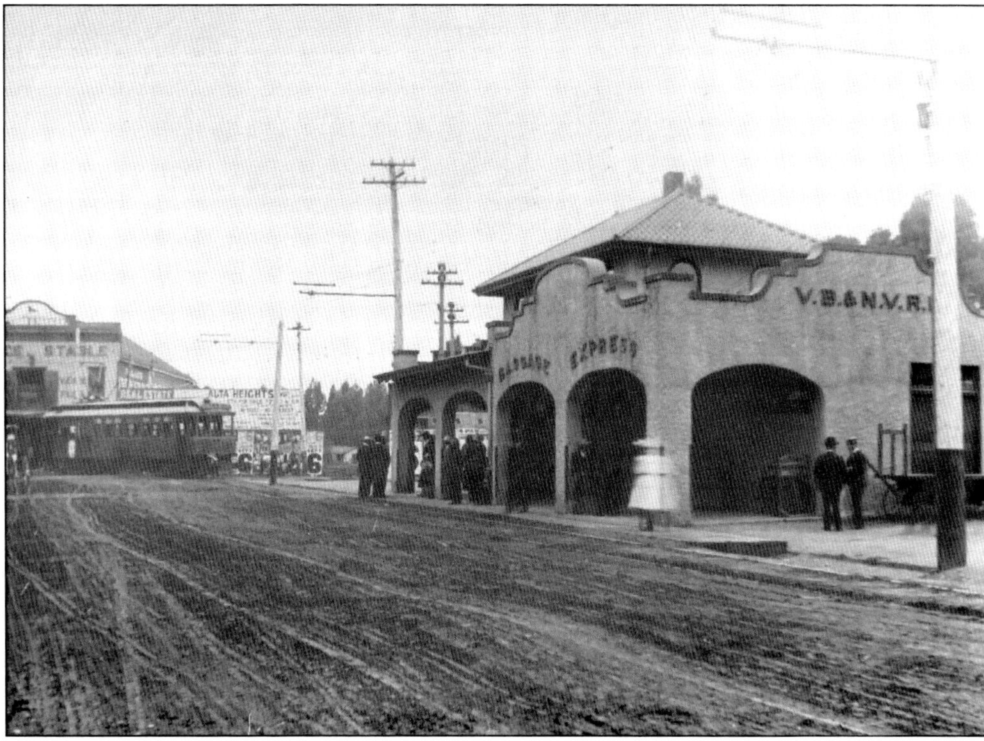

Men line up at the baggage express to board an oncoming train at the VB&NV Railroad Station. The Crowey Building on East First Street was remodeled into a substation to provide power for operation of the electric cars. Power was transmitted under the Napa River by submarine cable to the new substation in East Napa.

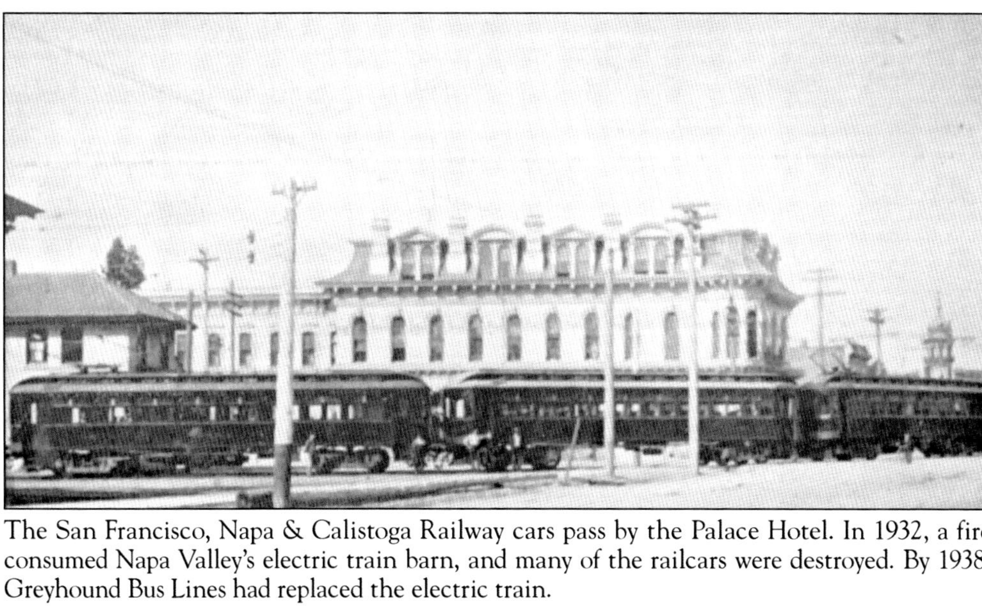
The San Francisco, Napa & Calistoga Railway cars pass by the Palace Hotel. In 1932, a fire consumed Napa Valley's electric train barn, and many of the railcars were destroyed. By 1938, Greyhound Bus Lines had replaced the electric train.

Seven

FLOODWATERS

THE RIVER STRIKES BACK

The river was not a quiet presence for Napa City. While one of its greatest assets, it became its greatest liability due to flooding. Floods are a natural function of rivers, but they had become a damaging and costly curse for the people living and working near the river. Like many other California rivers, Napa River has experienced repeated flooding. In winter months, the river flooded annually in the early years. Severe flooding occurred in 1890, 1896, 1907, 1940, 1955, 1986, 1995, 1996, and 2005. Since 1862, more than 27 major floods have inundated the Napa Valley, resulting in loss of life and property. With more than 53 tributaries feeding into the Napa River, winter rains and saturated soil caused the river to swell. With nowhere for the water to go, the river overflowed its banks and inundated the city. In fact, the first warehouse, which was built on the south side of First Street at the Steamboat Landing, was soon carried away in a flood. Not only did the river flood in the winter, but rains also made the mud streets nearly impossible to cross. These mud canals required men to stuff their pant legs into heavy boots. Imagine the inundations created by carriage and wagon wheels that, when dried in the summer, left the dirt roads rutted and dusty. Bridges built low to the water often exacerbated the problem when logs and other debris floating downstream became stuck, creating a dam. Water spewed out into Napa City streets. Over the past 150 years, much of the effort to manage the flow of rivers has centered on the construction of levees and dams to capture and hold back high flows. Flood-control districts and city, county, and environmental groups sought new strategies for flood management, bringing together both natural and man-made approaches. The current flood management and river restoration project, which has become a national model with its living-river principles, is discussed in chapter nine.

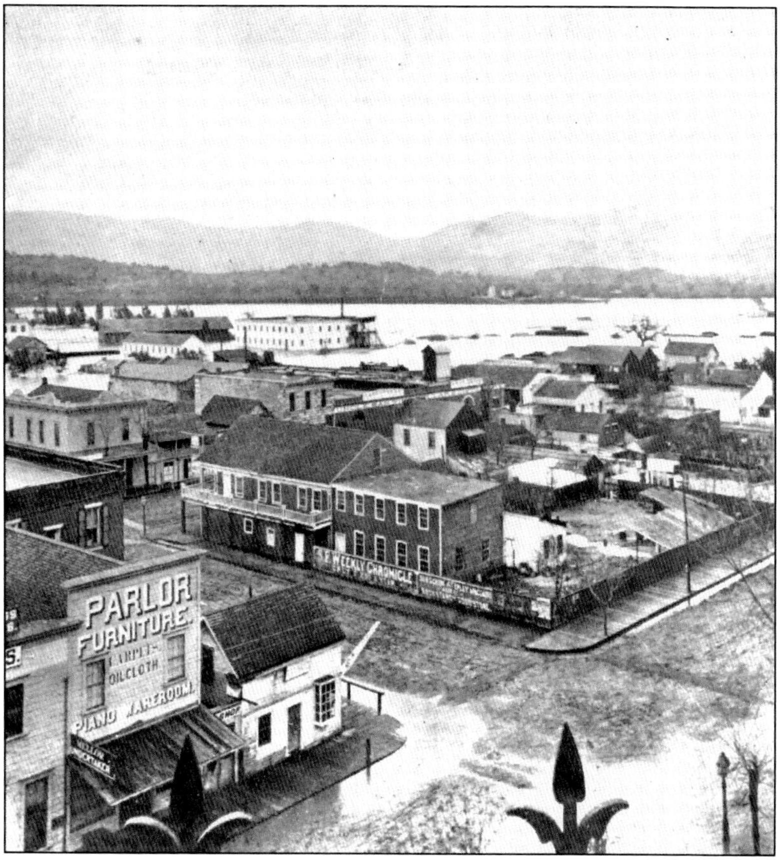

This photograph looks out over Napa City from the top of city hall down Third Street as the Napa River floods the town in 1885.

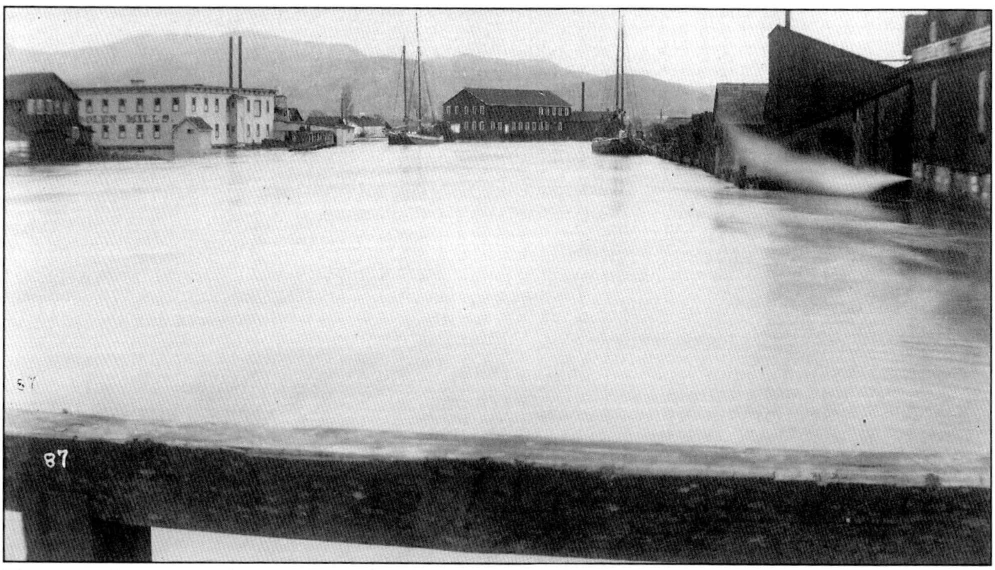

Torrents of water can be seen from the First Street Bridge looking downriver during the flood of 1890. The Napa Woolen Mills is the white building to the left on the east side of the river. The Union Tannery is in the center. Uncle Sam's Winery is visible on the right by the pipe shooting water. (Courtesy of Napa Valley Museum.)

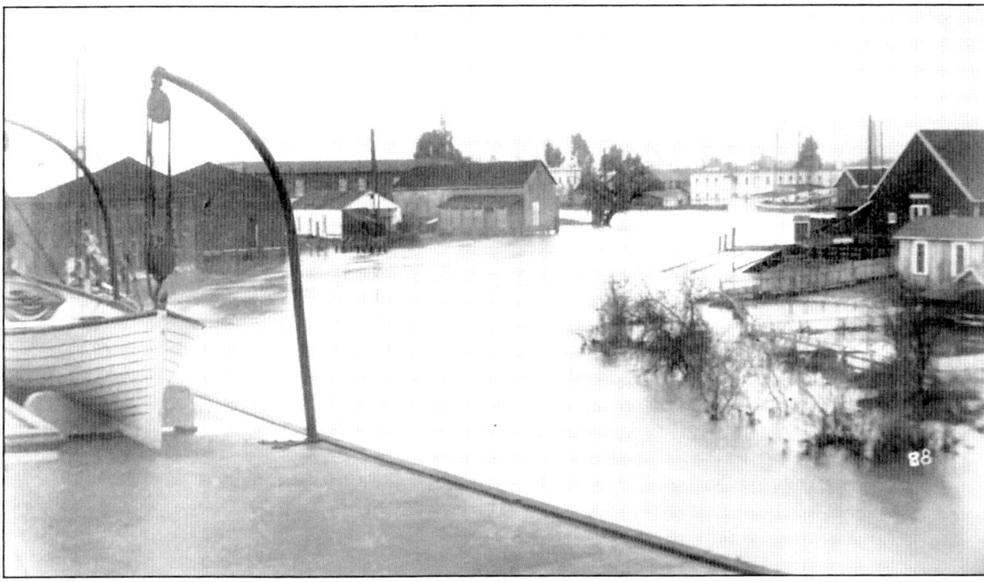

Likely taken from Alfred Hatt's plank wharf during the flood of 1890, the Woolen Mill can be seen in upper right of this photograph. (Courtesy of Napa Valley Museum.)

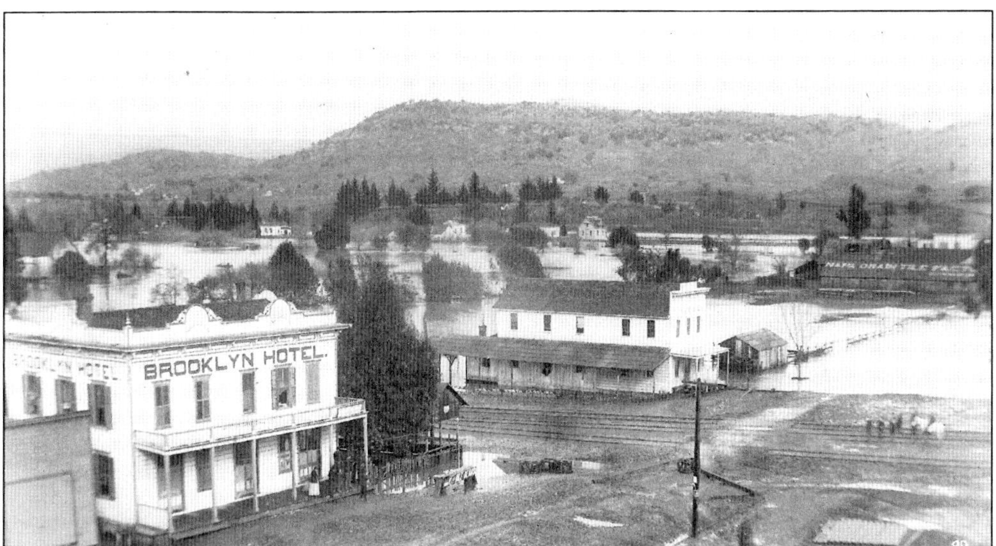

The Brooklyn Hotel, located on the 800 block of Third Street, served as a boardinghouse for Italian workers in the late 1880s. It was located on the east side of the Napa River in a neighborhood known as Little Italy. (Courtesy of Napa Valley Museum.)

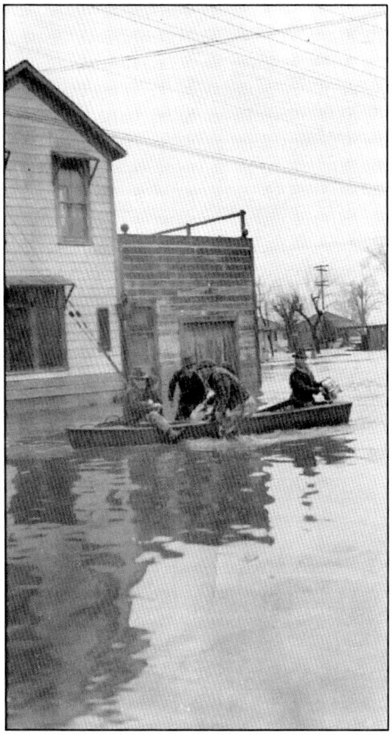

Two men push a rowboat and its passengers down Brown Street in this image, which was most likely captured during the 1907 flood.

In this aerial photograph of the 1940s flood, looking northwest over the downtown, Main Street can be seen to the left. (Courtesy of Napa Valley Museum.)

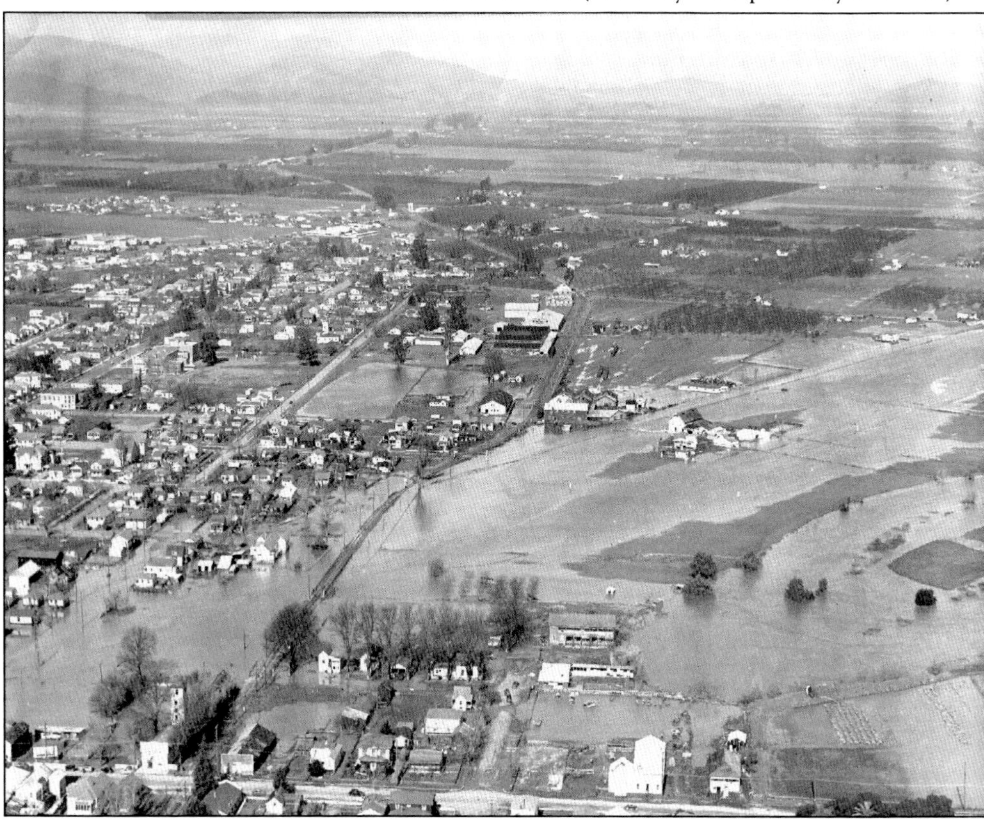

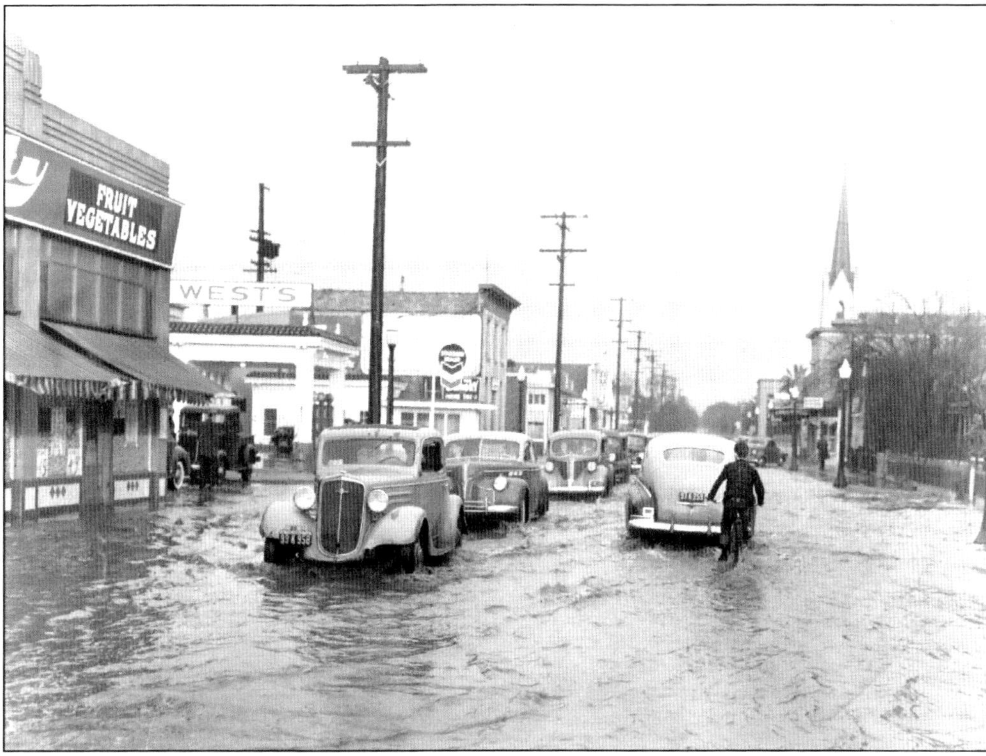

Vehicles make their way through floodwaters on Third Street during the 1940s flood. The Presbyterian church is visible on the right in the image above. Below, a car travels behind a pickup on Soscol Avenue during the same flood.

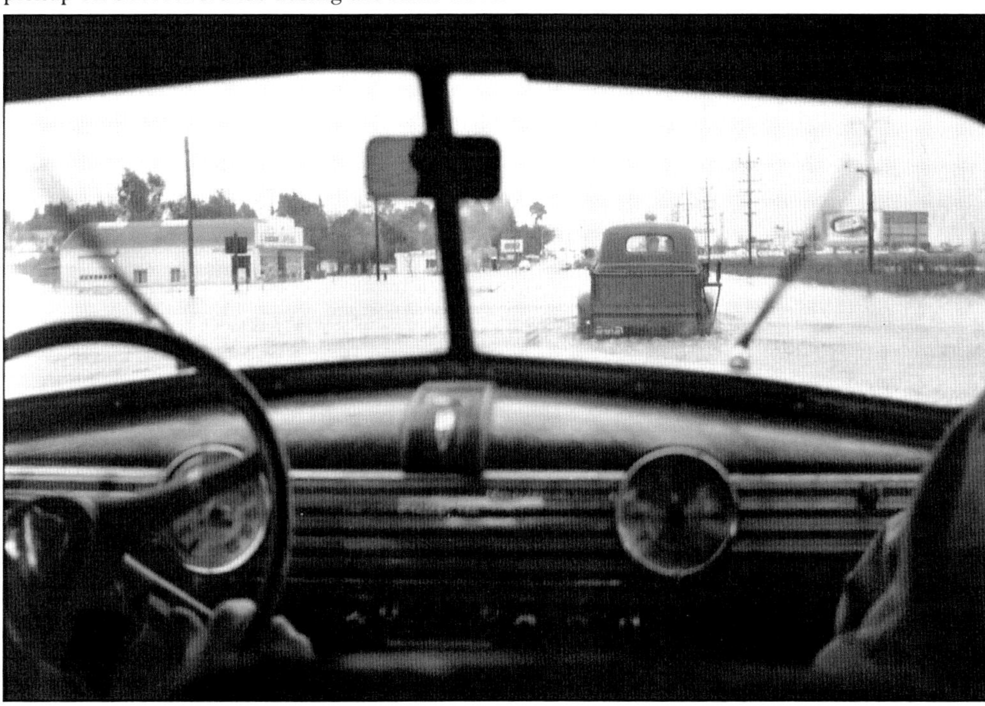

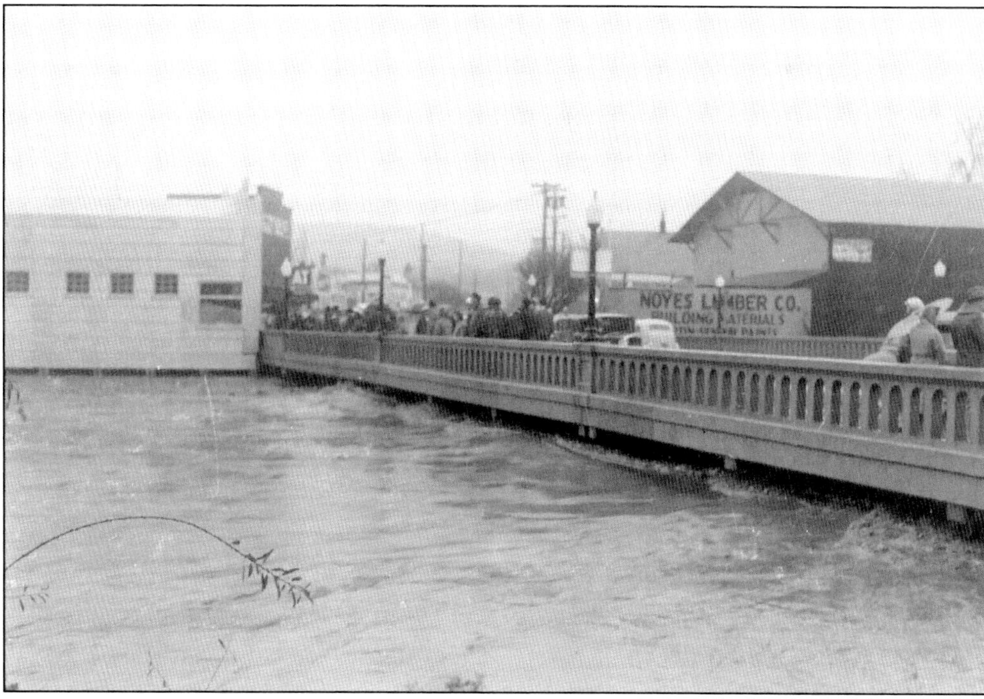

In this 1940 photograph, many spectators marvel at the height of the river from the Third Street Bridge during the flood stage. Newspaper stories perpetuated the reputation of Napa as a city that floods.

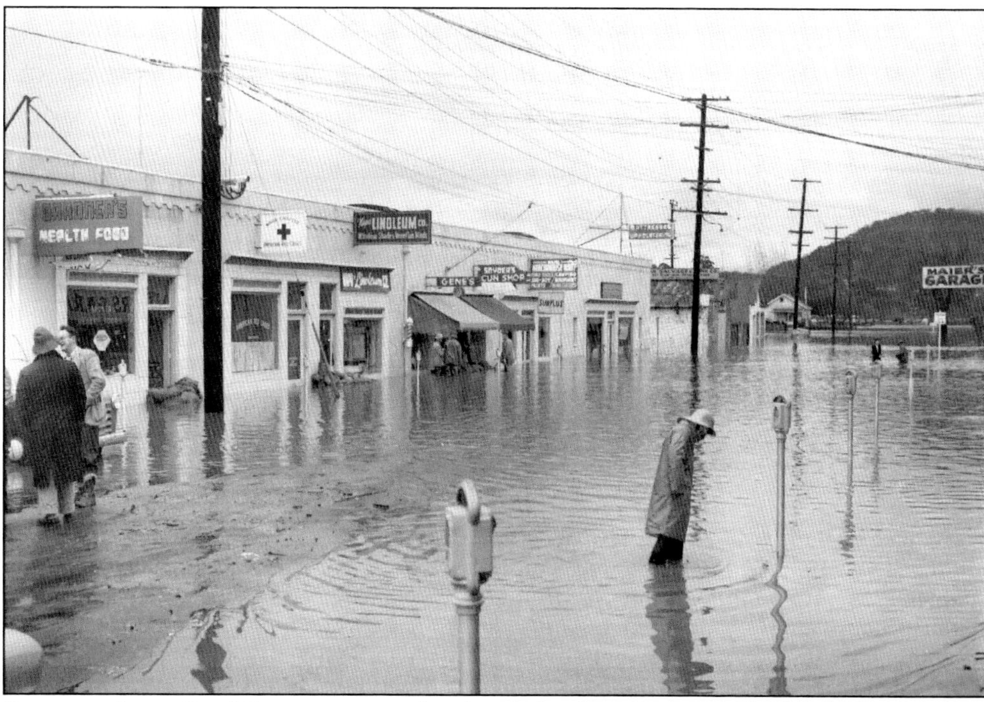

Businesses lining Pearl Street were inundated with floodwaters during the flood of 1955.

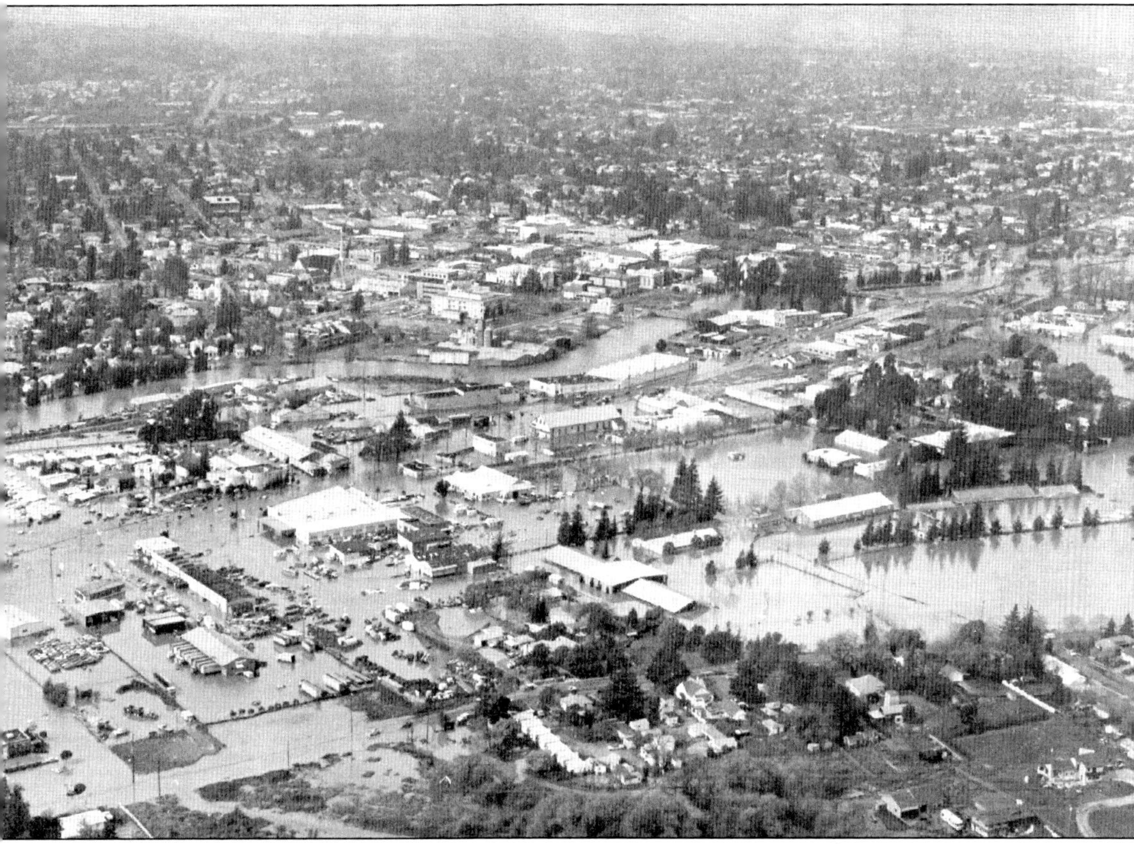

The flood of 1986 was one of the more damaging events, causing more than $140 million in losses. More than 7,000 residents were evacuated. The riverbed is 20 feet deeper in places than it was a half century ago. Boxed in by berms deprived of room to overflow, the river runs faster.

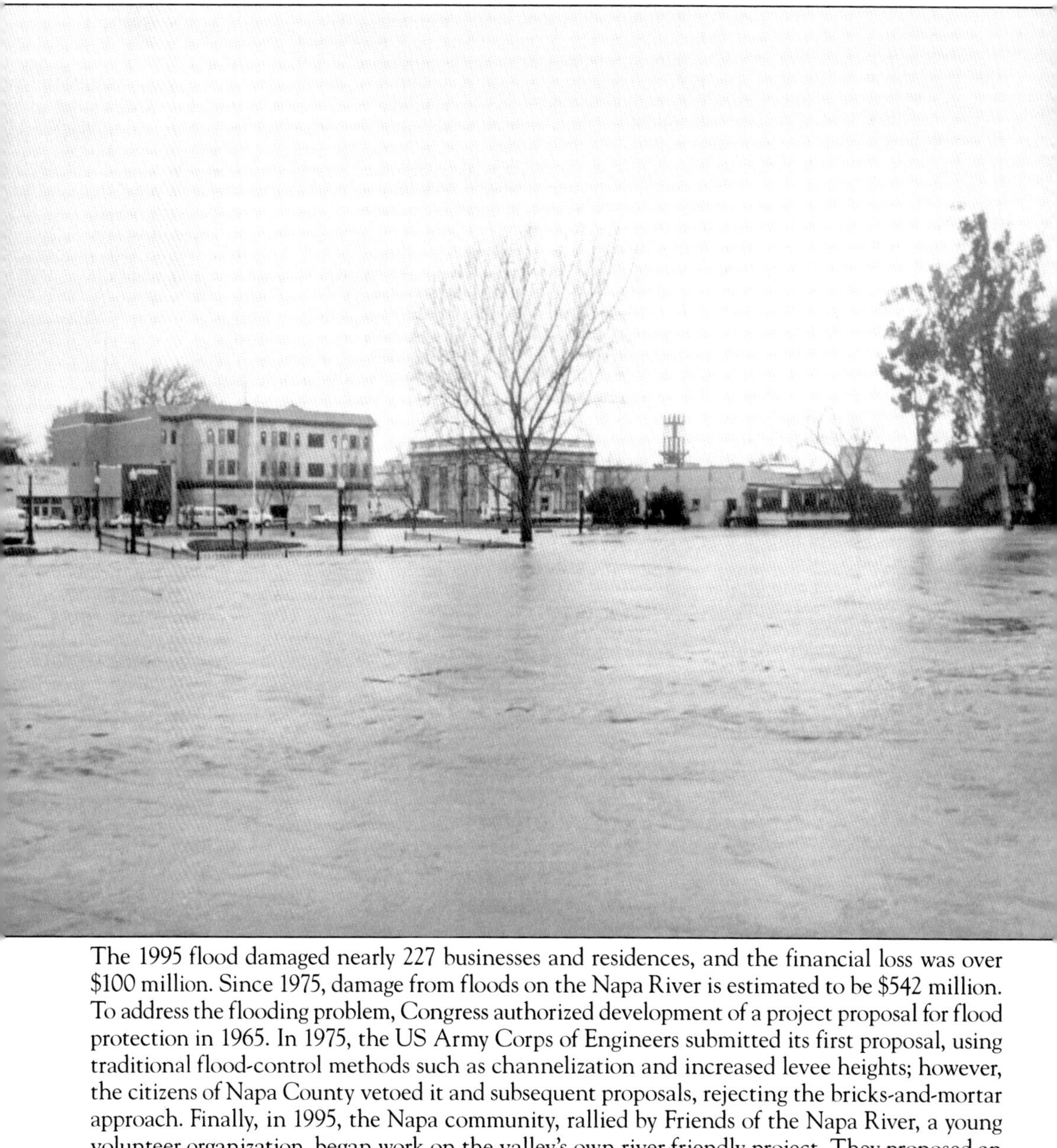

The 1995 flood damaged nearly 227 businesses and residences, and the financial loss was over $100 million. Since 1975, damage from floods on the Napa River is estimated to be $542 million. To address the flooding problem, Congress authorized development of a project proposal for flood protection in 1965. In 1975, the US Army Corps of Engineers submitted its first proposal, using traditional flood-control methods such as channelization and increased levee heights; however, the citizens of Napa County vetoed it and subsequent proposals, rejecting the bricks-and-mortar approach. Finally, in 1995, the Napa community, rallied by Friends of the Napa River, a young volunteer organization, began work on the valley's own river-friendly project. They proposed an environmentally sensitive flood project approved by the federal government, which would transform the way the Corps of Engineers had practiced flood control for the past 150 years.

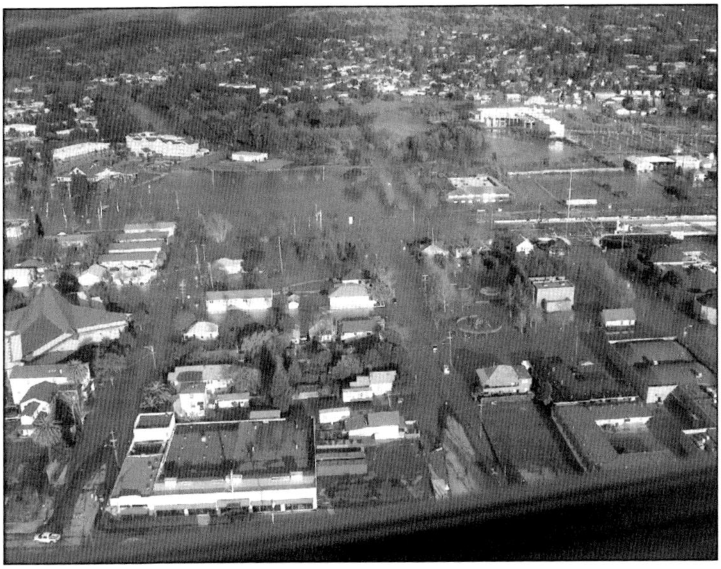

Muddy water flooded central Napa on New Year's Eve in 2005, causing an estimated $115 million in damage. The degraded riverbanks are deeper, steeper, less stable, and vulnerable to erosion. During floods, major erosion occurs. (Courtesy of the Napa County Flood Control and Water Conservation District.)

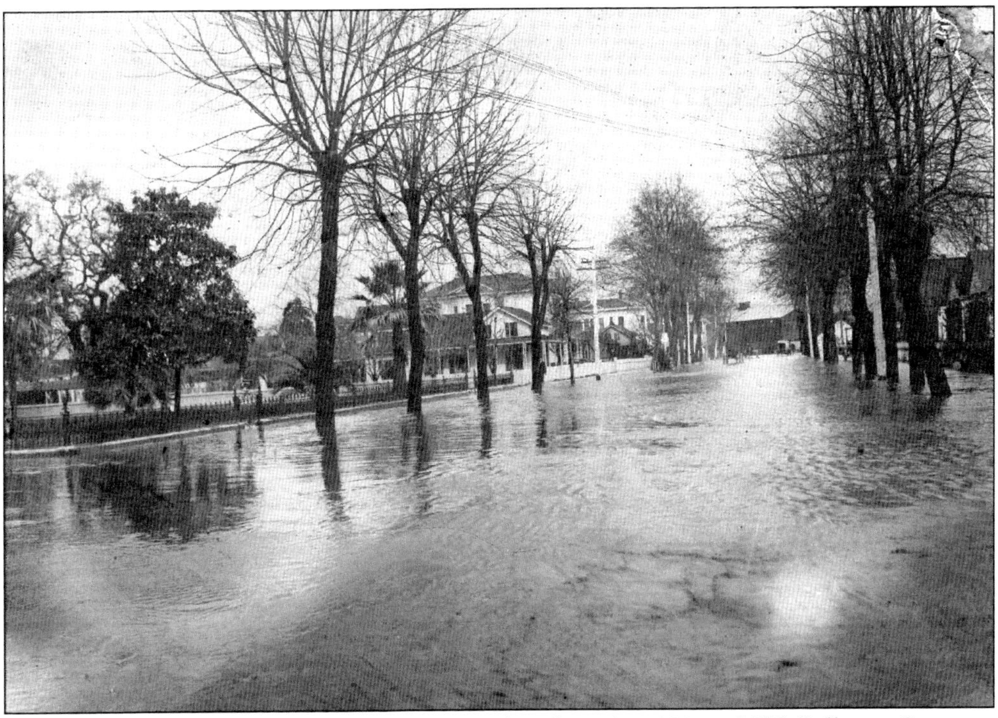

Severe flooding of the city streets was commonplace from the 1890s to 2005. Stillwater Sciences, an environmental firm hired to investigate the cause of flooding on the Napa River, determined that from 1940 to 1998, several causes were evident: "the abandoning of the floodplain and channel entrenchment, man-made causes such as the draining and diking of the valley floor, groundwater pumping, channel straightening, bank stabilization, levee construction, dredging downstream of the city of Napa, gravel bar skimming, and the loss of bed-load supply due to dam construction."

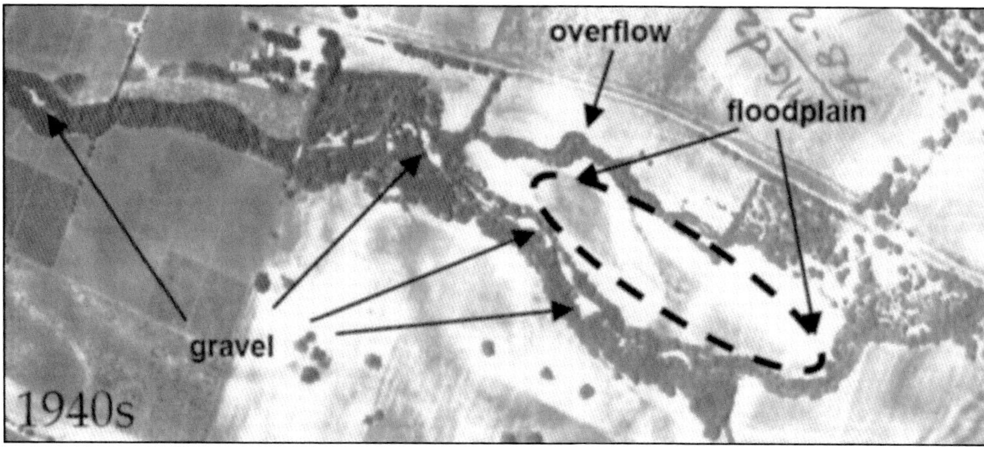

This aerial photograph shows Napa Valley fully developed by agriculture in the 1940s. Above the city of Napa, the river can be seen as a gravel-bedded stream with island bars and multiple channels. (Courtesy of Stillwater Sciences.)

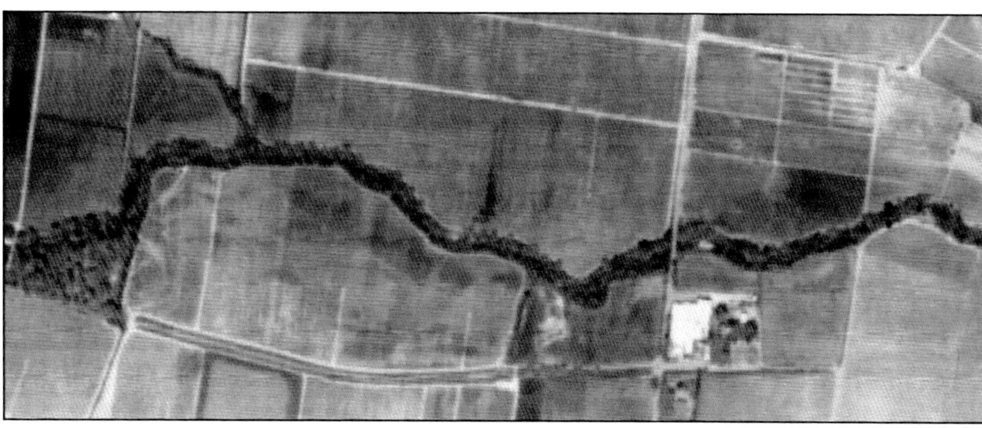
As secondary channels were changed to no longer carry flood flows, these flows were all directed into one channel. By 1998, the Napa River was a single-thread channel with an active floodplain. (Courtesy of Stillwater Sciences.)

Eight

An Under-Appreciated Waterway

The Napa River in the 20th Century

The development of the railroads and, later, trucking competed with the river for shipping freight. The Monticello Steamship Company, a partner of the interurban, began to transport autos during the 1920s. There were no bridges on the bay and Carquinez Straits in 1922, but many motorists wanted to drive their cars aboard a Monticello boat and cross to Vallejo, then travel into the Napa Valley in their own cars. Replaced by the highways, the ferries operated until the 1920s, when the steamer *Zinfandel* made its last run. The construction of the Golden Gate and Bay Bridges during the 1930s greatly reduced ferry service. The subdivision and shopping-mall culture post–World War II drew people away from downtown Napa. Cars and trucks now bypassed Napa's urban center on the new Highway 29. Along the Napa River, Sawyer Tannery and the production of hides kept shipping alive into the mid-20th century. Longtime Napa resident and businessman Al Giovannoni remembers swimming at the end of Oak Street when he was a boy in the 1930s. The kids had rigged up a diving board, and he and the neighborhood children of the Abate family enjoyed jumping in. He also recalls big, heavy boats, likely freighters, docking at the end of Division Street, carrying hides for Sawyer Tannery in the 1940s. He calmly relayed, "Dyes in the river used to be different colors." He fondly remembers "catching fish like mad" in the sewers near the first bridge at the end of Coombs in the Riverpark subdivision, including carp, striped bass, whitefish, and catfish. He also recalls Standard Oil on the east side of the river with two or three oil company wharfs. The industrial machinery of the Napa leather colony began to come to a close in the mid-20th century. While crops from the farms in the Carneros region and outlying area were still shipped primarily by barge, the river was replaced by new roads for automobile and truck traffic as the main transportation artery.

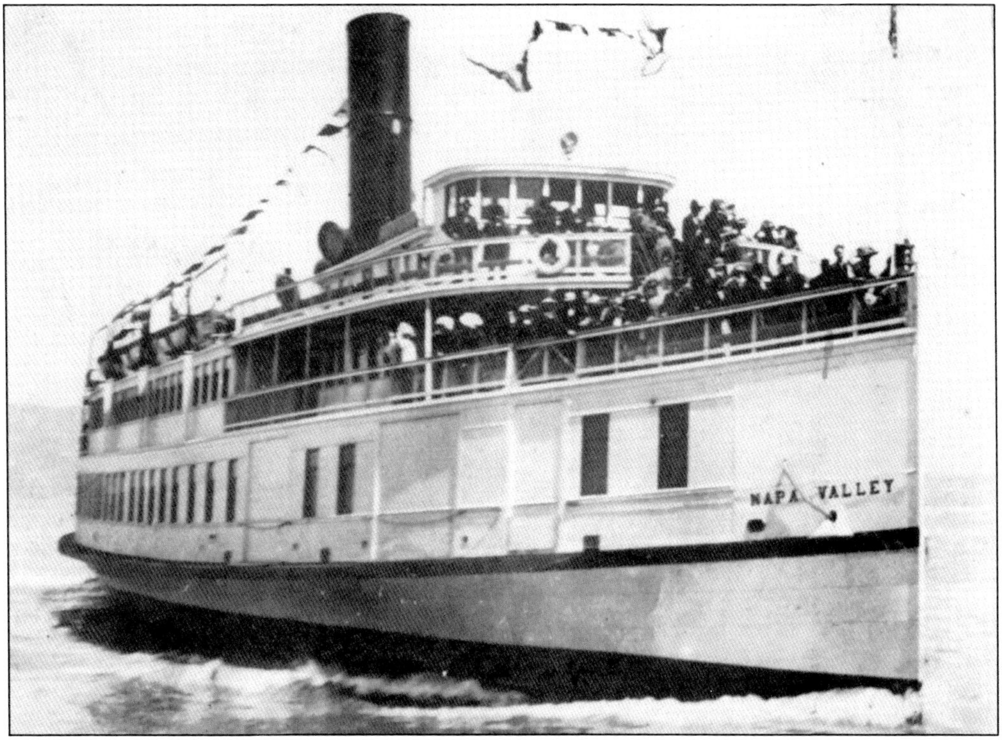

In 1922, Monticello rebuilt two of its largest steamers, the *Napa Valley* and *Asbury Park*, widening them so that they could carry many more automobiles and trucks. It was not unusual for passengers to crowd a ship's upper deck to gain a good view of the San Pablo Bay, as demonstrated below. (Above, courtesy of the California History Room, California State Library, Sacramento, California.)

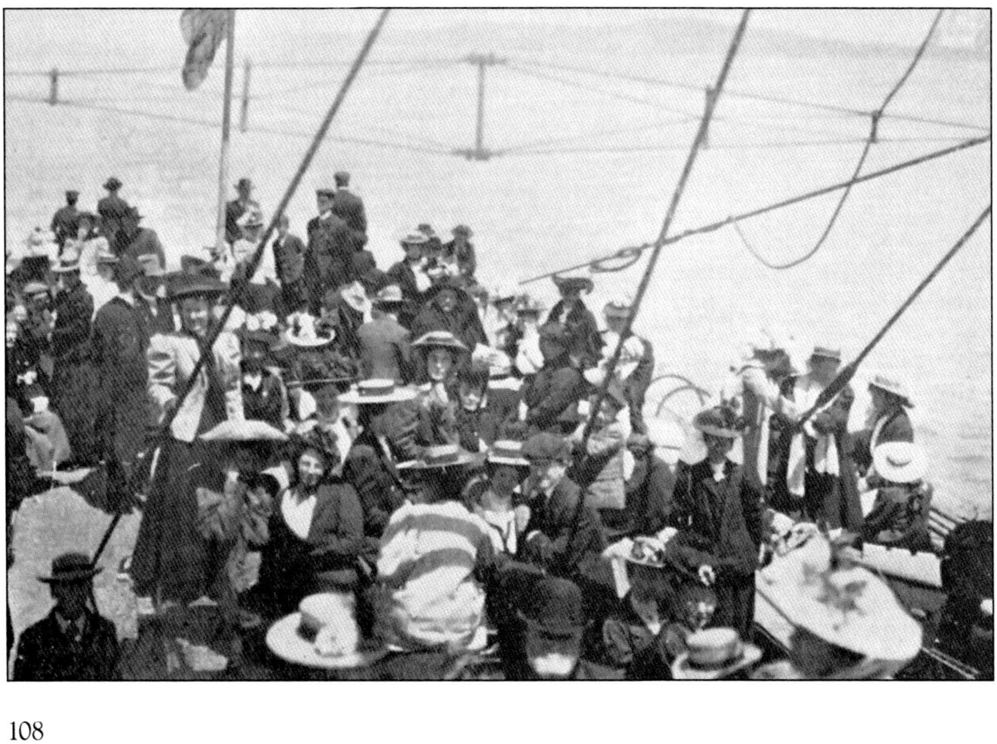

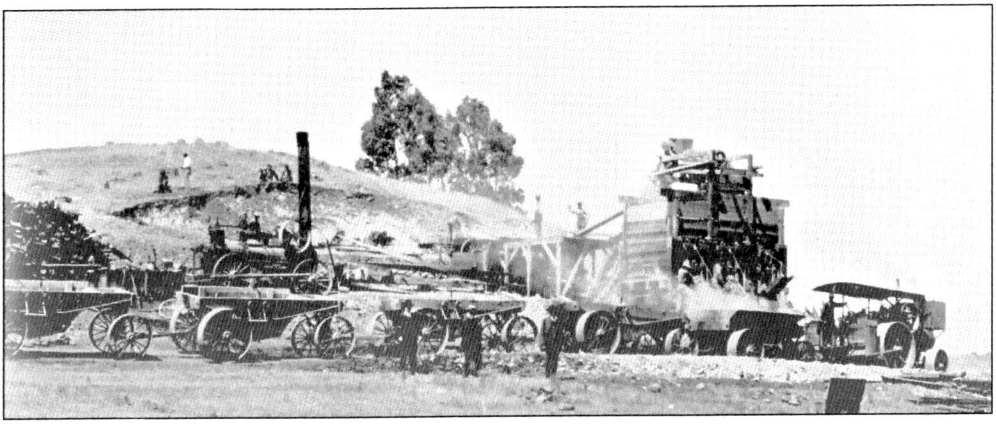

Rock-crushing, road-building equipment created a pathway for autos heading into the Napa Valley.

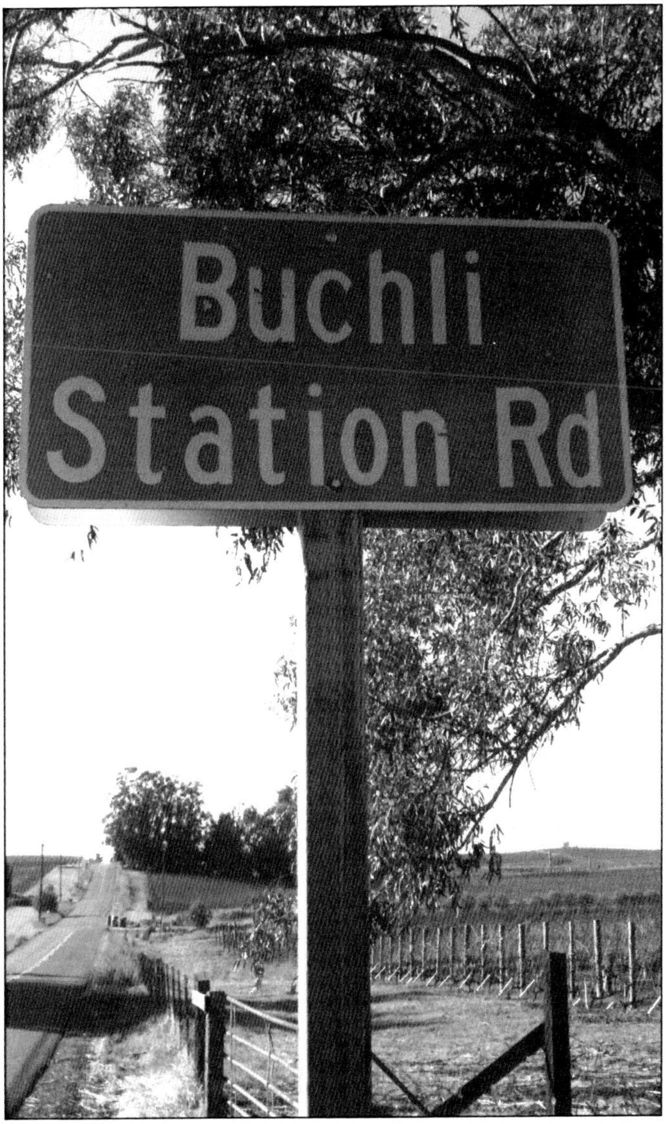

According to Walt Crivelli, a dairy farmer and cattleman who farmed oats on Bandy and Russ Islands in the Napa Delta during the 1930s and 1940s, "The only way off [the islands] was by water." In a 1984 interview with Geets Vincent, Crivelli noted, "We had to barge cattle across. We used to unload off Dutton's Landing and met the railroad at Buchli Station. Trucks came down too. If the weather weren't bad, you could move 400 tons of hay on old beet pulp barges."

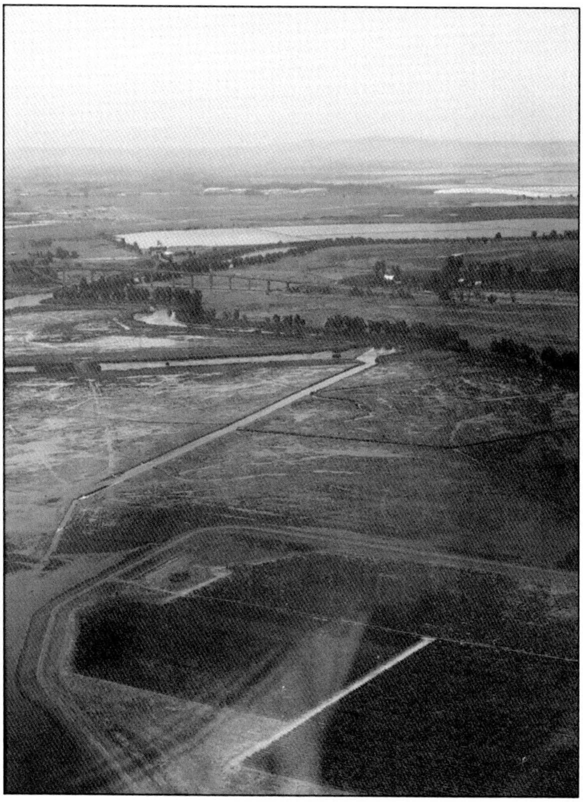

Looking out over the floodplain south of Imola in this 2008 photograph, mud and silt are exposed during a low tide on the Napa River. The Napa Airport is to the far left but not visible. Tom Dudenhoffer, a Napa fisherman and expert on the river, stressed the need for a GPS-based map of the Napa River, as it has not been plotted: "There is a dangerous jetty out there that is submerged in high tide creating a dangerous situation for boats. Many people mistakenly believe that sailing during high tide is the safest, but it is the opposite. During low tide ship wrecks are visible as well as other hazards." (Courtesy of Bernhard Krevet, FONR.)

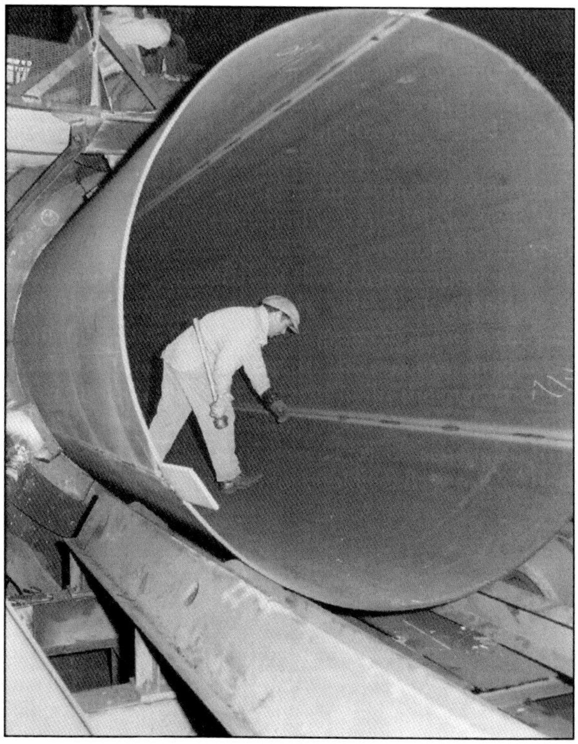

An ironworker inspects a pipe inside the Kaiser Steel Plant. Pollution has been an ongoing problem throughout Napa River's history. Between the tanneries and their hide and tallow operations, and later the municipal water runoff into the river, the river has been a dumping ground. In the 1920s, Basalt Rock Company ran a rock quarry, and in 1938, it began to build its own barges on the river site now known as Napa Pipe. It was poised to help the war effort by producing barges, tugboats, and other small ships for the Navy. The federal government created a neighborhood of 400 plywood houses named Shipyard Acres. Its purpose was to provide housing for out-of-state men and women working back-to-back shifts to support the war effort. The neighborhood was dismantled sometime during the 1950s, but some of these houses still remain in the Cuttings Wharf area.

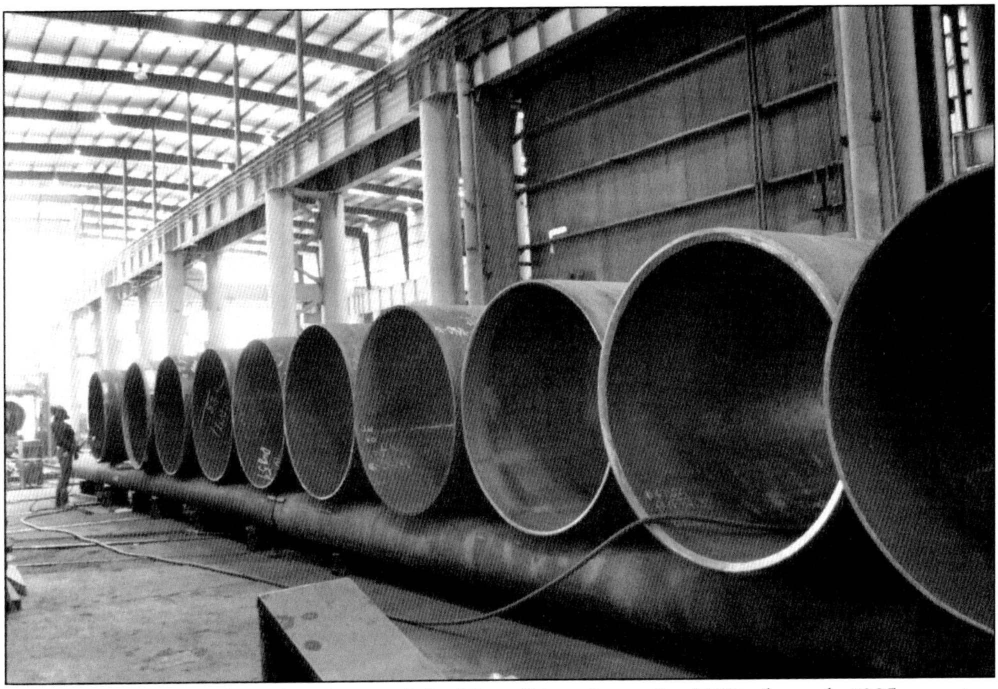

Kaiser Steel operated on the shores of the Napa River from the 1950s through 1985, creating heavy steel products. Pipes were one of many products manufactured there.

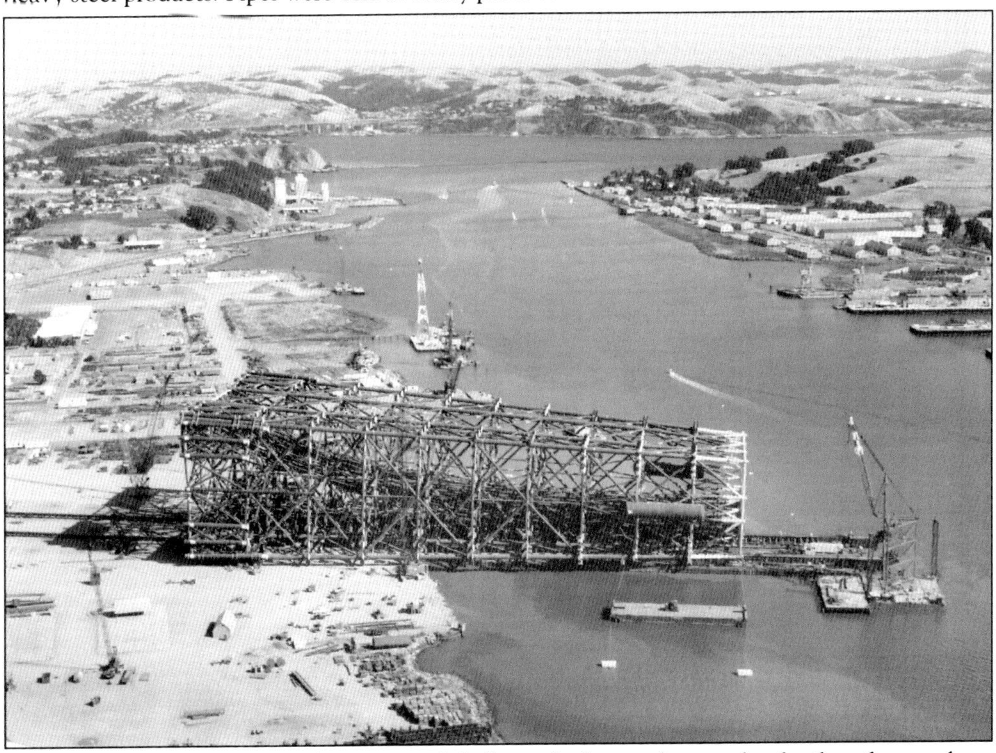

The Kaiser Steel Plant built deepwater oil-drilling platforms, thousands of miles of natural gas pipelines, and the Bay Area Rapid Transit (BART) Transbay Tube.

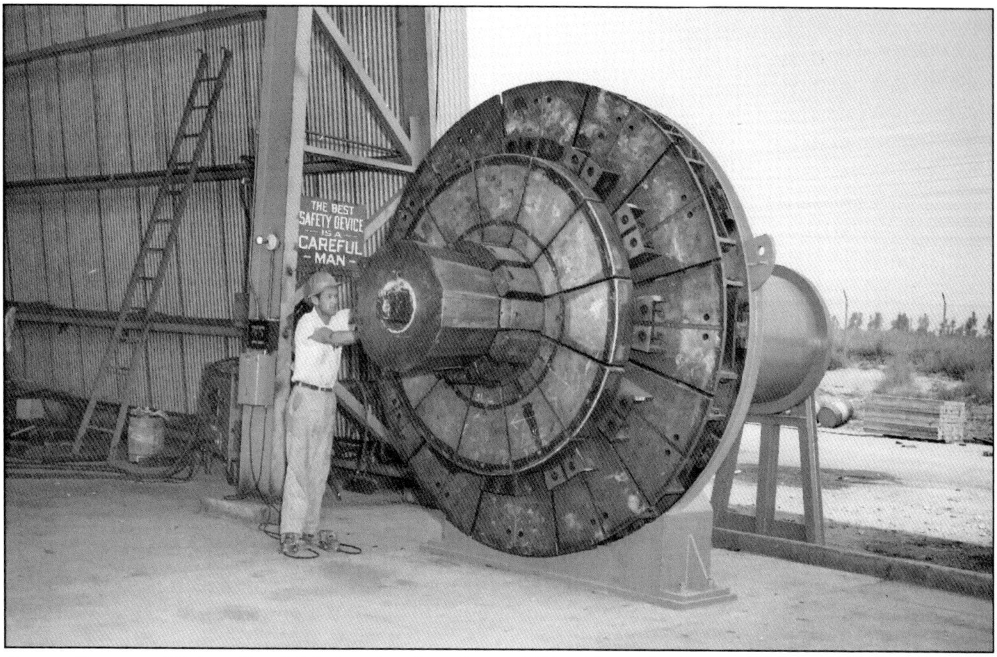

According to a Kaiser Steel fabrication brochure, "The Napa facility could handle the heaviest plate in the industry." Here, an ironworker inspects a ring expander. The navigable Napa River channel offered direct flotation of many of its products. Kaiser Steel was a major employer. When it closed, along with the Mare Island shipyards, Napa felt the economic impact.

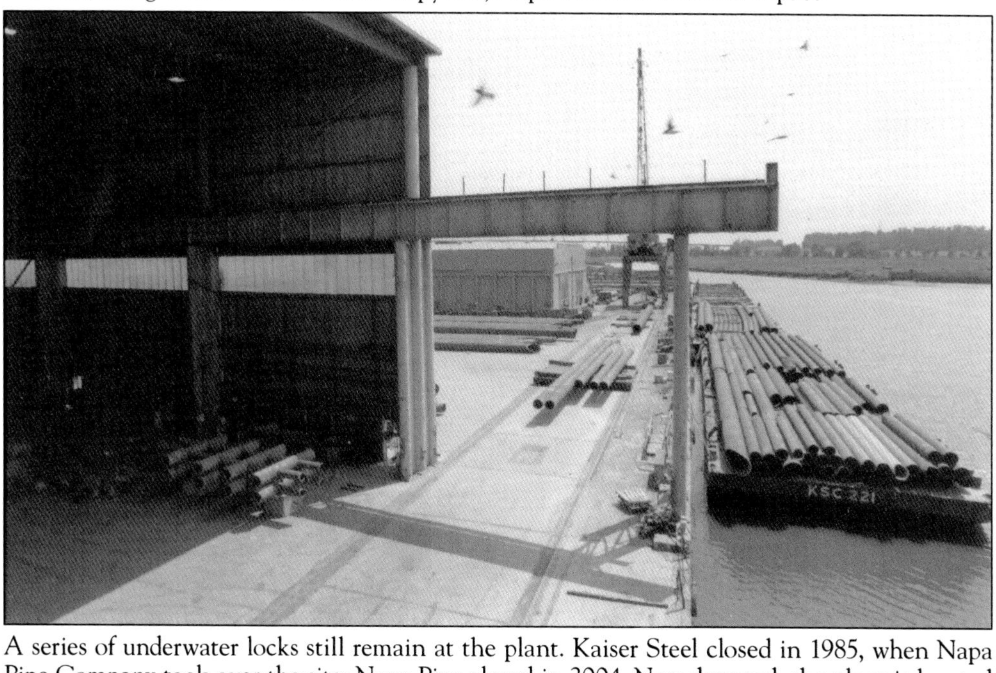

A series of underwater locks still remain at the plant. Kaiser Steel closed in 1985, when Napa Pipe Company took over the site; Napa Pipe closed in 2004. Now deserted, the plant is located on a 152-acre site and contains overhead crane systems, drydocks, and seawall facilities. With today's revitalized and protected river, the site is proposed for nonindustrial uses, including a large residential project with a commercially developed riverfront.

Nine

The Centerpiece of Downtown Renewal
A Living River Strategy

By the mid-1990s, the urgency of restoring the river and protecting the community from damaging and expensive floods had become a dynamic force throughout Napa City and County. Under the banner of a living-river strategy, a county-wide community coalition was formed to create a flood management and river restoration project, partnering with the Napa County Flood Control and Water Conservation District and the US Army Corps of Engineers. By 1998, this group had created a groundbreaking, environmentally sensitive strategy, and in the spring of that year, it was put up for a county-wide vote. The project won by narrow margin in a special election. With the local community funding half the project, a half-cent sales tax was put in place; it would generate over $120 million over 20 years to achieve the joint goals of flood management and river restoration throughout the Napa River watershed. In the years since the vote, the lower reaches of the Napa River have been the scene of dramatic action as the project grows to achieve the joint goals of a healthy river, flood protection, and natural functioning. In the process, hundreds of acres of wetlands have been created, levees removed, and river terraces built; the quality of fish and wildlife habitat has also improved. With the threat of flooding reduced, the urban center of the city of Napa is already enjoying a renaissance. The Napa River Project, scheduled to be finished by 2014, has become a national and international model for ecologically sensitive flood management and river restoration.

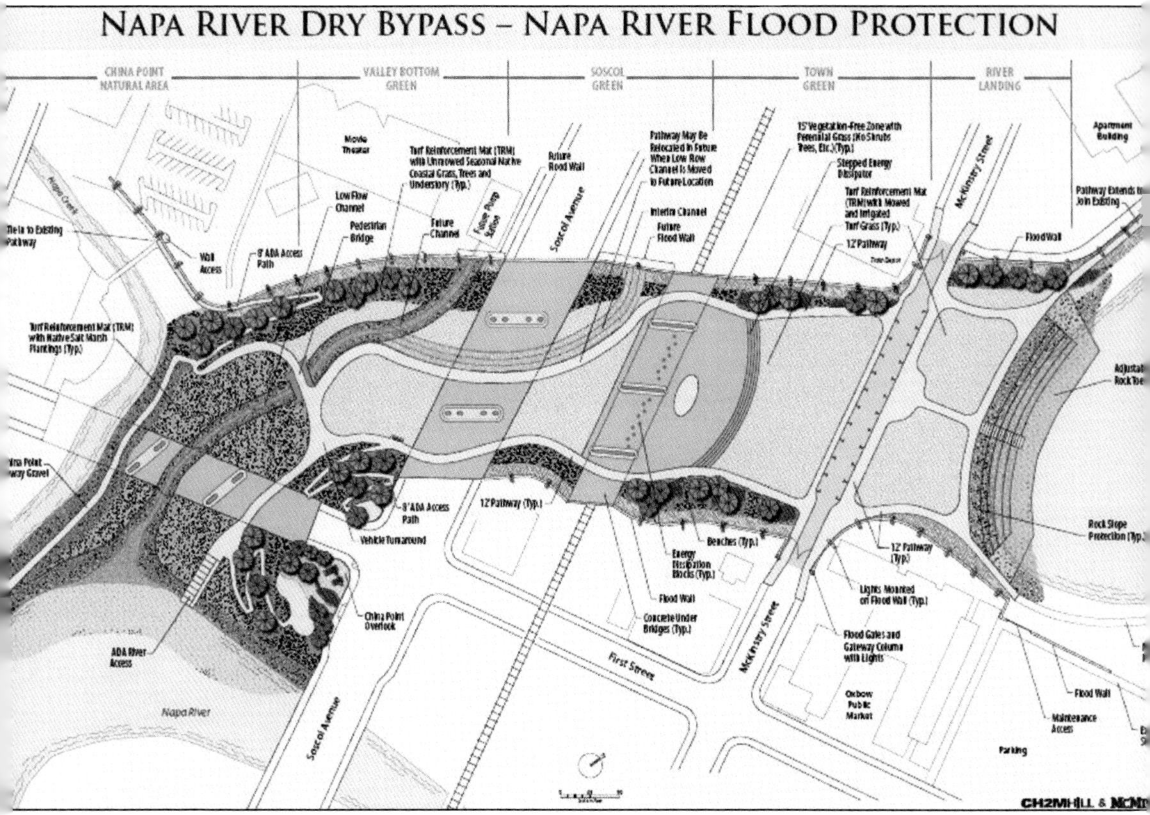

Removing and replacing bridges that impede floodwaters and the creation of a dry bypass channel at the river oxbow are key features of the design. (Courtesy of Napa County Flood Control and Water Conservation District.)

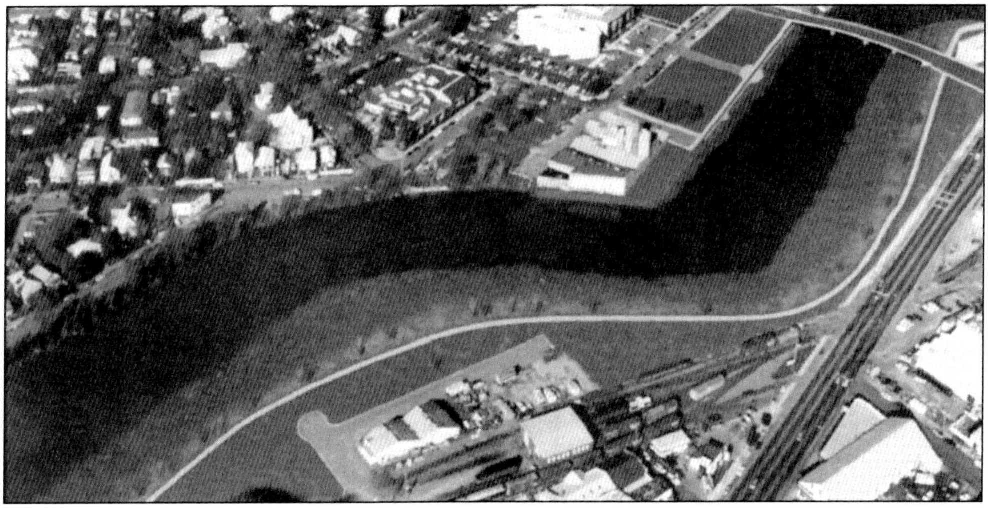

To create new floodplains and wetlands along Oil Company Road immediately flanking the river on the east, the project mandates the removal and cleanup of toxic waste that has accumulated over decades. The project is immense. According to Bill Campbell, "It features levee removal, riparian restoration, channel modifications, bank stabilization, a dry bypass channel . . . maintenance roads, and recreation trails." Watershed and flood control operations manager Rick Thomasser estimates the total cost to be $400 million, with over $120 million in funding coming from state subventions and the remaining costs shared by the US Army Corps of Engineers and local sales tax revenues. (Courtesy of Napa County Flood Control and Water Conservation District.)

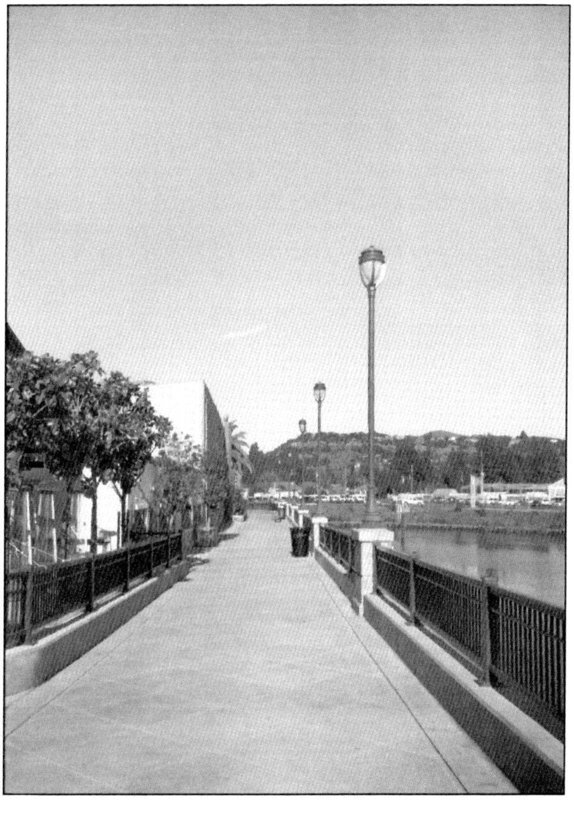

Today, as visitors come to downtown Napa, they can stroll along the river trail, extending on the west side from downtown Joe's Restaurant to the Napa Mill and Hatt Building. It features large, two-tiered promenade areas overlooking the river and new outdoor community gathering places. The trail also extends north from Lincoln Avenue to Trancas Street and will eventually be connected to the current terminus at the First Street Bridge. Soon, the Napa River Trail will extend all the way down Riverside Street past the Sawyer Tannery. On the eastern side of the river, a planned trail will stretch from the Third Street Bridge south to meet up with the trail that now runs past Napa Valley College and Kennedy Park, already a favorite of walkers, birders, and bicyclists. In all, a seven-mile river trail system will eventually connect to trails in American Canyon and Vallejo. (Author's collection.)

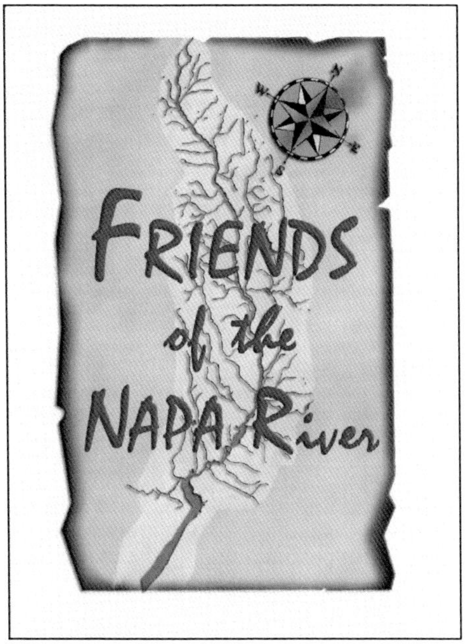

There are many organizations to be credited with the preservation of the Napa River. Friends of the Napa River is one such organization. FONR was established as a nonprofit organization in early 1994 with the mission to be "the community's voice for the protection, restoration, responsible development and celebration of the Napa River and its watershed." The organizers have worked together through the years on many different issues concerning the Napa River, including flood protection, boating, fish habitat, watershed restoration, trails, festivals, and riverfront development. Friends also served as cochair of the community coalition that spearheaded the flood project. (Courtesy of Bernhard Krevet, FONR.)

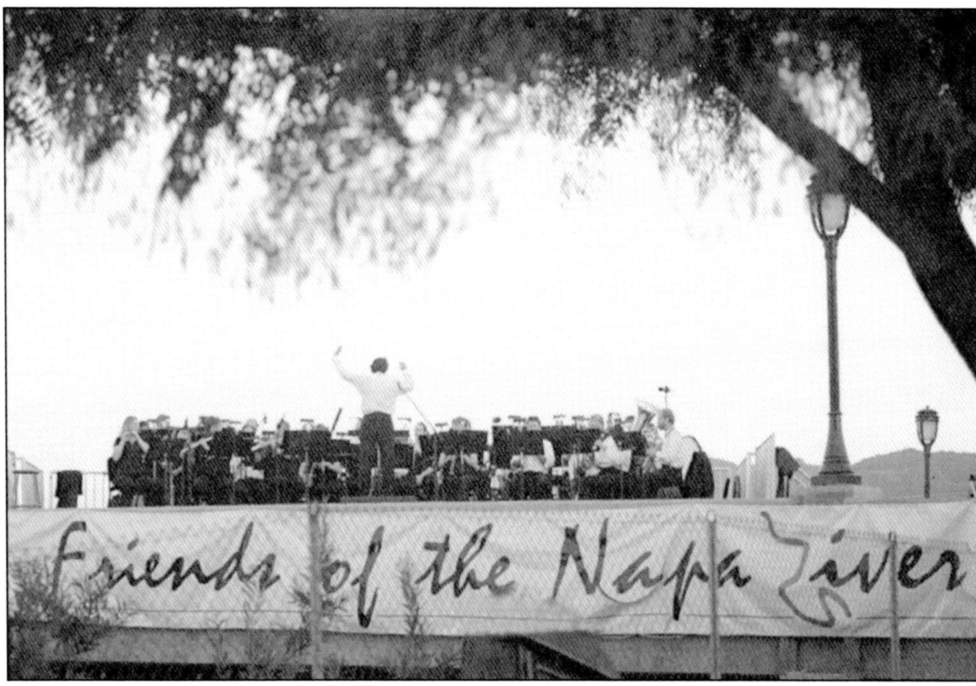

The primary goal of Friends of the Napa River has been to heighten the community's awareness of the river as a valuable but impaired resource. The group advocates for the Napa River at governmental meetings when decisions are being made that affect the river. They sponsor the annual river festival featuring the Napa Valley Symphony on the Sunday of Labor Day weekend. In addition, they sponsor cleanups and watershed hikes and participate on local committees concerning water, flooding, urban and land-use planning, and recreation. Many members have been involved over the years with the blueprint of the flood-control project in Napa, along with a county-wide coalition, to bring the most enlightened plan possible to Napa. (Courtesy of FONR.)

RUTHERFORD DUST SOCIETY

NAPA VALLEY

For the past seven years, a river restoration team of the Rutherford Dust Society, a coalition of property owners that mostly own vineyards along the banks of the Napa River, has worked with a wide range of stakeholders to develop a long-range sustainability program for the Napa River. Upriver, the Rutherford Reach area provides a critical spawning habitat for Chinook salmon and supports threatened steelhead trout. In a press release from executive director Paul Wagner, landowner coordinator Gretchen Hayes notes, "The Napa River watershed is an anchor watershed for steelhead in the San Francisco Bay Area, and has been ranked as having the highest restoration potential in regional studies conducted by the Coastal Conservancy. Repair of the fish barrier will have immediate benefits for steelhead, Chinook, and at least fourteen other native freshwater fish species. The Rutherford Dust Society and its Project Partners, including Napa County and the Napa County Resource Conservation District, have gained Congressional acknowledgment for their pioneering restoration work on the Napa River."

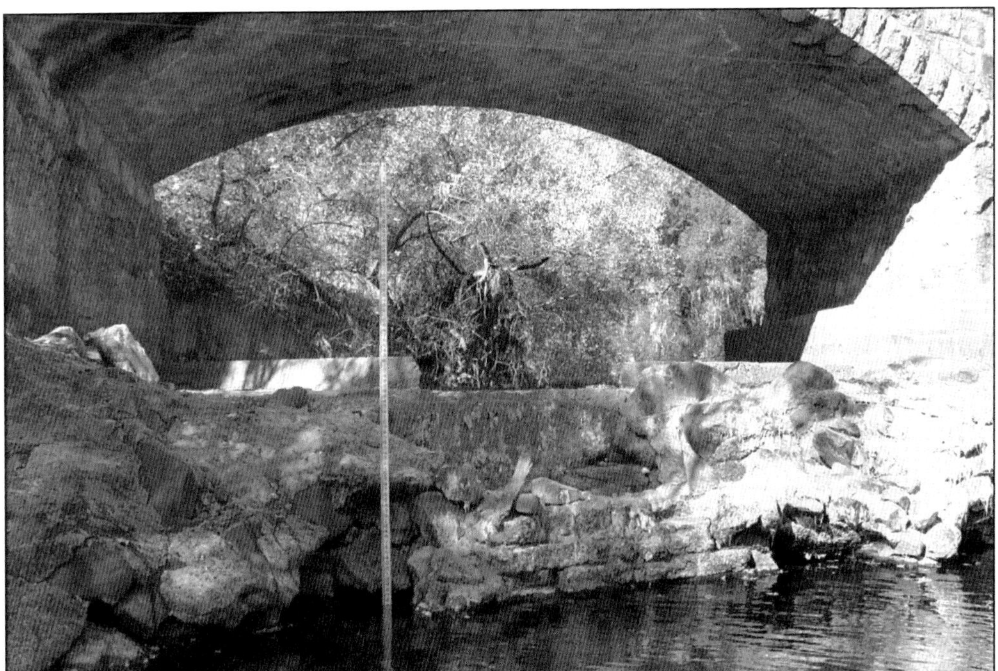

In November 2011, an area of 60 miles of prime spawning ground in the Napa River and its tributaries were opened thanks to the completion of a million-dollar project that eliminated a concrete apron that had blocked fish from spawning under the Zinfandel Lane Bridge, which is located upstream in St. Helena. (Courtesy of Napa County.)

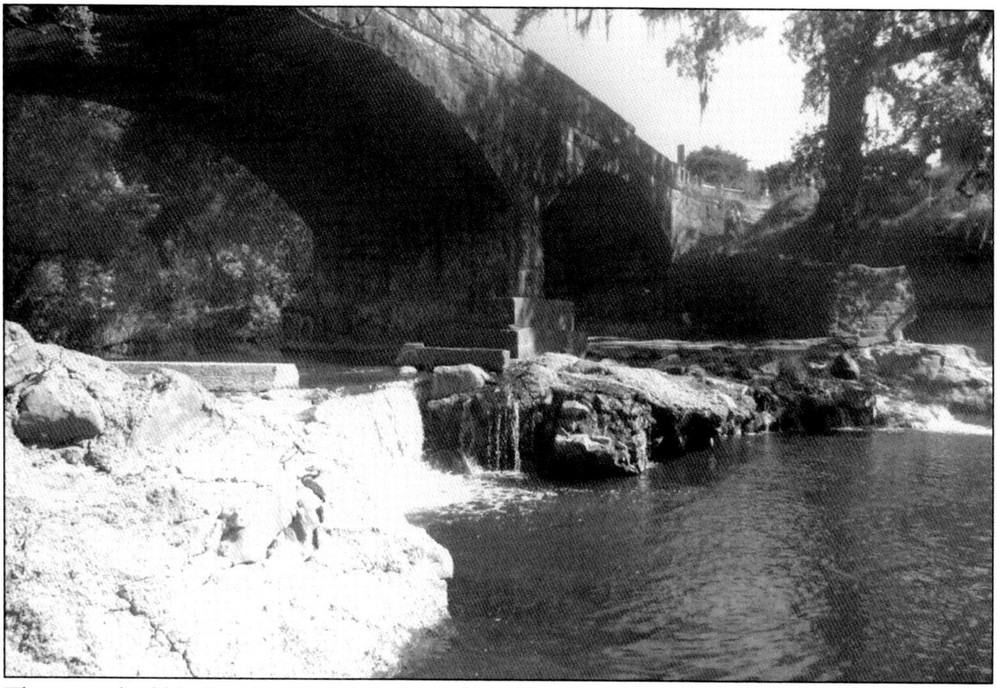

The apron had blocked Chinook salmon and steelhead trout from swimming upstream to their preferred spawning grounds. Before removal of the barrier, many fish banged their heads against the concrete apron and were killed. (Courtesy of Napa County.)

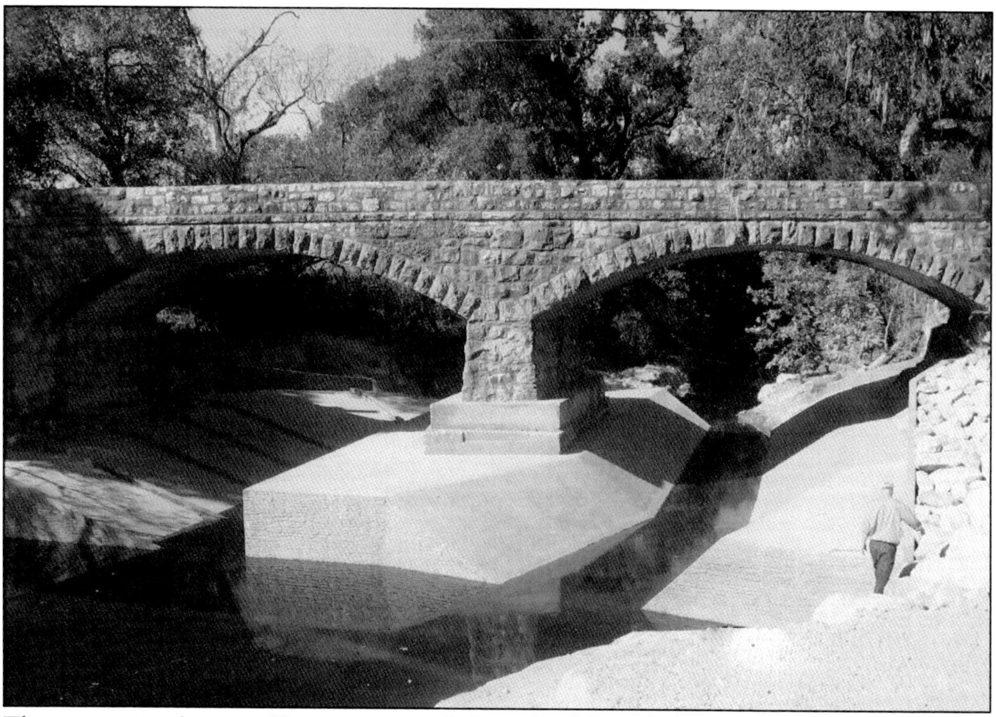

The renovation frees up 50 percent more habitat for fish and also serves the dual purpose of preserving the 1913 Zinfandel Bridge. (Courtesy of Napa County.)

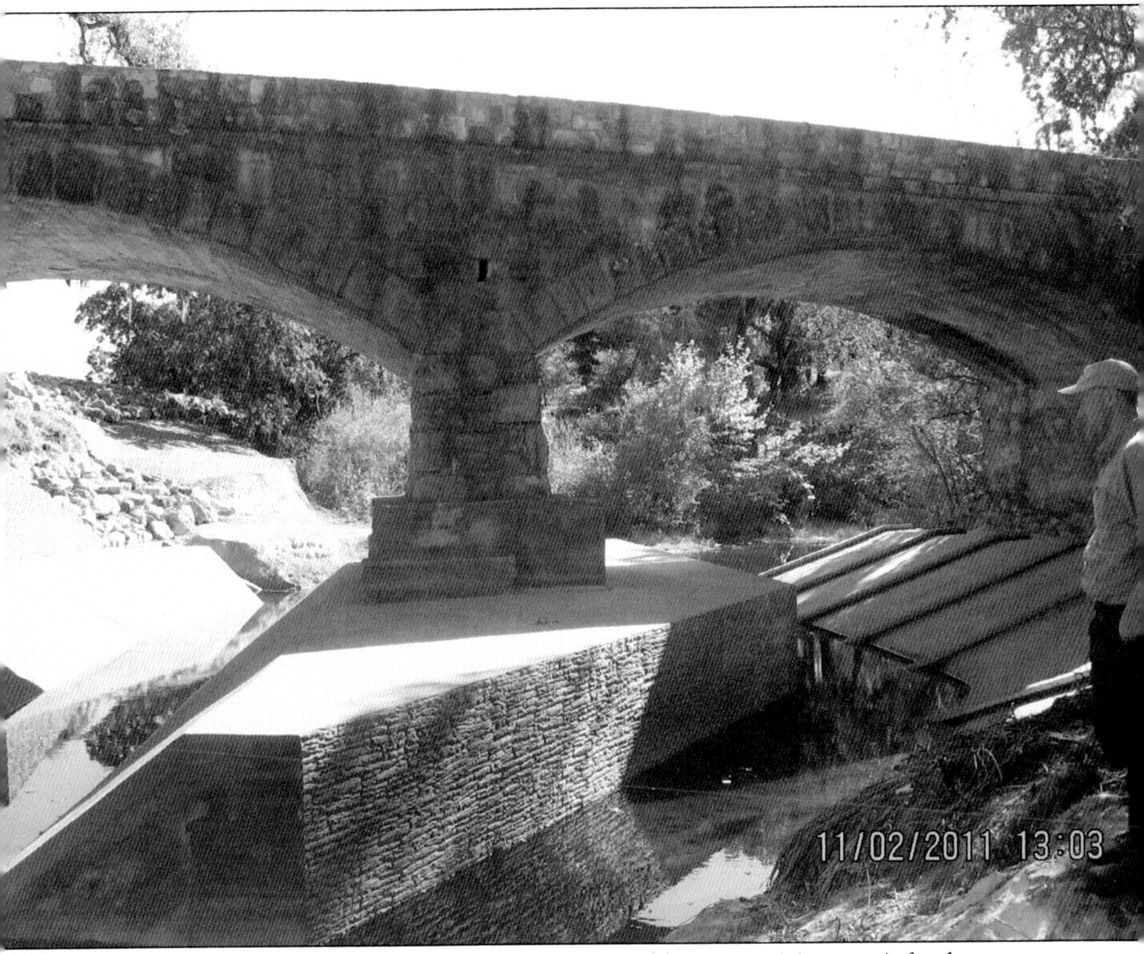

The Napa River Flood Protection Project was financed by county Measure A funds, a grant from the California Coastal Conservancy, the US Army Corps of Engineers, and the Gasser Foundation. (Courtesy of Napa County.)

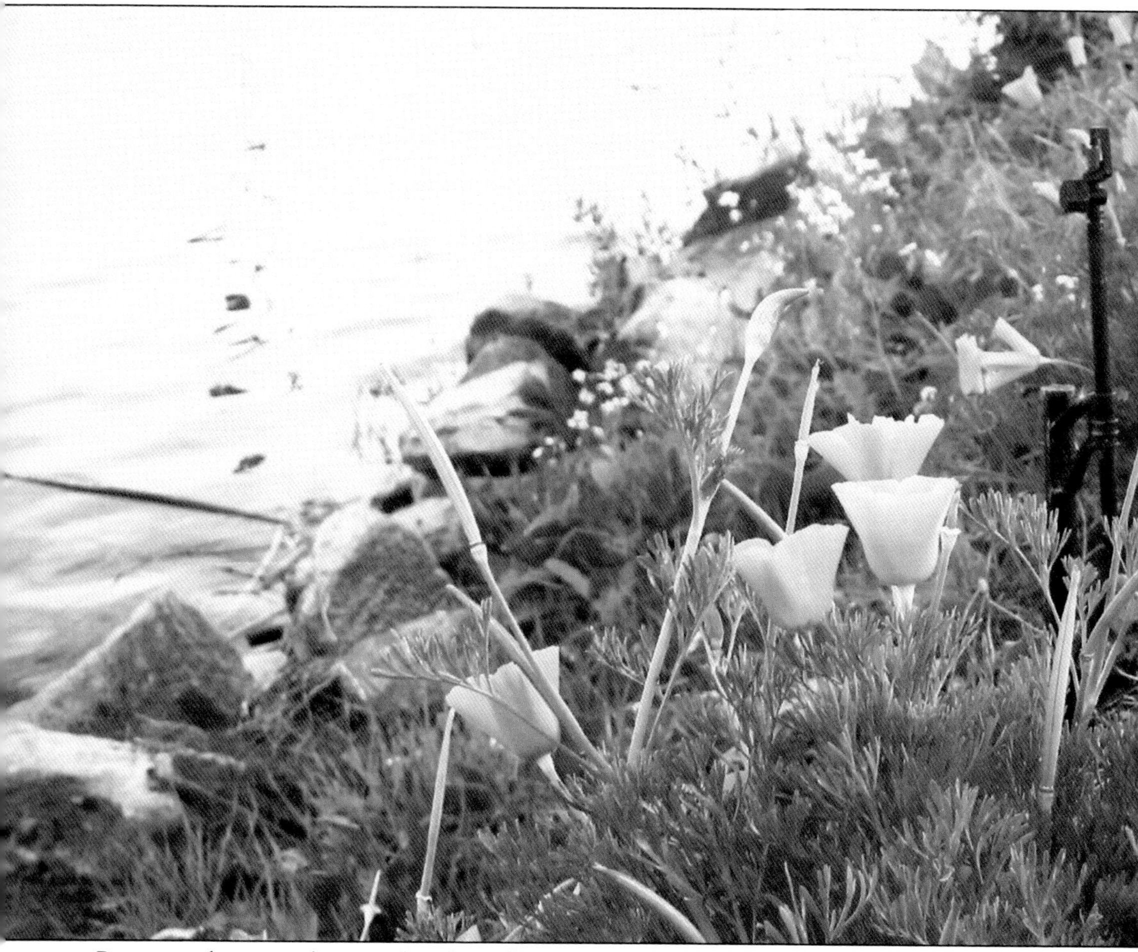

Progress is being made every day along the Napa River.

Ten

The Renaissance of the Napa River
Healthy and Vital Once Again

The river is changing not only downtown and upstream, but also downriver where it enters San Pablo Bay. In the Carneros region, over 7,000 acres of former salt evaporative ponds, also known as "concentrators," were used to make concentrated brine that was dried by the sun to make industrial-grade salt through the 1980s. In 1994, the ponds were acquired from Cargill by the Wildlife Conservation Board for the Department of Fish and Game, according to Tom Huffman's article, "The Napa-Sonoma Marshes: Then and Now." Twelve of these evaporative ponds are in the process of being restored by the opening of the levees, which allows bay waters to dilute the salt concentrations. Through levee breaches, water and sediment have begun to circulate with the tide cycles for the first time in over 40 years with spectacular results. Shorebirds and waterfowl are frequenting these ponds. A diverse ecosystem of tidal salt and brackish marshes with freshwater and seasonal wetlands is the goal, explains Huffman. Today, over 128 species of birds have been identified along the Napa River, and in the nearby marshes, over 25 species of waterfowl have been spotted, including the endangered California clapper rail, the threatened California black rail, the salt marsh yellow throat, and the western snowy plover, explains Larry Wyckoff in "When Winemaking Meets Wildlife, It Can Be a Beautiful Thing: The Napa-Sonoma Marsh." Today, the Napa River remains an active waterway. On any given day, it is quite remarkable to observe the variety of boat traffic on the river, most of it now recreational. Sailboats, powerboats, hand-launched canoes, and kayaks can be seen. Many families fish and picnic there, watching the parade on the river. After decades of turning their backs, the people have returned to the river.

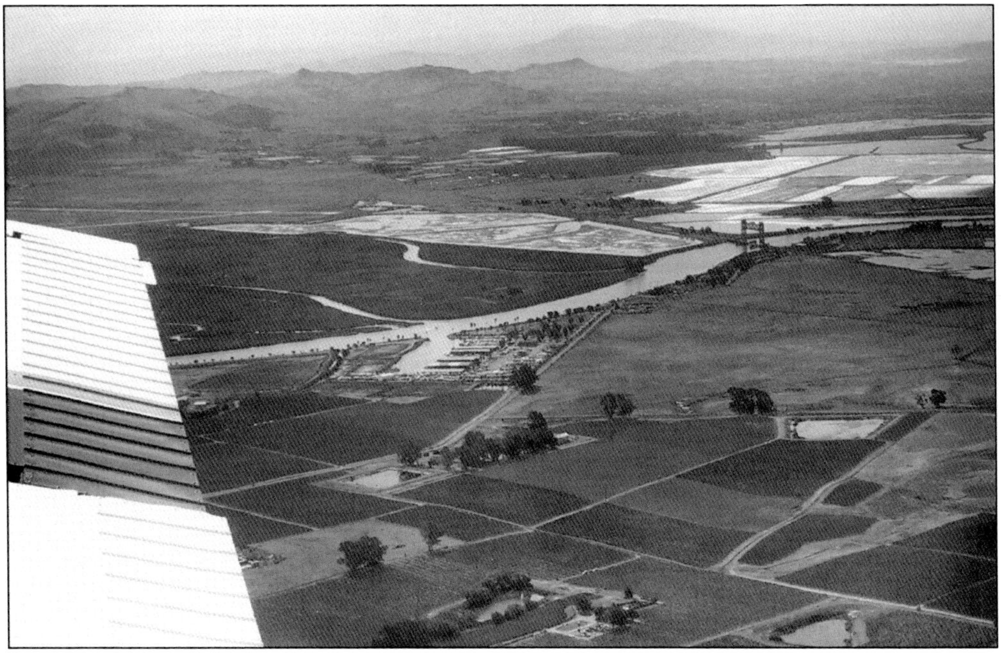

Salt ponds can be seen to the upper right in the distance of this aerial photograph of the Napa River. Brazos Bridge on Edgerly Island is also visible to the right. (Courtesy of Bernhard Krevet, FONR.)

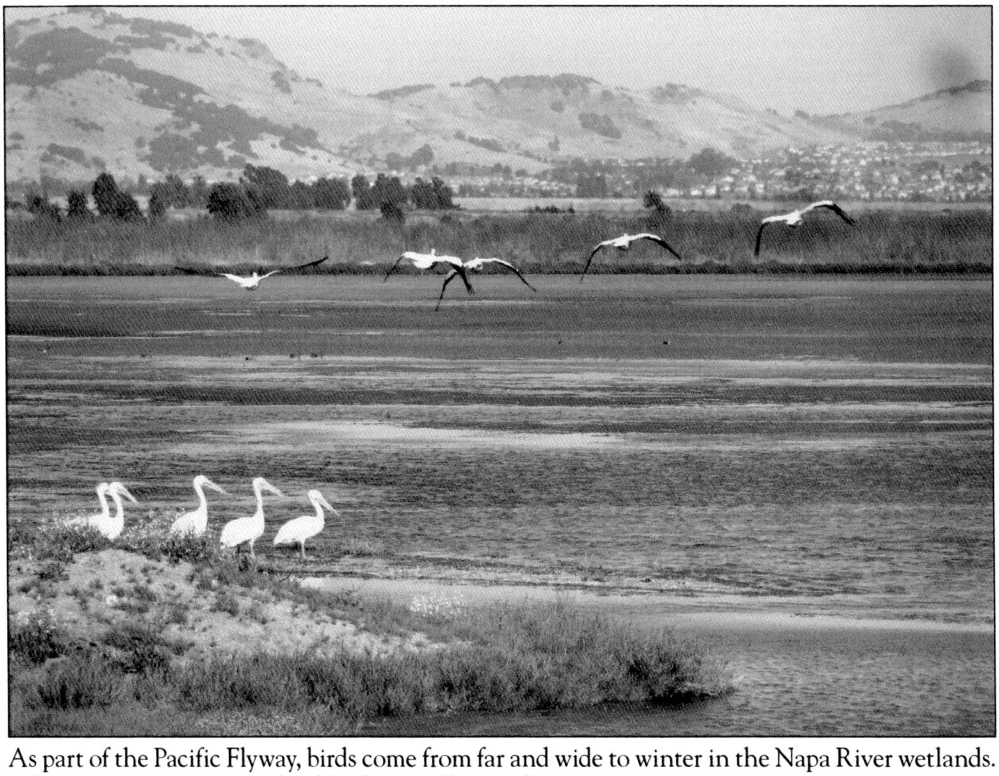

As part of the Pacific Flyway, birds come from far and wide to winter in the Napa River wetlands. Pelicans are a common sight. (Author's collection.)

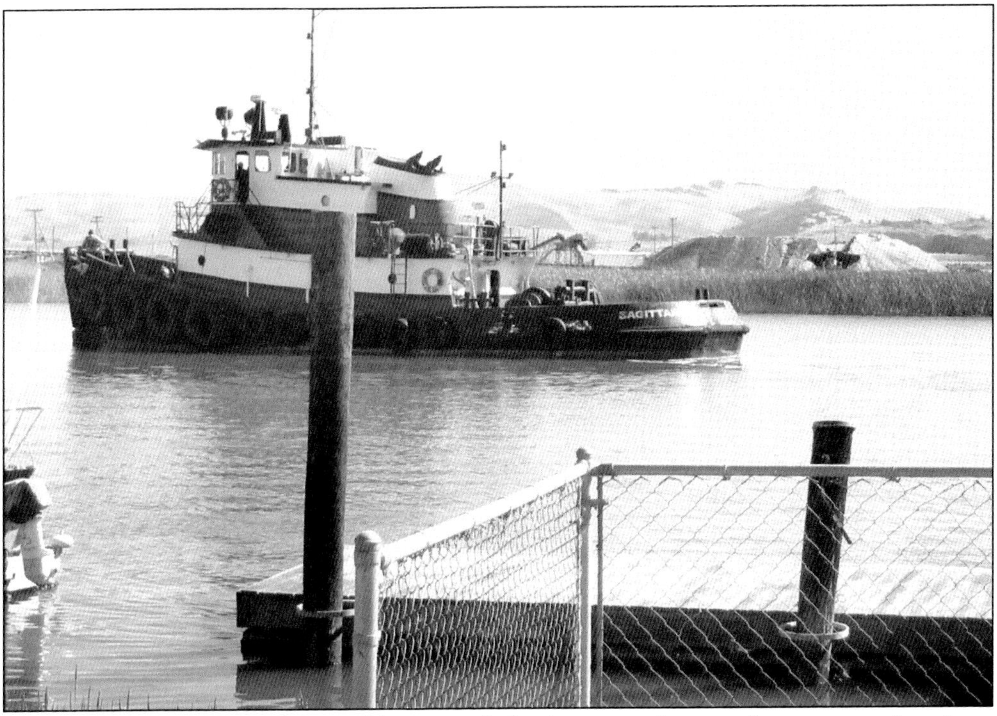

Tugboats, the modern-day workhorses of the bay, are frequently seen on the river. (Author's collection.)

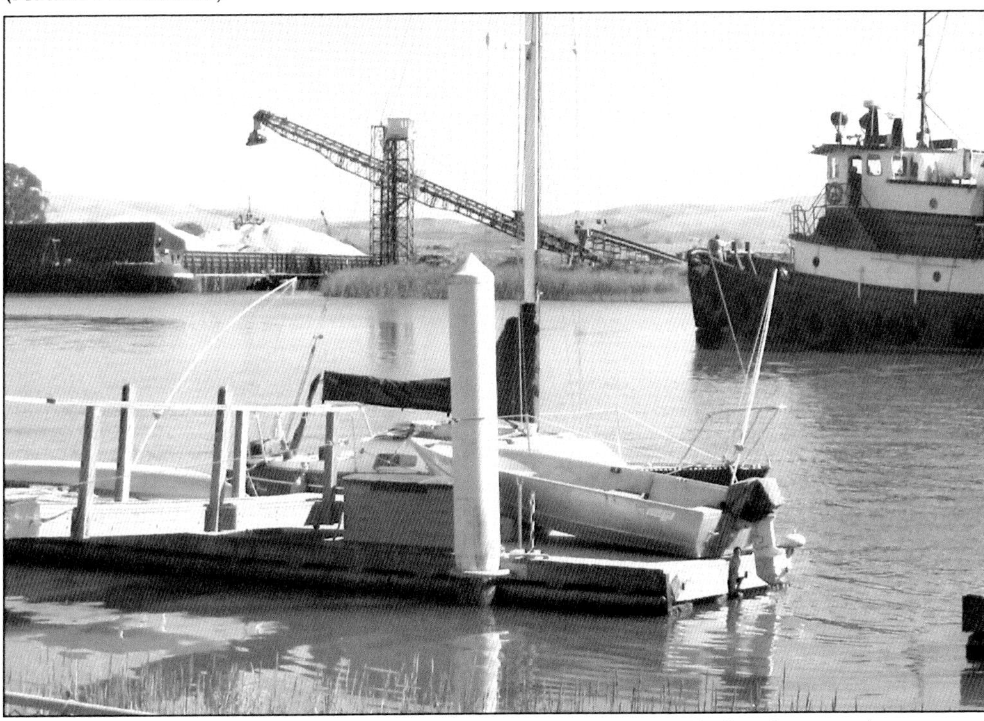

Salt has been harvested and loaded onto a barge. Salt removal will allow levees to be reopened and wetlands to be restored. (Author's collection.)

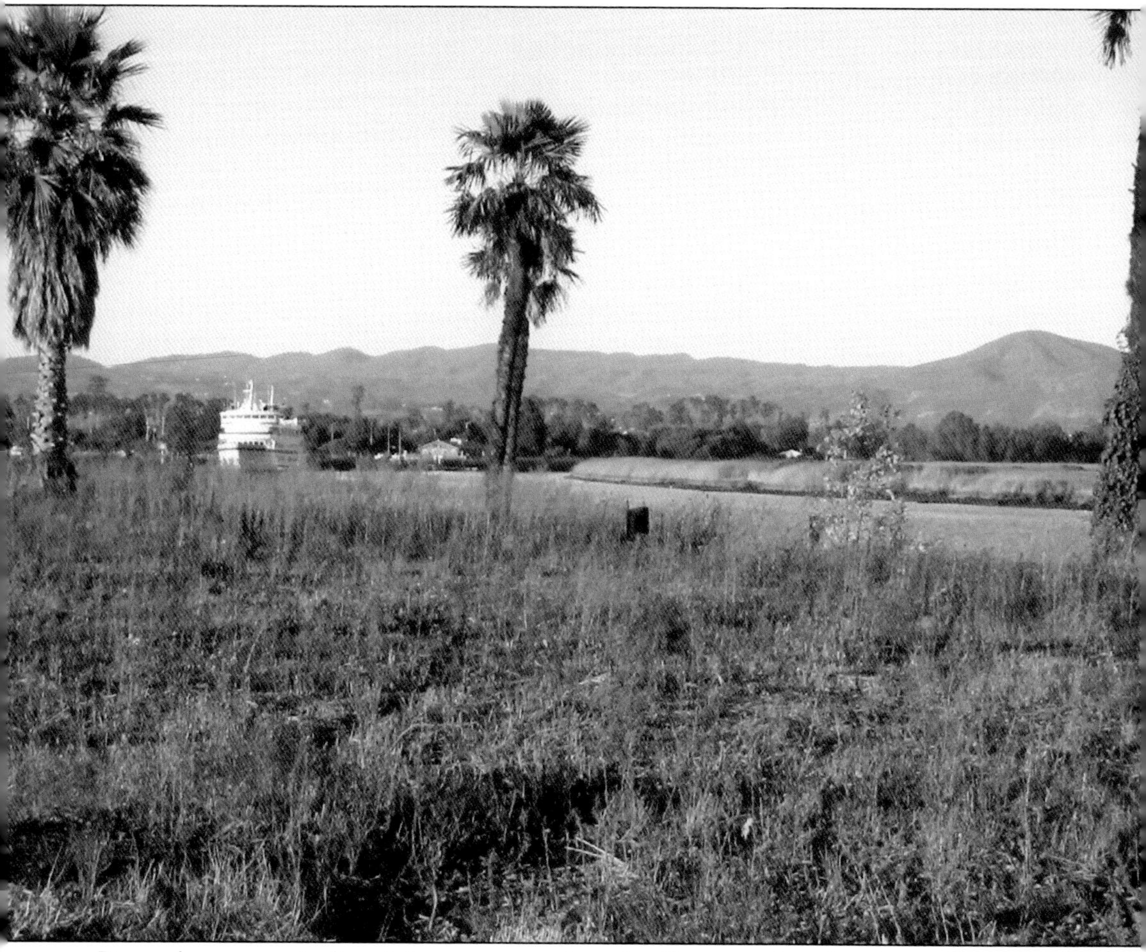

During harvest, cruise lines bring passengers from San Francisco for a day of wine tasting in the Napa Valley. (Author's collection.)

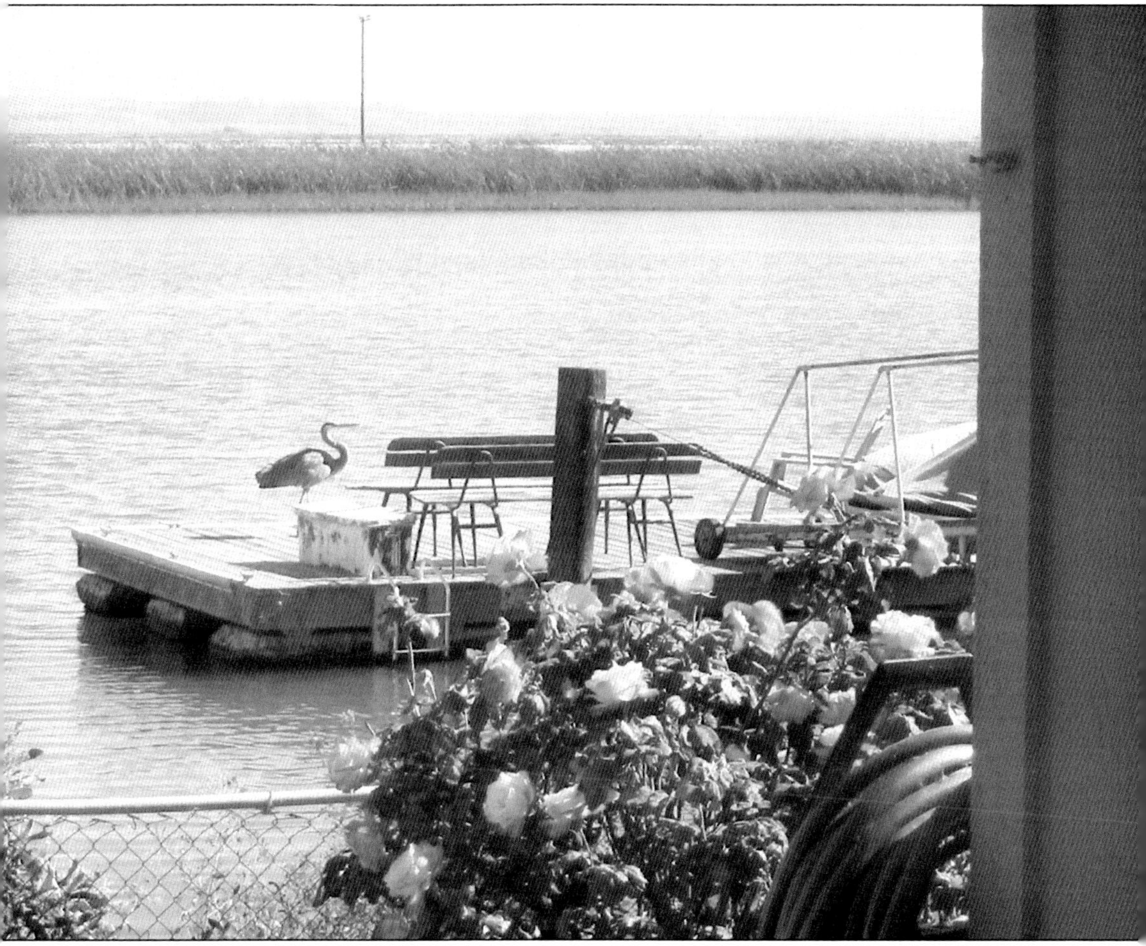

The Napa River is truly a gem in the midst. As the river is revitalized through living-river principles and protection efforts, residents and visitors reap the benefits, as does the wildlife that makes the river its home. As Napa's rich history continues, its river has been returned to the integral role it has always played in the area's ecosystem, culture, and economy. In this photograph, wildlife is abundant. Herons often fish off piers and docks to the spectators' delight. (Author's collection.)

BIBLIOGRAPHY

Campbell, Bill, "Napa County 'Living River Strategy' to Provide Flood Protection." *Wetlands Activity Update*. June 28, 2002.

Coodley, Lauren. "A Tannery in Town—Afterthoughts." *Napa Valley Marketplace Magazine* April 2006.

———. "Retracing Juliana's Path" *Napa Valley Marketplace Magazine*. June 2008.

Courtney, Kevin. "Early Settlers Found a Shangri-La, then they Drained and Boxed it." *Napa Valley Register*. August 29, 2010.

———. "Shipyard Acres Gone, Homefront Memories Remain." *Napa Valley Register*. November 12, 2002.

"Detailed Mapping of Artificial Fills, San Francisco Bay Area, California." *US Geological Survey Final Report*, September 2008.

Dietrich, William, and Stillwater Sciences. "Napa River Basin Limiting Factors Analysis." Berkeley, CA. June 14, 2002.

Dillon, Richard H. *Napa Valley Heydey*. San Francisco: Book Club of California, 2004.

Duarte, Jesse. "Fish Blockage Cleared from Zinfandel Lane." *Napa Valley Register*. November 23, 2011.

Duddenhoffer, Tom. Interview. July 20, 2011.

Eastman, Bright and Rebecca Yerger. "Transportation." *The Valley of Legends*. Napa, CA (1987).

Evans-White, Jules. "Rolling along the Oat Hill Mine Trail." *The Napa Valley Register*. February 21, 2010.

Giovannoni, Albert. Interview. July 11, 2011.

Gregory, Tom. *History of Napa and Lake Counties*. Los Angeles: Historic Record Company, 1912.

Greig, Jack R. "The Vessels of the Napa River 1844–1890." *Gleanings*. Napa, CA: Napa County Historical Society. February 1984: 2, 3.

Grossinger, Robin et al. "The Historical Ecology of Napa Valley." *San Francisco Estuary Institute Report* (2008).

Gunn, Harry Lawrence. *History of Solano and Napa Counties*. Chicago: The S.J. Clarke Publishing Co., 1926.

Hall, Albert Smith. "Institutional Records Digitization Project: Reminiscences of Early Pioneers: 1900–1904." Online Archive of California, www.oac.cdlib.org

Hanrahan, Virginia. *Napa County History 1823–1948*. Napa, CA: Napa Chamber of Commerce, 1948.

Harris, Paula. "Napa Rising: Arts Blossom in Once Neglected Riverfront Town." *Metroactive Arts*. January 31, 2002.

Huffman, Tom. "The Napa-Sonoma Marshes: Then and Now." *Outdoor California* (January February 1999).

JRP Historical Consulting. "Historic Resources Inventory and Evaluation Report Napa Plant Site Restoration Project Area, Napa County, California." Davis, CA. February 2006.

Loring, Charles M. "Early Steam Navigation on the Napa River." Napa County Historical Society. Napa, CA. April 13, 1967.

Menefee, C.A. *Historical and Descriptive Sketchbook of Napa, Sonoma, Lake and Mendocino.* Napa City: Reporter Publishing House, 1873.

Olin, K.G. "The Cabin Boy Who Became a Multimillionaire." *The Swedish Finn Historical Society Quarterly.* January 1998: 1, 7.

Olney, John M. "The Stories Underlying the Niebaum-Coppola Estate" *Napa Valley Winery Histories.* August 19, 2005.

"On the Water: To California by Sea". *Smithsonian National Museum of American History*, www.americanhistory.si.edu/onthewater

Palmer, Lyman L. *History of Napa and Lake Counties, California: Comprising Their Geography, Geology, Topography, Climatography, Springs and Timber.* San Francisco: Slocum, Bowen & Co., 1881.

San Francisco Call. San Francisco: 1895–1913, March 13, 1898, chroniclingamerica.loc.gov.

———. San Francisco: October, 2 1895. "Napa River Examined." California Digital Newspaper Collection.

Setty, Cecelia Elkington. *Atlas Peak: A History of a Napa County Settler.* Napa, CA: self-published, 2004.

Southport Land and Commercial Company. "History of the Company," www.southport-land.com/history.html.

Stone, Floyd. *1847 & 1848 Excerpts from the San Francisco Star.* Napa, CA, 1991.

Tobias, Arthur, Ed.D. "Pirates for the Republic 16 May 1843," users.rcn.com/robertbrecht/tobias/PDFs/engaged_text.pdf

Toledo, Charlie, Jim Big Bear King, Norma Knight, Colleen McCloud and Clink McKay "Native Americans" in *The Valley of Legends: Historical Fact Sheets.* Napa, CA (1997).

US Army Corps of Engineers, Napa County Flood Control and Water Conservation *District "A Citizen's Guide to the City of Napa, Napa River, & Napa Creek Flood Protection Project."* Napa, CA.

US Department of Commerce. "NOAA-NWFSC Tech Memo-27: Status review of West Coast Steelhead." February 1994.

US Department of Fish and Wildlife Service under the direction of the Anadromous Fish Restoration Program Core Group. "Working Paper on Restoration Needs." May 9, 1995.

Vincent, Geets. "Reflections on the Water." *Late Harvest.* California Indigenous Arts Organization (1984).

Wagner, Paul. "Funding Approved for Zinfandel Lane Fish Barrier." April 15, 2011.

Wheeler, Doug. "The Napa River Flood Management Effort." *California Biodiversity News*, Summer 1998, biodiversity.ca.gov/newsletter/v5n4/chair.html.

Wyckoff, Larry. "When Winemaking Meets Wildlife, It Can Be a Beautiful Thing: The Napa Sonoma Marsh." *Outdoor California*, September–October 2002.

Yerger, Rebecca A. "A Warehouse of History and Memories: A Historical Sketch of the Hatt Napa Mill." June, 1999.

For additional Napa River resources, visit www.napariverbook.com